D0899340

Boomerang!

How Our Covert Wars Have Created Enemies Across the Middle East and Brought Terror to America

Mark Zepezauer

Common Courage Press   Monroe, Maine

Copyright © 2003 by Mark Zepezauer
All rights reserved.
Cover by Matt Wuerker.
Cover Design by Erica Bjerning.
Indexing by Jim Wilhite

ISBN: 1-56751-222-4 paper
ISBN 1-56751-223-2 cloth

**Library of Congress Cataloging-in-Publication Data is
available on request from the publisher**

Common Courage Press
Box 702
Monroe, ME 04951

800-497-3207

FAX (207) 525-3068
orders-info@commoncouragepress.com

See our website for e versions of this book.
www.commoncouragepress.com

First Printing
Printed in Canada

Dedicated to my precious daughter Iris Anne Zepezauer,
who deserves the better world for which we struggle.

Contents

Acknowledgments

Above all I want to thank my wife, Nan, for her unflagging love and support in the face of this book's lengthy and difficult gestation. I am indebted to Professor David Gibbs of the University of Arizona History Department for reviewing the manuscript. David Blaisdell and Paul Reeder also gave helpful suggestions in the early stages. I will always be grateful to David Wood for persistently finding holes in my arguments, to Bruce Avery for helping to hone both the thesis and the prose, and to Peter Buckley for his courage and stamina in seeking a better world. My adorable parents, Frank and Joan Zepezauer, have been lifelong sources of love and support and have influenced my worldview in ways none of us suspect. My wonderful in-laws, the entire Lagemann clan, have all bounced ideas off me and vice versa. This book would not have been possible without invaluable babysitting from Sandy, Laurie and especially Lia, Huevos Mexicanos from Café Poca Cosa, Steve Earle's latest album, Sopranos reruns on DVD, and any number of unnamed patent attorneys. Thanks must go to Chaz Bufe of See Sharp Press for allowing me to delay a book owed to him in order to get this one finished. Kudos to Matt Wuerker for a mighty fine cover cartoon. And finally, the patient and indefatigable Greg Bates has helped to shape the text of this book into something far more coherent and penetrating than it would otherwise have been.

Introduction

Our Commitment to Creating Hell On Earth

In the wake of the 9/11 disasters, many Americans learned for the first time that the terrorist leader Osama bin Laden and his Afghani hosts, the Taliban, were both armed and trained by the CIA, back in the 1980s, for covert warfare against the USSR.[1] Later, our terrorist friends seem to have decided that one "corrupt Western superpower" is pretty much like another; hence the current *jihad* against us. But this is only the latest example of our behind-the-scenes skullduggery coming back to haunt us.

Saddam Hussein started his career with an assassination attempt against a leftist Iraqi leader on a CIA hit list.[2] Manuel Noriega was on the CIA payroll for many years before it was deemed necessary to invade Panama in order to arrest him.[3] In recent years, the U.S. sent troops to Somalia to untangle the chaos left by our support of a corrupt regime,[4] to Haiti to reverse a coup by CIA-trained death squad leaders[5] and to East Timor to address the devastation wrought by years of U.S. military support.[6] Just days before the tragedies in New York and DC, NATO was sending troops into Macedonia after Albanian rebels used U.S.-provided weapons to attack that nation's government.[7]

Professional intelligence agents have a word for this sort of thing: blowback.[8] It invokes the image of blood splattering back on the gunman after a point-blank shooting. But for the CIA, it's just the price of doing business. If anti-Castro

Cubans later blow up a Venezuelan passenger jet,[9] well, these things happen. If Nicaraguan paramilitaries finance their civil war by selling cocaine in the U.S.,[10] hey, you've got to take the good with the bad.

U.S. leaders have maintained a similar nonchalance over the blowback from Afghani operations. Zbigniew Brzezinski, who started the $6 billion effort during the Carter Administration, recently asked, "What was more important...a few stirred-up Muslims or the liberation of Central Europe and the end of the Cold War?"[11] Survivors of terror attacks by the "stirred-up Muslims" might question how casually armchair warriors can create a monster and write off subsequent monstrosities.

This book is an attempt to explain what the people of the Muslim and Arab states are so stirred up about; why our foreign policies in that part of the world have boomeranged back on us. As such, I don't spend much time looking at the good things the United States has done around the world. Nor do I consider, as others have, the difficult policy choices arising from the nastiness of our adversaries during the Cold War. These issues are not germane to the question of why we are so widely despised. Victims of U.S. bombing runs, or of tyrants kept in power by our tax dollars, rarely stop to reflect on the virtues of the Peace Corps or the details of Soviet Politburo debates.

Likewise, it has been fashionable of late to look at Arab and Muslim rage as a function of their corrupt and incompetent leaders, who have made such a mess of that part of the world.[12] Be that as it may, what's more relevant is the extent to which our country has installed and/or maintained such leaders in power. As citizens of the U.S., we have a responsibility for the actions of our own leaders.

To focus on the seamier aspects of our actions abroad

does not mean, as some will doubtless charge, that I hate America or sympathize with our enemies. To the contrary: I love my country enough to want us to stop making unnecessary enemies abroad. To do so we will have to learn from our history. At the dawn of the Cold War, an internal government memo by George Kennan—a respected diplomat in charge of long-term planning for the State Department—spelled out the basis of our foreign policy direction. It was written about the Philippines and Southeast Asia, but it could apply to any of the countries in this book:

"We [Americans] have 50% of the world's wealth but only 6.3% of the population. This disparity is particularly great between ourselves and the peoples of Asia. In this situation, we cannot fail to be the object of envy and resentment. Our real task in the coming period is to devise a pattern of relationships which will permit us to maintain this position of disparity without positive detriment to our national security. To do so we will have to dispense with all sentimentality and daydreaming... We should cease to talk about vague, and for the Far East, unreal objectives, such as human rights, the raising of living standards, and democratization. The day is not far off when we are going to have to deal in straight power concepts..."[13]

And that's exactly what we did. We devised a "pattern of relationships" throughout the Arab and Muslim world which was designed to maintain our wealth and disparity—chiefly through the control of one particular commodity: oil. Our number one priority in dealing with these states was not democracy or human rights, and certainly not the living standards of the inhabitants. It was to make sure that U.S. firms and U.S. client states controlled the bulk of the planet's oil supply. States that don't have oil, such as Turkey, Israel and Egypt, are useful to us primarily for helping to keep in line those that do.

It is this attitude that has turned friends into enemies. It has made a self-fulfilling prophecy of the "envy and resentment" to which Kennan referred. There are those who argue that our tactics, however unseemly, were necessary for building the strength of our economy, or for prevailing in the Cold War. Whether or not that's true, there is a price to be paid. In blood.

Some of that blood was spilled in the eastern United States on September 11, 2001; far more of it has been spilled in the countries profiled in this book. And that attitude has far outlived the Cold War. Another internal planning document, prepared by Paul Wolfowitz (then, as now, Undersecretary of Defense) under the supervision of then-Defense Secretary Dick Cheney, spelled out the direction of our foreign policy in 1992, following the dissolution of the Soviet Union.

At that point, according to Wolfowitz, our real task was to "establish and protect a new order" which would account "sufficiently for the interests of the advanced industrial nations to discourage them from challenging our leadership," while spending enough on our military to be capable of "deterring potential competitors from even aspiring to a larger regional or global role." And, of course, "in the Middle East and Southwest Asia, our overall objective is to remain the predominant outside power in the region and preserve U.S. and Western access to the region's oil."[14] And that's pretty much the way it's worked out.

It seems never to have occurred to our policy planners that we might make do with a bit less oil or wealth. Thus, over the past half-century, we've rigged elections, bolstered tyrants, sponsored assassinations and coups, and sold weapons to both sides in regional conflicts. We've been an inconstant ally, playing the game of divide and conquer, repeatedly abandoning former friends to suffer the consequences of our alliance.

We've studiously looked the other way while our clients commit appalling human rights abuses. We've helped the Israelis to keep down the Palestinians, the Turks to oppress the Kurds, the Saudi royal family to keep slaves and live in opulent palaces. We've sent our own troops into Lebanon, Iraq, and Afghanistan, killing some of the enemies we've made, and anyone else who gets in the way. And we've kept the people of Iraq under punishing sanctions for over a decade, contributing to the deaths of more than a million people who never did a thing to harm us.[15]

The survivors of those dead innocents, or those who pull their loved ones from bombed-out buildings in Afghanistan, are no less devastated than the people of New York. They, too, burn with a white-hot rage, and call for retaliation against those who killed their families. Further, they know exactly who is responsible; the bombs, and the planes that drop them, are marked "Made in the USA."

But how many Americans know about our shameful history of dealing in "straight power concepts," let alone the million-plus dead in Iraq? If they did, it might go a long way towards explaining how anyone could hate us so much. To be sure, neither our policy towards Iraq, nor the rest of the history described below, is any justification for the 9/11 attacks; to explain is not to condone. People have the right to take up arms in self-defense, but no nation, no group has the right to target non-combatants. Sadly, too often, our nation has been guilty of just such crimes. And unless we learn from our history, as the philosopher Santayana put it, we are doomed to repeat it. If we stay on the path of disregarding human rights and the living standards of others—in order to maintain our own disparity of wealth—our children and grandchildren may well pay the price.

Part I

ENEMY STATES

CHAPTER ONE

Iran

Equal and Opposite Reaction

The history of America's relationship with Iran illustrates the distance between the claim that we stand for democracy and freedom throughout the world and what the U.S. actually does when that principle is stacked up against another interest: controlling the spigot of the world's oil supply. In 1953 the U.S. toppled Iran's popular prime minister, Mohammed Mossadegh, putting the Shah of Iran firmly in control. By 1979 our support of the Shah had turned most Iranians into bitter enemies of the United States. They chased him out of power and installed a fundamentalist Muslim regime that bedevils us to this day.

The reason the U.S. toppled the Mossadegh regime boils down to one word, the same word that governs most of our policy in the region: oil. When Mossadegh became prime minister, Iran had one-quarter of the world's proven oil reserves. And yet his country received more income from the sale of its carpets abroad than from its petroleum.[1] The British Empire held a controlling interest in the Anglo-Iranian Oil Company (AIOC), and they were not shy about exerting that control.

When Britain assumed control of AIOC in 1913, Iran's share of royalties was 16%, and was based only on the sale of its crude, not on the more profitable refining business. The Iranian government was never allowed to audit the books to ensure they were getting a fair deal, nor were any Iranians involved in the management of the company. Even the drinking fountains—on Iranian soil—were marked "not for Iranians."[2]

But by 1951 the Saudis had cut a deal for a 50-50 split of the profits for the jointly owned company with the U.S., and a similar arrangement had been made in Venezuela. The British, however, were unwilling to go quite that far—until it was too late. When negotiations bogged down, the Iranian legislature voted to nationalize the AIOC.[3] Mossadegh was then swept into office on a wave of nationalist fervor, determined to use oil revenue to construct highways and railroads and improve the educational system.

The Iranian prime minister offered Britain compensation, including a continuing 25% of net profits, as well as retention of all British employees.[4] His Majesty's government responded with a threatening flotilla of gunboats, followed by an economic blockade and a boycott of all Iranian oil products, enforced by oil companies worldwide. Rather than modernizing his country, Mossadegh presided over its decline into chaos.

As the crisis deepened, both Iran and Britain turned to the U.S. for assistance. The Truman Administration was uninterested in helping the British get their oil company back, but when Dwight Eisenhower became president in 1953, his secretary of state, John Foster Dulles, saw Iran as yet another pawn in the Cold War. Iran's communist party, the Tudeh, received little support from Moscow, and was illegal in Iran.[5] But Dulles saw Mossadegh as insufficiently keen to suppress the Tudeh, and feared the economic decline caused by the British boycott might strengthen the party's hand. Then, too, Dulles and his brother Allen (head of the CIA) were also corporate lawyers who represented a number of major oil companies.

The CIA budgeted up to $19 million[6] for a change of government in Tehran, and decided to back the weak and inexperienced Shah of Iran. The Shah was at that point little more than a figurehead, more or less irrelevant during Iran's first experience with democracy in the years following World War II. He had assumed the throne as a teenager in 1941, when his father, who had tilted towards Nazi Germany,[7] was chased from the country by allied forces. (This didn't prevent the younger Shah from buying a 25% share in the infamous Krupp arms factory, still headed by Nazi war criminals, during the 1950s.[8])

According to recently released CIA documents, the U.S. "extensively stage-managed the entire coup, not only carrying it out but also preparing the groundwork for it." This groundwork included harassment of religious leaders, including bombing the home of one of them, in order to turn the mullahs against Mossadegh.[9] The Shah precipitated the crisis by dismissing Mossadegh as prime minister, replacing him with Fazlollah Zahedi, who had also been a Nazi collaborator.[10] The prime minister refused to leave office, maintaining that he served at the pleasure of parliament, not the Shah. Mossadegh ordered that Zahedi be arrested, but he was sheltered by the military, many of whom were receiving CIA bribe money.[11] The Shah, meanwhile, grabbed his wife and a bag of jewels and fled to Switzerland.[12]

Street demonstrations broke out against the Shah and in favor of Mossadegh. But the CIA budget paid for mobs of counterdemonstrators, intensifying the crisis and creating a pretext for military intervention. The pro-Shah demonstrators began trashing pro-government newspapers, parties and buildings. A captured radio station announced, falsely, that

Mossadegh had been ousted and Zahedi installed in office. A tank was sent to fetch Zahedi and convey him to the seat of power, but it took a nine-hour battle between loyalist and coup forces before the government finally fell.[13] Hundreds were killed in the streets of Tehran,[14] and while the Tudeh forces might have made the difference, Mossadegh repeatedly refused their assistance, and they did not take to the streets. This rather weakens the CIA's claim that it was toppling a "pro-communist" government.[15]

The Shah returned from exile and immediately began consolidating his rule by cracking down on both the Tudeh and the pro-democracy forces, while paying off the Islamic parties to support his rule.[16] But while placating the mullahs on the one hand, with the other hand the Shah alienated them with a program of rapid Westernization. With no natural constituency of his own, he launched an ill-considered land reform program to court the peasantry. But breaking up the old estates antagonized the wealthy landowners, as well as the clerics who took tribute from them. Worse, the program never followed through to teach the peasants how to manage their own land. Many went bankrupt and ended up in urban shantytowns—where Islamic agitators took up their cause.[17]

The clergy were not happy about the Shah's challenges to their powers, and began to speak up more forcefully. The Shah responded as he always did: with violence. More than sixty mullahs were detained, while theology students were illegally drafted into the armed forces. In March 1963, the Shah's fearsome security forces attacked the Faizeiyejh Theological School, arresting dozens of students and killing two. The survivors ran to the nearby home of Iran's most respected cleric, the Ayatollah Khomeini.[18]

In response, Khomeini gave a major speech in which he

called the Shah a "miserable wretch," and announced that "it will be difficult for us to tolerate you much longer.... The nation will not allow you to continue this way." Predictably, the Shah had Khomeini arrested, and just as predictably, the streets of Iran's cities erupted in fury. In three days of rioting, 86 people were killed, and it took martial law to restore order. Though the Shah would sit on the Peacock Throne for sixteen more years, this was the beginning of the end for him. Ironically, his U.S.-backed purge of leftists and centrists left open no other avenue for dissent besides Islamic militancy.

Khomeini challenged his authority again the following year, denouncing a treaty which allowed U.S. citizens immunity from Iranian laws. For this affront, the Ayatollah was sent into exile in neighboring Iraq. There he continued to spread the word of militant Islam through writings and audiocassettes, widely distributed in his homeland.[19]

Shah Reza Pahlavi entered a downward cycle of ever-greater repression of the Iranian people, which stirred up ever more opposition to his rule. By 1976, Amnesty International announced that Iran had the worst human rights record on Earth, no small distinction on this particular planet.[20] The secret police, SAVAK, trained by Israel and supplied by the U.S., were infamous for the use of torture and assassination. And meanwhile the Shah's personal corruption grew ever more blatant. Iran's vast oil wealth was squandered on palaces and ceremonies, used to enrich a small class of cronies and collaborators, and funneled into massive weapons purchases from the U.S.[21]

Throughout the last years of the Shah's reign of terror, as opposition grew and the security forces massacred more and more demonstrators in the streets, U.S. support never wavered. In 1978 President Jimmy Carter toasted Reza Pahlavi, reading off some speechwriter's inane prose: "Iran under the leadership of the Shah is an island of stability in one of the more troubled areas of the world. This is a great tribute to you, Your Majesty, and to your leadership, and to the respect, admiration and love which your people give to you."[22] Within a year the Shah's leadership would be over, and some ten to twelve thousand of his people would be dead at his hands.[23] Hundreds, perhaps thousands of protestors were killed on a single day, September 8, 1978, known as Black Friday in Iran.[24] From that point on any compromise with the Shah's regime became impossible.

Opponents of the Shah, both left and right, coalesced behind the figure of Khomeini. His call for a government based on the tenets of Islam appealed to the traditionalists, while his opposition to the American presence strengthened his nationalist credentials. Unfortunately, Ruhollah Khomeini turned out to be every bit as ruthless, intolerant, cynical, humorless and bloodthirsty as the man he replaced in 1979. Neither the far left nor the center had the muscle to overthrow the monarchy on their own, and many held romanticized views of the exiled cleric that ran into the brick wall of reality once he gained power.[25]

The gallows and torture chambers were never retired. The Shah's own torturers were the first to be executed; like many successful revolutionaries, the mullahs spilled more blood to prevent a counterrevolution.[26] But the killing didn't stop there. As Khomeini gradually drained power from the civilian government, opposition began to grow. The Islamic republic entered the familiar cycle of repression, dragging the country into a virtual civil war. Democratic centrists, the remnants of the Mossadegh regime, were purged from the government, and a new constitution was rammed through in an election fraught with irregularities.[27] On the left, many survivors of the Tudeh party had rallied behind a theology that combined Marxism with Islam. But the leftist mullahs were purged as well; only Khomeini's theology could reign. Before long Marxist guerrillas were in open conflict with the regime.[28]

Two things happened to help the conservative mullahs strengthen their grip on power: the hostage crisis and the war with Iraq. In February 1979 the U.S. embassy was seized by militant Muslim students, angered when the Shah was admitted to an American hospital for medical treatment. Against President Carter's better judgement (and the vehement warnings from the U.S. embassy in Tehran), the Shah's friends, Henry Kissinger and David Rockefeller, successfully lobbied to bring him to the U.S.[29] Iranians feared a repeat of the 1953 CIA plot that re-installed the monarchy (though in reality Reza Pahlavi was rapidly dying of cancer). Shredded documents from the "nest of spies" were painstakingly reassembled, making public the details of CIA collaboration with the Shah's secret police.[30] Nationalist sentiments were further inflamed when the U.S. launched a failed military rescue of its 53 hostages; the regime played it up as the first battle of a planned counter-coup, foiled by Islamist troops (though in reality the U.S. helicopters had crashed in an unexpected sandstorm).[31]

In frustration, the U.S. cozied up to Iraqi dictator Saddam Hussein. He was thirsty for revenge over a 1975 territorial dispute with the Shah. The U.S. hoped that a war with Iraq would force the Khomeini regime to bargain for the hostages to gain spare parts for the Shah's U.S.-built arsenal.[32] Both sides figured the war would be short and relatively painless; in reality it would last eight years and cost over a million lives.[33]

Khomeini was indeed willing to bargain for military equipment. But unfortunately for the Carter administration, according to investigative journalist Robert Parry, the bargain was made with a group of ex-CIA officers who supported the Reagan-Bush presidential campaign.[34] Abolhassan Bani-Sadr was the civilian president of Iran in the first year of the revolution. In his memoirs, he explained that Khomeini's anti-American rhetoric was just show business for the masses, and that behind the scenes the Ayatollah had no problems dealing with the "Great Satan." For instance, in 1983 the U.S. secretly provided lists of leftist infiltrators in the Iranian government, which Khomeini used for mass roundups and executions.[35]

According to numerous witnesses,[36] representatives of the mullahs met in Paris with William Casey (later named CIA director) and other Reagan campaign officials in October 1980.[37] This was done behind Carter's back and also behind Bani-Sadr's back, and though both caught wind of what was happening, they were unable to stop it.[38] Iran agreed to keep the hostages until Carter was defeated for re-election, in return for $40 million in military equipment.[39] Shipments of U.S. arms through Israel commenced shortly after Reagan was inaugurated.[40] About the same time Bani-Sadr was forced from office and fled Iran under threat of assassination. The nationalist fervor surrounding the embassy seizure allowed Khomeini and the mullahs to purge centrists from the government; soon clerics controlled both the judiciary and the military.[41]

Meanwhile the war with Iraq rallied Iranians behind the regime, discrediting the armed resistance, which was receiving backing from Baghdad.[42] U.S. diplomats had told Iran that for geopolitical reasons, they would not allow Iraq to prevail.[43] Unfortunately, for the same reasons, the U.S. would not allow Iran to prevail. At various times, the U.S.

covertly offered both material and intelligence to both sides, while publicly maintaining neutrality. The war dragged on through years of bloody stalemate, with both sides unwilling to negotiate so as not to seem weak at home. Alarmed by Khomeini's willingness to export his theocratic revolution, the U.S. and its allied Gulf monarchies funneled billions of dollars of military aid to Iraq.[44] By 1987, the U.S. was willing to intervene overtly on the side of Saddam Hussein.[45]

As both Iraq and Iran had been attacking vessels in the Persian Gulf, American flags were raised over Kuwaiti tankers, and American battleships retaliated massively against any Iranian moves. The U.S. destroyed Iranian oil platforms after a frigate was damaged by mines.[46] Then in July 1987 the USS Vincennes shot down an Iranian passenger jet, killing all 290 civilians on board. The captain claimed that the plane appeared to be menacing his ship in international waters; later investigations showed it was on a regularly scheduled flight—in Iranian airspace—at the time of the shootdown.[47] Vice President George Bush announced at the UN, "I don't care what the facts are; I will never apologize for the United States of America!"[48] As if to underscore the point, the captain of the Vincennes was later given a medal for valor.[49]

A year later, Khomeini reluctantly accepted a UN cease-fire resolution. The war had cost Iran over $125 billion, and of the one million dead, three-quarters were Iranian lives.[50] For Khomeini, it had cemented his hold on power, whereas for the U.S. and its allies it had mostly contained his Islamic revolution—at least for the time being. Once Iran had learned that hostages were a valuable commodity, it used proxy forces in Beirut to seize more of them, and the Reagan Administration had duly bargained further military aid for their release, one at a time.[51] But wearied by eight years of war, Iran saw diminishing returns and little success in an expansionist foreign policy. After Khomeini's death in June 1989, the remaining hostages were released.[52]

Since then, Iran has continued to support anti-Israeli forces in Lebanon, but has also tried to reach greater accommodation with the West.[53] The more moderate Khatami regime was elected in 1997 and overwhelmingly re-elected in 2000, but the mullahs still maintain veto power over the legislature and continue to dominate the judiciary.[54] Following the 9/11 attacks, Iran has both condemned the U.S. war on Afghanistan and offered to help rescue downed pilots on its territory.[55] While the U.S. has maintained a trade embargo, other nations have been willing to resume business as usual with Tehran, and U.S. oil companies are impatient to get back in the game.[56] But Iran was lumped in with North Korean and Iraq as an "axis of evil" in President Bush's 2002 State of the Union address, setting back reformist forces in Tehran by almost a decade.[57]

The blowback from U.S. interventions in Iran will reverberate for years to come. Our policies, meant to establish "stability" for a secure oil supply, have instead left a legacy of bitterness in Iran, destabilized its neighbors (including Afghanistan),[58] strengthened Saddam Hussein, and given both literal and rhetorical weapons to enemies of the United States. The disregard for the disastrous (and largely foreseeable) consequences of these policies should be recalled every single time that we are tempted to intervene abroad. But among many consistent threads through U.S. foreign policy is a complete indifference to the carnage wreaked by our interventions, a point we see illustrated by the 1991 war against Iraq—a war that continues in many ways to this day.

CHAPTER TWO

Iraq

We Think It's Worth It

The United States went to war against Iraq in 1991 to reverse Saddam Hussein's invasion of Kuwait. Iraqi forces left Kuwait 42 days later,[1] but for the people of Iraq, the war continues. Some 200,000 Iraqis died during the Gulf War;[2] in the decade since, more than a million have perished.[3] The U.S. has bombed Iraq hundreds of times[4] and led international sanctions in hopes of toppling Saddam's regime. Ironically, these efforts have served only to strengthen him.[5] Meanwhile Iraqi civilians are paying the price for living within the same borders as the dictator Washington built up in the first place. Today, as the U.S. asserts its right to "take out" Saddam, it's worth recalling that the old ghoul's path to power was paved by an earlier decision to "take out" one of his predecessors.

Saddam Hussein first made a name for himself in a CIA-backed assassination attempt against General Abdel Karim Qassim, then in charge of Iraq.[6] In 1958, Qassim had overthrown and executed the unpopular British-backed monarch, King Faisal. The CIA was taken by surprise, and U.S. leaders watched in dismay as the Qassim regime pulled out of the pro-Western Baghdad pact, founded the Organization of Petroleum Exporting Countries (OPEC) and asserted Iraq's longstanding claim of sovereignty over Kuwait. Soon the U.S. let it be known that it wouldn't mind if Gen. Qassim went to an early grave as well.[7] One of those who answered the call was young Saddam, then a minor officer of the Ba'ath Party.[8]

The assassination attempt was not successful, and Saddam went into exile in Cairo, where he kept in contact with the U.S. embassy. He returned in 1963, when the still-popular Qassim was successfully liquidated in a Ba'athist coup.[9] Saddam and his colleagues quickly went to work on a bloody purge of 700 Iraqi leftists, using hit lists helpfully provided by, who else, the CIA.[10] Over the next dozen years, through a series of murders, purges, and shifting alliances, Saddam worked his way up through the ranks. He became head of security, then vicepresident, and finally, in 1979, supreme leader of Iraq.[11]

Like many Middle Eastern leaders, Saddam liked to do business with both the U.S. and the USSR.[12] Generally the superpowers felt that if you were friends with one, you were the enemy of the other. But this was no big problem, since everybody was more than happy to switch sides as events warranted. In 1975, Iraq was friendly with the Soviets, from whom they received military support. Consequently, the Kurdish minority in northern Iraq, previously friendly with the Soviets, was then allied with the Americans. At that time neighboring Iran was a U.S. client state, involved in a border dispute with the Iraqis. The Shah of Iran prevailed on Washington to arm the Iraqi Kurds as a way of putting diplomatic pressure on Baghdad.[13]

This worked out well for everyone except the Kurds. Once Iran and Iraq came to terms over their border dispute, the U.S. withdrew support for the Kurdish insurgency. Double-crossed by Uncle Sam, the Kurds were mercilessly slaughtered by Saddam Hussein's security forces. Asked to explain all this before a congressional committee, Secretary of State Henry Kissinger offered the immortal words "covert action should not be confused with missionary work."[14] As if to prove Kissinger's point, everybody switched sides again just a few years later.

When the Shah of Iran was overthrown by an Islamic rebellion in 1980, it was time for the U.S. to make friends with Saddam Hussein. The new Islamic revolution in Iran, headed by the Ayatollah Khomeini, was making other U.S. allies nervous—notably the Saudi royal family, who feared similar uprisings in their own country.[15] Saddam met with Saudi leaders and with CIA agents in Amman, where King Hussein had long been on the Agency's payroll. He got a "green light" for an invasion of Iran, and was promised economic and military support from the oil-rich Gulf sheikdoms.[16] What resulted was a bloody eight-year war between Iraq and Iran that would leave over a million dead.[17]

A big part of the problem was that Washington was offering support to both sides. When Iranian militants seized hostages in the U.S. embassy, the Carter Administration hoped that war with Iraq would force Khomeini to come to terms with the U.S. in order to procure needed spare parts for the Shah's U.S.-built arsenal. But at the same time, Carter's Republican opponents were cozying up to Iran, hoping they would hold on to the hostages long enough to humiliate Carter, so he would be defeated in the upcoming election—which he was. The day Ronald Reagan took office, the U.S. hostages were released, and just a few weeks later, U.S.-approved arms shipments to Iran were underway.[18]

When these were publicly revealed in late 1986, the resulting scandal became known as the Iran-Contra affair, since the Reagan Administration used profits from arms sales to Iran to finance the secret "contra" war against Nicaragua. But Reagan also aided Saddam Hussein, "bleeding" both sides in hopes of weakening any potential rivals to U.S.

client states in the region.[19] When Iran got the upper hand, U.S. warships were sent into the Persian Gulf to intervene on behalf of Saddam. Iranian ships were attacked in the name of "protecting oil shipments,' though the main threat to Gulf shipping came from Iraq.[20] Even when Iraq attacked the USS Stark in 1987, killing 37 sailors, Washington shrugged it off, determined to keep pressure on Iran.[21]

During the Iran-Iraq war, the U.S. covertly supplied Saddam with weapons of mass destruction, including chemical and biological arms.[22] "Agricultural" loans to Iraq were used as a cover for military aid. The U.S. branch of an Italian bank funneled $5 billion in questionable (taxpayer-backed) loans to Baghdad,[23] and U.S. firms shipped toxic agents like Anthrax and Botulism, all with government approval.[24] Saddam put these weapons to use, employing both chemical and biological weapons against Iranian troops, as well as Kurdish rebels. The Kurdish village of Halabja was attacked with nerve gas, killing 5000 and injuring 200,000 more, most of whom are suffering to this day from the effects.[25] Despite protests by human rights groups, Washington looked the other way[26]—though President Bush later cited the atrocity as one of the reasons to go to war against Iraq in 1991.

Once the Iran-Iraq war ended in stalemate in 1988, it began to seem to the U.S. and its allies that Iraq, in particular, had been insufficiently bled. Saddam now had the most powerful military in the Gulf region, with over a million battle-hardened men in uniform.[27] Thus it was just about time for everybody to switch sides once again.

Henceforth, U.S. policy towards Baghdad employed both carrots and sticks. Covert military aid continued, but loan amounts dropped off, owing to investigations of the

banking scandals.[28] Washington suddenly began to take public notice of human rights abuses in Iraq. And the wealthy
little kingdom of Kuwait began playing hardball with its
powerful neighbor. Though Saddam had nearly gone broke
protecting the Gulf sheikdoms from revolutionary Iran, the
Kuwaitis demanded accelerated repayment of wartime
loans.[29] Worse still, the Kuwaitis had been "slant drilling"
underneath the border into Iraq's valuable Rumaila oilfield,
draining $14 billion in crude. A company owned by Brent
Scowcroft, President Bush's national security advisor, had
sold the special drilling equipment to the Emir of Kuwait.[30]
As an old crony of Henry Kissinger, Scowcroft was presumably not involved in "missionary work."

Under Ottoman rule, Kuwait had been a province of
Iraq, but was broken off by Britain in order to prevent
Baghdad's access to any usable seaports.[31] Squeezed by the
Emir, Saddam began to look at Kuwait's oil revenue as the
answer to his problems. Those problems had grown even
worse when Kuwait violated OPEC production quotas,
sharply driving down the price of crude oil. With their extensive investments in the West, the Saudis and Kuwaitis could
ride out lower oil prices, but Iraq's war-torn economy was
hurt even further.[32]

As tensions escalated, Washington continued its two-
track policy. A well-connected Washington think tank
encouraged Saddam to treat Kuwait more aggressively,[33]
while at the same time the director of the CIA was advising
Kuwait to "take advantage of the deteriorating economic situation in Iraq."[34] Publicly, U.S. officials gave mixed signals.
After Secretary of Defense Dick Cheney said that America
would come to Kuwait's defense if it were attacked, the
White House backed away from the statement.[35] State
Department spokespersons announced more than once that

no treaty would obligate the U.S. to assist Kuwait.[36] When Congress sought to impose sanctions on Iraq for human rights violations, the White House opposed the measure.[37] And U.S. Ambassador April Glaspie told Saddam that Washington had "no opinion" on his border disputes with Kuwait.[38]

The Kuwaitis seemed unafraid of their more powerful neighbor. At an emergency Arab League summit, they responded to Iraq's negotiating offers with insulting replies. "If they don't like it, let them occupy our territory," one Kuwaiti told Jordan's King Hussein. "We are going to bring in the Americans."[39] And so they did. After Iraqi troops invaded Kuwait, the Bush Administration began a buildup of U.S. military forces in the Persian Gulf, which continues to this day. Cheney traveled to Riyadh, carrying forged satellite photos, which showed an alarming buildup of Iraqi forces on the Kuwaiti-Saudi border. In actuality, no such buildup had occurred. But the Saudis, fearing that they, too would be invaded, invited U.S. troops onto their territory—much to the dismay of Islamic dissidents.[40]

The U.S. resisted all attempts to mediate a peaceful resolution to the crisis. The president and his advisors regarded a negotiated Iraqi withdrawal from Kuwait (being mediated by Soviet leader Gorbachev) as a "nightmare" scenario.[41] "Don't you realize that if [Saddam] pulls out, it will be impossible for us to stay?" asked Scowcroft of General Colin Powell, who favored the peace initiative.[42] In a recent interview, former Secretary of State James Baker admitted that his last-ditch negotiating session with Iraqi diplomats in January 1991 was strictly for show. "I'll tell you this," Baker told PBS, "the meeting with Tariq Aziz in Geneva permitted us to achieve congressional support for something that the President was determined to do in any event."[43] Or as Baker's boss told his advisors, "We *have* to have a war."[44] Administration insiders have identified Bush's main motivations as twofold: to wipe out Iraq's military capabilities and to wipe out the "Vietnam syndrome."[45] This was Beltway jargon for the American public's irritating reluctance to support overseas military adventures.[46] At the end of the Gulf War, Bush exulted, "By God, we've licked the Vietnam syndrome once and for all!"[47]

The Pentagon candidly spelled out the bottom line in a post-war evaluation: "In the Middle East and Southwest Asia, our overall objective is to remain the predominant outside power in the region and preserve U.S. and Western access to the region's oil."[48] Pursuant to this, the U.S. had been planning war games scenarios against Iraq for 18 months before Saddam's invasion.[49] A 1990 U.S. Army white paper had discussed Iraq as a prime candidate to replace the Warsaw Pact as a target for future military expenditures.[50] In the end, estimates of Iraq's military capabilities proved to be wildly overinflated, though by that time they had served their purpose.[51]

By the time the U.S. began its ground war against Iraq, Saddam had withdrawn his elite Republican Guard units back to Baghdad, leaving the Kuwaiti front to be defended by frightened young conscripts, many drawn from dissident Kurdish and Shi'ite regions.[52] Many of them were killed while trying to surrender. Thousands were buried alive by U.S. bulldozers in the middle of the night,[53] or burned to a crisp while retreating from Kuwait City.[54]

Meanwhile, allied bombing had utterly devastated the civilian infrastructure of Iraq, destroying power plants, water facilities and hospitals. As this constitutes a war crime under international law,[55] U.S. authorities were careful to note that such destruction was "accidental." Such accidents took out 38 schools, 28 hospitals, 31 sewage facilities, four of the seven major water pumping stations, and all 11 of Iraq's major electrical power plants, along with 119 substations. In fact, the possibility of "punitive raids" on such targets had been widely discussed, both publicly and privately, by U.S. war planners. "If there are political objectives that the UN coalition has," one of them told the *Washington Post*, "...it gives us long-term leverage."[56]

Of course, attacking civilian targets for the purpose of "leverage" for "political objectives" is the very definition of terrorism.

As the war ended, many of Iraq's neighbors were happy to have seen Saddam taken down a peg, but didn't want to see him out of power. Though allied propaganda had encouraged Shi'ites and Kurds to revolt against Baghdad, the war effort pointedly stopped short of assisting them, and they were once again double-crossed and left to Saddam's revenge.[57] Civil war in Iraq—so the reasoning went—might lead to rebellions in Kurdish areas of Turkey and Syria, and the triumph of the Shi'ites in southern Iraq would only strengthen Iran once again.[58] So Saddam was left in power, with his military might decimated and his economy in a shambles. The balance of power in the Gulf now favored the monarchies, bolstered by new U.S. military bases.

Iraq's oil revenue was used to pay reparations to the Emir of Kuwait, who held hundreds of billions of dollars in overseas investments.[59] While the once-prosperous Iraqis suffered and died under the sanctions, U.S. firms made fortunes in the reconstruction of Kuwait. In his post-presidential 1993 "victory tour" of Kuwait, George H. W. Bush brought along his sons Marvin, Neil, and future president George W. Bush. The younger Bushes worked to secure a contract for their friends at the Enron Corporation in rebuilding a Kuwaiti power plant. Best of all, the Gulf war essentially ratified Kuwait's de facto annexation of the Rumaila oilfield, the very theft which had provoked Iraq in the first place. This new territory had the effect of doubling Kuwait's oil output for U.S. and British companies based there.[60]

But for the people of Iraq, caught in the middle of this power play, the worst was yet to come. Economic sanctions prevented Baghdad from repairing water treatment plants or importing needed medicines.[61] Declassified Pentagon documents show that even as the war was being pursued, it was recognized that the destruction of Iraq's water supply "could lead to increased incidences, if not epidemics, of disease."[62] Through the 1990s, the U.S. and Britain kept a tight lid on Iraqi imports, and cynically blamed Saddam for the resulting suffering.[63] Iraq's children were hardest hit, dying of malnutrition and easily preventable diseases at the rate of 5000 a month—the equivalent of a 9/11 disaster every 30 days. After eleven years of sanctions, more than 1.2 million Iraqi civilians have perished, more than half under the age of 18.[64]

In 1996, asked by reporter Leslie Stahl about the death of "half a million children," then-UN Ambassador Madeleine Albright did not dispute the figure. Instead she offered, "I think this is a very hard choice, but the price—we think the price is worth it."[65] While this comment made little impact in the U.S., it has been widely repeated throughout the Muslim world.

Several UN officials in charge of overseeing the sanctions program have resigned in protest, charging that Washington and London have engaged in a program of deliberate genocide against the people of Iraq.[66] At the same time,

Scott Ritter, who was a member of UN teams sent to verify Iraqi cooperation with disarmament resolutions, stated that Iraq had been "essentially disarmed."[67] UN weapons inspectors departed in 1998 in anticipation of a major new bombing campaign by the U.S. Saddam subsequently refused to allow them to return, charging that the CIA was using the group as a cover for espionage operations. Washington later admitted that the charge was true, but bombing of Iraq continues on a routine basis.[68]

Saddam has been kept not too weak and not too strong, in a cynical effort to preserve a balance of power that favors U.S. interests by keeping Arab nations divided and squabbling. Not surprisingly, U.S. policy against Iraq has stirred up massive resentment in the Arab world. It seems exceedingly unlikely that U.S. citizens would allow a foreign power to slowly kill off a half a million innocent American children without doing something to strike back.

In the aftermath of the war in Afghanistan, persistent reports reveal Bush Administration plans to initiate another full-scale war against Iraq as soon as possible.[69] These plans have been delayed due to the opposition of the entire Arab League as well as most of our Western allies.[70] But like his father, the president is determined to have a war; U.S. policy is that we are committed to "regime change" no matter how much Saddam cooperates with the UN[71] (which of course gives him little incentive to do so). Press leaks (later debunked)[72] have tried to link Saddam to the al-Qaida network, though in fact they are sworn enemies.[73] But if history is any guide, the search for a pretext will continue. On the other hand, to find out what happens to bloodthirsty dictators who do play ball with the U.S. (at least when it counts), it may be instructive to take a look at Syria.

CHAPTER THREE

Syria

A Wicked Sense of Humor

Syria was the target of one of the CIA's first interventions, in March of 1949.[1] The Agency had been in existence for less than two years, an independent Syria for less than three. But the U.S. decided that an independent Syria was not in our interests—or rather it was not in the interests of our oil companies. So on their behalf, the CIA sponsored the 1949 military takeover, the first of more than a dozen coups which would destabilize Syria over the following twenty years.

Syria had been occupied by the French since 1920, in the wake of World War I. Under political pressure from the U.S., Britain and the Soviets, French troops were supposed to withdraw following World War II, but the French bombed Damascus in May 1945 in an effort to intimidate Syrians into allowing the occupation to continue. Nevertheless the French were eventually persuaded by the UN to withdraw completely by April 1946. A constitutional government under President Shukri al-Quwatli was established, though it was plagued by corruption and infighting.[2]

Corruption within the Syrian army contributed to a rout at the hands of Israel in their first war of 1948-49. Before the French and British had carved up the Middle East in 1916, the territory known as Syria included present-day Lebanon as well as parts of what is now Israel and Palestine. Expansionists in Israel had attacked Palestinian areas in April and May 1948, before full-fledged war broke out (see chapter 9). Many of the new Arab states intervened on behalf of the Palestinians, though the Syrians may have had expansionist motivations of their own.[3]

During the war with Israel, the CIA approached the Syrian army's Chief of Staff Husni Zaim about the possibility of an "army-supported dictatorship." The problem the U.S. wanted to solve was that President Quwatli was insufficiently supportive of a pipeline deal sponsored by a consortium of oil interests known as Tapline. Zaim took over in a bloodless coup, dissolved the parliament and arrested leading politicians, and suddenly Syria and Tapline came to an understanding.[4] Zaim also offered to initiate peace talks with Israel, but received a cold shoulder from the Ben-Gurion government.[5]

But Zaim too was deemed to lack the required deference to U.S. interests. Prior to the coup, CIA agents referred to him as Husni or "our boy." Once he assumed office, however, Husni demanded to be addressed as "Excellency," and declined to consider U.S. suggestions for appointment of ambassadors and cabinet ministers. A few months after his ascension, he was overthrown and executed.[6] Subsequent CIA-backed coup attempts in Syria were less successful. As researcher Douglas Little has put it, while Syrians had long been pro-American, our interventions there "helped reverse a century of friendship."[7]

Syria got a new constitution in 1950, and another in 1953 under its third military dictator, Col. Adib Shishakli. He had overthrown Zaim's successor in 1951, and received discreet U.S. support, but was forced out in 1954 by mounting popular opposition. Elections were held that year, with nationalist and socialist parties increasing their appeal. The pan-Arabist Ba'ath Party, which was also active in neighboring Iraq, became the most influential.[8] The Ba'athists were socialist, but anti-Communist, and also looked with suspicion on U.S. alliances in the Middle East. Syria tried to purchase American military equipment, but balked at having strings attached. Subsequently Damascus obtained arms from Czechoslovakia, which Washington regarded as unacceptable.[9]

So in 1956 the CIA scheduled and financed another coup in Syria, hoping to install "conservative" elements who would purge officers with "leftist tendencies." The coup had to be postponed after the Suez crisis in October, but was later set for the spring of 1957. The CIA was keen to get Shishakli re-installed, but the coup plans were leaked before they could be realized. Syrian intelligence penetrated the plot, and learned that the U.S. was prepared to offer hundreds of millions of dollars in aid, in exchange for a peace treaty with Israel. The Syrians instead expelled the CIA officers and publicly denounced U.S. meddling—to the great indignation of the U.S., which expelled the Syrian ambassador in retaliation for the affront.[10]

Relations with Washington grew chillier as Damascus turned to the East Bloc for additional military equipment. The U.S. sent warships to the Syrian coast, and encouraged Turkey to send 50,000 troops to the border for "maneuvers."[11] But Damascus also feared the growing influence of its own Communist Party, and in 1958 entered into a union with Nasser's Egypt known as the United Arab Republic (UAR). All political parties were banned except for the ruling National Union. But Syrians chafed under increasing Egyptian influence, and political leaders were wary of Nasser's popularity throughout the Arab world. The UAR was abruptly broken up by a coup of conservative Syrian officers in 1961.[12]

Elections were held, yet another constitution written, and political parties re-emerged. But elements of the Ba'ath party seized control in 1963, banning all other parties, and the Ba'athists have not let go to this day.[13] Struggles and intrigues within the Ba'ath party dominated an unstable Syria throughout the 1960s, with a succession of coups and coup attempts, clashes with the Israelis, and waxing and waning influence of the USSR.

The disputed border area known as the Golan Heights was the subject of many disputes with Israel, and the Israelis knew they could always provoke a Syrian response by sending in soldiers on tractors, disguised as farmers. Then the Israelis would retaliate with warplanes.[14] In 1967, Syria went to war against Israel after the latter had attacked Egypt, with Damascus ultimately losing control of the Golan Heights. Israel expelled all Syrian farmers from the area and repopulated it with Israeli settlers. The U.S. had given the green light to Israel's war plans, and regarded the attacks on Syria and Egypt as a great victory against "Soviet influence."[15]

Syria's most recent coup took place in November 1970, led by a ruthless and cunning officer named Hafez al-Assad. Assad became one of the most bloodthirsty dictators in the history of the modern Middle East, and methodically eliminated rivals to become the undisputed ruler.[16] But Assad's human rights record didn't stop the U.S. from cutting deals with him from time to time. At first, Secretary of State Henry Kissinger ignored Syrian and Egyptian diplomatic efforts to regain lost territory, which led to yet another war against Israel in 1973.[17] In the aftermath, Kissinger negotiated the return of a small patch of land to Syrian sovereignty. He subsequently offered that he found Assad to have "a first-class mind and a wicked sense of humor."[18]

Then in 1976, Assad invaded Lebanon, with Kissinger's tacit approval,[19] intervening on behalf of Christian forces against the Palestinians. Assad distrusted Palestinian leader Yassir Arafat, regarding him as a rival for greater influence in Lebanon. Seeing the PLO crushed certainly suited U.S. interests fine at the time, so Assad was welcomed into Lebanon with a wink from Washington. But no alliance with Assad lasted for long; soon he intervened on the Palestinian side against the Christians.[20] His own interest was in seeing that no one faction became too powerful at the expense of the others. Syria has dominated Lebanon ever since, playing various militia groups against each other and controlling the lucrative drug trade in the Bekaa Valley.[21]

In 1982 Hafez al-Assad faced an insurrection from Islamic forces based in the northern city of Hama. Weeks of merciless government assaults on the city resulted in an estimated 15,000-25,000 dead, mostly civilians who had nothing to do with the rebellion. *New York Times* columnist Thomas Friedman visited the area soon after and found it utterly flattened, "as though a tornado had swept back and forth over it for a week."[22] Assad's ferocity deterred Islamists from challenging his regime; it also scattered them into neighboring countries, including Lebanon and Afghanistan. Like the Saudis, Assad came to a tacit understanding with Muslim extremists; as long as they didn't threaten his longevity, he would turn a blind eye to their fundraising for activities elsewhere. And like the Americans, he also found them useful as proxy forces for his own interventions.[23]

Assad's brother Rifaat, widely rumored to be a CIA asset, was suspected of conspiring against him. A summit meeting with their aging mother resulted in Rifaat's exile to Lebanon, where he worked with drug traffickers as well as terrorist forces linked to Oliver North's Iran/contra operations. Rifaat's daughter was married for a time to the terrorist Abu Abbas and was later mistress to North's middleman Monzer al-Kassar. Rifaat himself was married to the sister of Syria's intelligence chief, who controlled opium production in the Bekaa Valley. Kassar played all factions adeptly, helping to negotiate the release of Western hostages in return for a blind eye to his trafficking operations.[24]

But strange bedfellows like Monzer al-Kassar proved to be a major liability after U.S. forces shot down an Iranian passenger jet in 1988 (see chapter 1). Six months later, Kassar and his colleague Ahmed Jibril helped to plan the bombing of Pan Am flight 103 over Lockerbie, Scotland. According to former Israeli intelligence agent Juval Aviv, the Syrians took the contract to avenge the U.S. shootdown of Iran's civilian airliner. Investigating the Lockerbie crash on behalf of Pan Am's insurance company, Aviv turned up compelling evidence of Jibril's involvement, as reported at the time in the mainstream media, including *Time*, *Barron's* and NBC news.[25] But the Syrian connection to Lockerbie became an embarrassment after Iraq invaded Kuwait. Hafez al-Assad was needed as an ally against Saddam Hussein. Assad was only too happy to tilt against Saddam, a rival Ba'athist who had sponsored rebellions and assassination attempts against him. President George H.W. Bush declared that "Syria took a bum rap [on Lockerbie]," and traveled to Geneva to shake Assad's bloodstained hand.[26] Henceforth—and to this day—the official line is that Libya was responsible for the bombing (see chapter 5).[27]

Authors John Loftus and Mark Aarons have supplied a fascinating explanation for Bush Senior's flip-flop on Syria: Assad was blackmailing him. According to the authors' interviews with retired intelligence agents, the Syrians had received videotaped confessions of kidnapped CIA agent William Buckley in Lebanon (see chapter 6). Under torture, Buckley supplied details about Bush's involvement in terrorist activities in the Middle East, including a Beirut car bombing. The Syrians were able to corroborate enough of the details to put considerable pressure on Bush.[28]

In any event, Assad sent an armored division to Saudi Arabia, though it ultimately saw little action. In return for supporting the U.S. in the Gulf War, Assad received cash infusions from the Gulf monarchies ($2 billion from the Saudis alone) and from the European Union; a free hand for his activities in Lebanon; and a promise of a U.S.-backed peace effort with Israel (which later came to naught).[29] He also gained good will in Washington just at the time when the Soviet Union, a longtime patron, was beginning to unravel. He used the political capital to install a pro-Syrian regime in Beirut, and employed allies like Islamic Jihad and Hamas to put pressure on Israel during the ultimately fruitless negotiations over the Golan Heights.[30]

Assad's flexibility and ruthlessness allowed him to stay in power longer than any other Middle East dictator, save for Qadaffy. Hafez al-Assad died of a heart attack in June of 2000 and was replaced by his son Bashar, his chosen successor. Bashar had to overcome some challenges from his Uncle Rifaat, but managed to establish his rule thanks to his late father's extensive internal security forces. The inexperienced Bashar was expected to try modernizing the Syrian economy, but has been cautious in implementing any changes. He has also been willing, like his father, to crack down on any challenges to his regime.[31]

Following the 9/11 attacks on America, Syria became

useful once more, and CIA officials traveled to Damascus to discuss co-operation in tracking down al-Qaida operatives.[32] Apparently these discussions were fruitful, as NBC has reported that Damascus has provided valuable intelligence as well as access to interrogations of a key al-Qaida figure they have in custody. In exchange, the U.S. has agreed to look the other way as Syria imports oil from Iraq in defiance of UN sanctions.[33]

But Syria is still on the U.S. State Department's short list of regimes said to be sponsoring terrorism, and like others on the list (notably Libya and Sudan), it is the subject of a good cop/bad cop strategy from Washington.[34] It remains to be seen if Syria will become an asset of America's latest war, or a target of it. Much the same could be said about another cooperative "terrorist" state: Sudan.

CHAPTER FOUR

Sudan

They Come to Take Our Oil

Sudan has been engaged in a bloody civil war, off and on, since 1955, on the eve of independence from Britain. The first phase lasted until 1972, after which a truce held for eleven years. The war resumed in 1983 and has continued ever since, intensifying in recent years. Though the Sudanese civil war has received little attention, over two million people have been killed.[1] Perhaps you will not be surprised to learn that oil is a factor in this slaughter.[2]

Of course, great powers have been trampling through the Sudan since long before any oil was discovered; that's what great powers do. Within a generation of the founding of the Islamic religion in the 7th century, Muslim invaders were exporting their new faith southwards down the Nile. Further incursions in the 15th century led to administration by the Ottoman Empire. Predictably, they had more success ruling in the familiar desert terrain than in the jungles further down. That set up the conflict between the Arabic north and the African south that continues to this day.[3]

British mapmakers, as usual, did not help matters. The British Empire trampled through in 1899, taking over both the north and the south; the borders were drawn wherever they ran into turf claimed by Italy, France or Belgium. The British "protectorate" did eventually recognize the cultural differences within their colony, and set up a Southern Sudan Policy in 1930. But when the time came to let go of its

African possessions, Britain found it politically convenient to placate Arab opinion and declare that "North and South are bound together."[4]

"Bound" turned out to be the appropriate term for the south, which was disproportionately underrepresented in the legislature. The north was more homogeneous, hence better equipped to take over a nation-state than the ethnically diverse black communities of the south (which include Christians, Muslims and animists). The southerners began armed resistance shortly before the British waved goodbye in January 1956. Authorities in Khartoum likewise began a new Islamization program, which resulted in fiercer resistance, followed by even harsher reprisals.[5]

Harsh reprisals led to more recruits for the liberation movements in the south, and despite air raids and massacres in the 1960s, more territory began to fall into rebel hands. The insurrections sought full independence from Khartoum, arguing that the south had never consented to be part of Sudan in the first place. Just to complicate matters, Arab governments like Egypt and Syria offered aid to the central government, while Ethiopia and Israel helped to back the south. And because you couldn't run a war in the 60s without inviting the Russians and the Americans, we sided with the south, and they went with the north.[6]

Foreign backing helped prolong the war, preventing either side from attaining complete victory. The stalemate was codified in the Addis Ababa agreement of 1972, which granted limited autonomy and better representation to the southern Sudanese. Seventeen years of war had left the country exhausted, with the south having paid mostly in blood and the north, in treasure. Peace was shaky, though, and was undermined by tribal rivalries in the south and a growing Islamic movement in the north. What virtually guaranteed further conflict, though, was the discovery in 1978 that Sudan sat atop vast seas of petroleum. Around this time the U.S. decided it might be better to be allied with the north. Within two years Sudan had become the sixth-largest recipient of U.S. military aid.[7]

This transition gave Khartoum considerable incentive to undermine southern autonomy and, before long, the Addis Ababa agreement wasn't worth the paper it was printed on. In 1983 the Nimieri government imposed Islamic law over the entire country. That same year the Sudan People's Liberation Army (SPLA) was founded, and the war that drags on today was launched. The rebels were motivated to attack foreign oil companies as assets of the Khartoum regime. Consequently, the government was motivated to pursue a scorched-earth policy of ethnically cleansing anyone who lived anywhere close to the oilfields.[8]

In 1989, just as negotiations for a new autonomy accord were about to begin, an Islamic revolution headed by General Omar el-Bashir swept into power. Even stricter Islamic law was imposed. The National Islamic Front (NIF) banned all other political parties, along with trade unions, and tightened restrictions on the press and on women's rights. More than 78,000 people were purged from the government and reports of torture in the prison system became commonplace. If that wasn't bad enough, the government had a habit of drafting children into the military, as well as selling southern prisoners into slavery.[9]

Black slaves from southern Sudan have been used as agricultural workers as well as domestic servants and concubines. They have also been sold to other Islamic countries, including Saudi Arabia. In the last six years alone Christian organizations have bought the freedom of some 40,000 southern slaves,[10] though critics argue that foreign money has simply inflated the cost of redeeming slaves; Arab abolitionists had been quietly doing the same work for years.[11] Despite these efforts, an estimated 100,000 Sudanese remain in bondage.[12]

But in a classic validation of the argument that human rights issues are used selectively (or ignored) based on other interests, none of these policies were enough to get the U.S. to switch sides once again and begin supporting the southern rebels. Instead that shift occurred only after the Bashir regime supported Iraq in the Gulf War—based on widespread sympathy towards Baghdad by his Islamic power base.[13] Relations soured even further with reports of paramilitary Islamist organizations based in Khartoum. Sanctions were imposed in 1995 after an assassination attempt on Egyptian president Hosni Mubarak.[14] The assailants fled to Sudan; the government claims they were expelled, although it's not clear to where.[15]

Osama bin Laden arrived in Khartoum in 1992, offered sanctuary after being expelled from his native Saudi Arabia for opposing the regime (and their embrace of U.S. military bases). He was attracted by the reputation of Hassan al-Turabi, chief ideologist for the NIF, and reputed brains of the Bashir regime. Turabi reportedly regarded bin Laden as "an eager but not particularly bright student."[16] But bin Laden's wealth allowed him to build up an extensive network of other Islamist veterans of the Afghan war, many of whom were attracted to the Sudanese revolution. Bin Laden's al-Qaida organization had been blamed for bombings against U.S. targets back in Saudi Arabia (see chapter 11). Under pressure from the Saudis and the U.S., Sudanese authorities expelled Osama bin Laden and 300 of his followers in 1996, after which he returned to Afghanistan (see chapter 13).[17]

When U.S. embassies in Kenya and Tanzania were destroyed by bombs in August 1998, bin Laden's group was accused of sponsoring the attacks. At this point, according to

the London *Observer*, authorities in Khartoum had been trying in vain for several years to share their extensive dossiers
on bin Laden with Western intelligence agencies.[18] Because
the U.S. and its African allies were providing cash and
weaponry to the SPLA, contacts with Sudanese government
agencies were forbidden. Even after the embassy bombings,
when Sudan arrested two bin Laden operatives and offered to
extradite them, the U.S. refused to cooperate. Instead, in
August 1998, we bombed Khartoum with 75 cruise missiles.[19]

The U.S. claimed, erroneously, that the target of our
cruise missiles was a factory owned by Osama bin Laden, used
in the production of chemical weapons. In fact, bin Laden
had long since sold the factory, which was then the sole supplier of needed pharmaceutical products to one of the poorest nations on earth.[20] Washington later quietly admitted
this when it agreed to settle a U.S. lawsuit filed by the factory's owner.[21] But there is no telling how many died—perhaps
tens of thousands—because medicines to treat malaria,
tuberculosis, diabetes and other diseases were no longer
available because of the bombing and the sanctions.[22]

Even Sudanese who opposed the NIF were outraged.
One dissident pointed out that it simply gave the regime "a
big shot in the arm." And as for bin Laden, "the Americans
have suddenly created a Muslim hero out of him, whereas last
week he was considered a fanatic nut," said an anti-funda-
mentalist Muslim.[23]

And of course the war continued to drag on, fueled, just
like the last one, by foreign backing. By then the government
was generating considerable revenue from oil production,
allowing it to procure more advanced weaponry.[24] Likewise
the SPLA has been receiving aid, with U.S. backing, from
nearby Eritrea, Uganda and Ethiopia. In response Khartoum
has armed and trained separatist militias in each of those

countries; these groups stage raids on the SPLA as well as on their home governments.[25]

The SPLA has also had a poor human rights record. Like the government, they have been accused of child conscription, drafting boys as young as eleven into military service. The group is dominated by the largest ethnic group, the Dinka, and other southern ethnic groups have complained of oppression by the Dinkas as well as by the northern Islamists. *The Economist* charged that the SPLA "has been little more than an armed group of Dinkas… killing, looting and raping." Its indifference, even animosity towards the people it was supposed to be "liberating" was all too clear.[26]

Human rights organizations have complained that U.S. policies have helped to prolong the Sudanese war. Roger Winter of the U.S. Committee on Refugees argues that "U.S. policy, since about 1991 or 1992, has been driven exclusively by the issue of international terrorism," rather than adopting a "solution-oriented" approach.[27] Former President Jimmy Carter stated in 1999 that "the people in Sudan want to resolve the conflict. The biggest obstacle is U.S. government policy. The U.S. is committed to overthrowing the government in Khartoum. Any sort of peace effort is aborted, basically by the policies of the United States. Instead of working for peace in Sudan, the U.S. government has basically promoted a continuation of the war."[28]

That same year, SPLA leader John Garang met with Secretary of State Madeleine Albright, who offered him food supplies if he would reject a peace plan sponsored jointly by Egypt and Libya. Six of the seven rebel groups had agreed to the plan; only the SPLA rejected it. The U.S. position was that talks should be between the north and the south only, rather than a multilateral conference with neighboring countries who were also parties to the conflict. But this fuelled suspicion that the U.S. was really only interested in an SPLA victory.[29] Funneling all famine relief through the SPLA enhanced its power, as well as freeing up more cash for weapons purchases. But international relief agencies complained that they were being prevented from bringing in food aid of their own to assist starving civilians in the south. More than 70,000 Sudanese died in the famine of the late 90s.[30]

Meanwhile, the British relief group Christian Aid has accused foreign oil companies of complicity in government atrocities, including depopulation of villages. The companies receive government protection and in turn provide the use of their airstrips and roads to government forces. These companies include Talisman Energy of Canada, Lundin Oil of Sweden, and the Chinese government's China National Petroleum Corporation.[31] U.S. sanctions have prevented any American companies from investing in Sudan since Chevron left in the late 80s, as the war heated up. But recent discoveries indicate that there may be much more oil in Sudan than previously believed—perhaps nearly enough to rival Saudi Arabia.[32]

For that reason, the Bush Administration has been pursuing a dual-track policy in Sudan. In order to get U.S. companies back in the game, one of three things would need to happen: either the SPLA would succeed in overthrowing the NIF; or the two factions could join in a coalition mediated by the U.S.; or the U.S. could simply switch sides again and lift sanctions on Khartoum. The first is unlikely due to the government's increasing revenues, but Washington continues to provide millions of dollars of aid to the rebels annually, and has encouraged new offensives.[33]

A mediated solution seems equally elusive given the bitterness of the civil war, but exhaustion has again set in and all sides can see that there is money to be made. The Bush Administration is being pulled both ways. Their allies in the evangelical movement support the Christian rebels in the south against the Islamic government, and have sponsored the Sudan Peace Act, legislation designed to prevent oil companies working in Sudan from trading in the U.S. Christian Aid has made similar calls. But the Muslim-Christian aspect of the conflict can be overstated; animists and Muslims combined outnumber the Christians in the south.[34] Moreover, the SPLA has displaced thousands of refugees of all religions in its territorial pursuits, many of whom have fled to the north.[35]

Meanwhile, the oil companies are looking for a settle-ment. As Vice President Dick Cheney, a former CEO of Halliburton, put it, "the good Lord didn't see fit to put oil and gas only where there are democratically elected regimes friend-ly to the United States."[36] So the administration appointed former Senator John Danforth, an Episcopalian minister, to negotiate a settlement, again derailing regionally sponsored efforts. The plan called for Danforth to visit Sudan in November 2001 and decide by the middle of 2002 on whether a negotiated settlement was possible. In the meantime, the U.S. would continue to fund the SPLA's operations.[37]

But the Bashir regime had long been under pressure from Egypt and Saudi Arabia to work for better relations with the U.S. Khartoum had purged al-Turabi from the gov-ernment, placing him under house arrest. The NIF had been willing to sign on to negotiations for several years, lacking only Garang to negotiate with.[38] When the SPLA agreed to participate in the Danforth effort, the Bashir government did as well, on September 10, 2001.[39]

The next day changed the dynamic completely. Khartoum took advantage of the 9/11 attacks to move closer to Washington. The NIF made arrests of several Islamic activists, again offered to share their intelligence files, and indicated that Sudanese airfields may be available for the war on terrorism.[40] For its part, the U.S. quietly agreed to Egypt's request that UN sanctions against Sudan be lifted; the U.S. abstained from the vote.[41] The administration also persuaded its congressional allies to hold off on the new sanctions in the Sudan Peace Act. But just in case, the U.S. has also extended its own existing sanctions for one more year, pending Danforth's recommendations. A cease-fire was declared in January 2002, but collapsed in February.[42] Another cease-fire was arranged in April, with international monitors, but persistent reports of fighting around the oil fields continue.[43] In July a "breakthrough" was announced for a framework on future peace talks;[44] in September the talks were "suspended" until the SPLA ceased military operations.[45] Throughout, the U.S. has continued to back the rebels with both overt and covert funding.[46]

And so the war in the Sudan continues. Nearly two million have been killed in the last round alone (since 1983), including one out of every five residents of the south. There are four million refugees displaced internally, with another half million in neighboring countries.[47] Eventually some sort of deal will be cut, but in the meantime, the chessboard is full of pawns. The people of the Sudan may not all comprehend the geostrategic reasons for their continued suffering, but they understand the bottom line. As one of them told a journalist after helicopter gunships drove him from his village, "We know that somebody comes from another country and takes our oil."[48]

Lately the geostrategic importance of oil has led the U.S. to reconsider its relationship with yet another pariah state: Libya.

CHAPTER FIVE

Libya

Whose Side Are You On?

Over previous decades, Libya has been one of Washington's most hated adversaries, accused of everything from stalking President Reagan to blowing up passenger jets. Under its eccentric leader, Col. Muamar Qadaffy,[1] Libya has been subject to U.S. airstrikes and years of sanctions, and is still regarded as a pariah regime. But the actual nature of the U.S. relationship with Libya is considerably more complex.

Prior to the coup that brought Qadaffy to power in 1969, Libya had been the playground of the U.S. and major European powers. The Libyans had endured a particularly brutal occupation by Italy from 1912 through 1943.[2] Thirty years of colonization by Italy killed approximately 250,000 (one quarter of the population), and turned another quarter million into refugees. The Libyan population was subject to concentration camps, poisonous gas attacks, aerial bombardment of civilian targets and widespread executions.[3]

The Allies liberated the country from Italian occupation during World War II, but soon afterwards the U.S., working behind the scenes, advanced a plan to have Libya jointly controlled until 1959 by France, Britain… and Italy. This was necessary to scuttle a Soviet plan which called for immediate independence and no foreign military presence, because both the U.S. and Britain wished to establish bases on Libyan territory. But the local reaction to any continued Italian presence was not favorable; riots and demonstrations broke out in the streets of Tripoli. The plan was narrowly defeated in the UN, with decisive votes coming from, as the Italian foreign minister sniffed, "delegations representing colored people and small nations."[4]

At this point the new U.S. fallback policy was summarized in a classified document: "The U.S. should support strongly the establishment of a united Libya which would achieve independence in some form at a definite date in the near future *but which would in effect be so tied to the United Kingdom as to assure enjoyment of adequate strategic rights* to the UK and, therefore, also to the United States" (emphasis added).[5] In other words, following World War II, just at the time the U.S. was projecting its image as a crusader for democracy, it was quietly but clearly moving to quash the independence of even a small country like Libya, seeking instead to preserve the reality if not the trappings of colonial control.

To this end, the U.S. supported Britain's installation of a puppet monarch, King Idris, through gerrymandering, arrests of opponents and other repressive measures. The occupying powers controlled the process of adopting the constitution, which gave Idris extraordinary powers. One-third of the legislative seats were appointed by the British client "King" Idris, another third by a key French ally, and the final third by a friend of the U.S., the Mufti of Tripolitania. The U.S., Britain and France then made any future humanitarian aid to the war-ravaged and poverty-stricken nation contingent on agreement to allow foreign military bases on Libyan soil. Not surprisingly, this demand was granted.[6]

In 1959 oil was discovered in Libya. The Libyan oilfields proved to be extraordinarily productive, and U.S. companies were soon making considerable profits from operations there. But this, along with resurgent Arab nationalism following the conflicts with Israel in 1956 and 1967, fueled rising resentment against the client monarchy. In the eyes of many observers, the demise of the Idris regime was just a matter of time. Nevertheless, the circumstances under which Qadaffy seized and consolidated power are somewhat unusual.

Some have claimed that the U.S. actively assisted Qadaffy's coup, hoping to replace a British client with one of our own.[7] Others argue that the U.S. was simply determined to cut its losses with the unpopular rule of the aging monarch, and chose to look the other way when the coup came. Under this view, the future of the oil business was deemed more important than maintenance of the military bases on the Mediterranean Sea, which Qadaffy soon shot down. As one government document put it shortly after the coup: "The return to our balance of payments and the security of U.S. investments in oil are considered our primary interests. We seek to retain our military facilities but not at the expense of threatening our economic return."[8]

Either way, when the weak but pro-Western King was overthrown by a junta of young nationalist officers, the U.S. did nothing to stop it. While Idris was abroad enjoying the spas of Europe, the officers invited the palace guard to a party and simply arrested them all in a bloodless coup. The leader, 28-year-old Muamar Qadaffy, inspired by the pan-Arabian rhetoric of Egyptian leader Nasser, proclaimed a military dictatorship based on "socialism, unity and freedom." The parliament was dissolved and relations with Nasser and other anti-Western regimes grew friendlier, while militant anti-Israeli rhetoric was turned up.[9]

The U.S. has invaded nations on far less provocation, and with far less oil wealth at stake. It's true that the U.S. Ambassador sent word back to Washington that while

Qadaffy was a radical nationalist, he was also dependably anti-Soviet. But while the Colonel did sometimes criticize the USSR and its allies, he also began, almost immediately, to seek East Bloc arms and markets for Libyan oil. Still, neither the U.S. nor Britain showed any interest in helping Idris regain his throne. The U.S., within a matter of days, recognized the Qadaffy regime. And not only did the U.S. warn Qadaffy of several coup plots against him, but the CIA actively assisted in preventing the plotters from returning to Libya.[10]

If the U.S. government's main concern was oil investments, it had a strange way of showing it. A consortium of oil companies issued an analysis of the Libyan situation shortly after the coup that correctly predicted that "once the regime is stable it will launch a frontal attack on the oil industry." Qadaffy proceeded cautiously at first, mindful of what had happened to other regimes that challenged Western economic power. What followed was, as journalist Jack Anderson described it, "a succession of testing probes, of retractable bluffs, of muted confrontations, of small penetrations followed by halts to assess reaction, resuming only when no counterattack surfaced, becoming truly bold only in the eighth month of the campaign after a dozen tests had shown that there *never would be* a counterattack" (emphasis in original).[11]

Young Qadaffy waged a deft war of attrition against the combined power of the largest multinational oil companies, skillfully playing one off against the others, breaking their heretofore united front against producer nations. The oil companies resisted, but the Nixon Administration reacted throughout with uncharacteristic passivity. Eventually, in early 1971, the companies caved in, giving Qadaffy much higher royalty rates than any other oil-exporting country.

And just as predictably, the other producer nations soon demanded the same kind of deal. This time the battle against the oil companies was led by Nixon and Kissinger's most trusted regional ally, the Shah of Iran.[12]

Once again the oil company executives asked for U.S. government backing for their negotiating position. This was agreed to, and then suddenly withdrawn on the eve of negotiations. Without the implicit threat of U.S. intervention to back them up, the companies once again folded their hands and acceded to the demands of the producer countries, represented by a cartel known as the Organization of Petroleum Exporting Countries, or OPEC. What happened after this was also predicted by oil company planning documents: Qadaffy soon demanded an even bigger slice of the pie, and another round of fruitless negotiations took place, followed by higher royalty rates for Libya, and then for the rest of OPEC.[13]

All of this has the whiff of Br'er Rabbit being tossed into the briar patch. The net result of all these bizarre maneuverings was to end forever the world where the price of oil was fixed at around a dollar a barrel for the foreseeable future. By the time of the oil shock of 1973, prices rose to an unprecedented $12 per barrel, even though production costs remained the same. The companies passed these prices along to consumers and began enjoying unheard of levels of profitability. Soon, they were cheerfully collaborating with OPEC behind the scenes in setting production and pricing levels. Meanwhile the Shah and other U.S. allies in the Persian Gulf were awash in oil revenues, which they then used to purchase unheard of amounts of U.S.-made weaponry, as well as stocks, bonds and other investments in the West.

Some have charged that this was Nixon and Kissinger's

true aim in the first place, as they needed a way to finance a military buildup in the Gulf while still engaged in Indochina.[14] Saudi oil minister Sheikh Yamani has stated, "I am 100 percent sure that the Americans were behind the increase in the price of oil."[15] Wittingly or not, by design or accident, Muamar Qadaffy was the main instrument of that transformation. Whether he was just a dependably militant leader who could be relied on to pursue higher prices, or whether there was something more collusive at work is not known.

But there are other anomalies in the picture of Qadaffy as the nemesis of the West. In 1975 he bought a 10% share of Fiat, the Italian automaker which was also a major defense contractor. This made the government of Libya the single largest shareholder besides the founding family, and also gave it several seats on the board of directors.[16] British Aerospace is another NATO contractor with interests in Libya.[17] During the 1980s Qadaffy's armed forces received both weapons and training from two well-connected CIA officers, Ed Wilson and Frank Terpil. The CIA later prosecuted the two as rogue elements (Terpil, still a fugitive, in absentia), but Wilson maintains to this day that their Libyan operations were officially sanctioned. There is, in fact, considerable evidence that the CIA was well aware of what their officers were doing in Libya, and that the Agency subsequently helped convict Wilson on false pretenses.[18]

But throughout the 80s Qadaffy came to be regarded more and more as America's public enemy number one, the man we loved to hate (this was at a time when both Saddam Hussein and Manuel Noriega were still valued allies). It's clear that Qadaffy could be as ruthless abroad as he was repressive at home; by no means is he without blood on his hands. He trains international guerrilla forces at a dozen camps throughout Libya, and has harbored notorious fugitives, including Carlos the Jackal and members of the Japanese Red Army. He has also assassinated opponents of his regime on foreign soil as well as at home.[19]

At the same time, the U.S. frequently exaggerated or falsified the extent of Libyan involvement with terrorist activities. Libya was blamed for attacks at the Rome and Vienna airports in 1985, but in testimony under oath, a Pentagon official conceded that evidence for that was "far less concrete" than for other terrorist operations. As with other such claims against Libya, there is much stronger evidence connecting the attacks to Syria.[20] Libya has also been accused of involvement with the massacre at the 1972 Olympics, a claim which Israeli intelligence has debunked.[21] And the claims of the Reagan administration that Qadaffy had sponsored hit squads to assassinate President Reagan were later admitted to be complete falsehoods.[22] On the other hand there is quite credible evidence that the U.S. sponsored several attempts to assassinate Qadaffy. One such attempt came close to success when U.S. warplanes bombed Tripoli in 1986. Numerous press accounts have shown that one of the aims of these air raids was to kill not only Qadaffy but also members of his family. In fact, his infant daughter was one of the casualties.[23]

U.S. warplanes based in the Mediterranean had frequently challenged Libya's claim to a 100-mile zone of sovereignty in the Gulf of Sidra. In August 1981, the U.S. shot down two Libyan jets defending what they regarded as their airspace. Other provocative actions took place in the years leading up to 1986, and in March of that year, U.S. aircraft carriers sank two Libyan coast guard vessels, killing all 72 sailors. U.S. officials were quoted as saying, "of course we're aching for a go at Qadaffy," and that if he "sticks his head up we'll clobber him; we're looking for an excuse." But the bombing raids of April 15, 1986, according to the U.S., were reprisals for Libyan involvement in the bombing of a Berlin discotheque ten days earlier.[24]

Again, earlier evidence pointed to Syrian involvement in the disco bombing. But if the Reagan Administration had proof of Libyan involvement within ten days, it's not at all clear why it took another fifteen years just to convict several Libyan nationals as accessories to the plot (a German woman was convicted of murder in November 2001). Even then, no convincing evidence was offered to prove the involvement of the government of Libya.[25] Still, none was needed in 1986. It was justification enough to say then that the U.S. had "suspicions" of Libyan involvement. The U.S. soon claimed to have had "intercepts" of Libyan radio transmissions prior to the Berlin bombing, though this later proved to have been a fabrication.[26]

Noam Chomsky has noted that the U.S. raids on Libya were "the first bombing in history scheduled for prime time TV, for the precise moment when the networks open their national news programs."[27] Though the U.S. claimed to be conducting surgical strikes against military targets, more than one hundred Libyan civilians were killed. And while the bombings were blatantly illegal under international law, the U.S. established a unique doctrine under which it claimed to be acting under "self-defense against future aggression."[28]

The U.S. also later claimed that, in revenge for these air raids, the government of Libya blew up Pan Am flight 103 over Lockerbie, Scotland two and half years later. However, just a few months before that tragedy, the U.S. military had shot down an Iranian passenger jet in the Persian Gulf. Early reports indicated that it was Iran and not Libya that was seeking revenge. Once again, evidence of Syrian involvement was circulating; indications were that the Syrian-backed terrorist Ahmed Jabril had gotten the contract from Iran. But in 1990, when Syria and Iran were needed to aid in the war against Iraq (which Libya opposed), U.S. investigators began to focus publicly on two Libyan intelligence agents for the Lockerbie bombing (see chapter 3).[29]

In 1992 the U.S. pressured the UN to place sanctions in order to pressure Libya into giving up the suspects for trial in Britain. Libya said it was willing to extradite the suspects for trial in an international court. Seven years later a compromise was reached under which the two Libyans were tried in the Netherlands. In early 2001, one of the Libyans was acquitted, while the sentence of the other, Ali Mohmed al-Magrahi, was confirmed on appeal. Magrahi was convicted on extremely slim evidence, as even the court admitted. The strongest evidence against him was that a shopkeeper in Malta identified him as the person who had bought some clothing supposed to have been in the bomb-laden suitcase, a scrap of which was later found among the wreckage in Scotland. The shopkeeper, however, had previously identified several others as having bought the clothing in 1986, changing his mind years later after Magrahi's photo had been widely publicized.[30] During the trial the U.S. government gagged a CIA officer and prevented him from testifying that, as he put it, he could "identify the men behind the attack," who would be found in Damascus and not "anywhere in Libya."[31]

In August 2002, after the notorious terrorist Abu Nidal was killed (or killed himself) in Baghdad, one of his former associates came forward to claim that the Abu Nidal organization was responsible for the Flight 103 bombing. Atef Abu Bakr said that Nidal had told him that "reports which link the Lockerbie act to others are false reports. We are behind what happened." A British member of Parliament who has long been skeptical of the Libyan theory called for a new investigation, so far in vain.[32]

Nevertheless, the people of Libya lived under international sanctions for seven years in order to pursue this verdict. The UN lifted sanctions after Qadaffy surrendered the suspects in 1999, while the U.S. still imposes its own sanctions dating to 1982.[33] Meanwhile Qadaffy himself has been quietly refurbishing his image, forging more economic links with Italian businesses (and even more quietly, with U.S. oil executives).[34] He quickly condemned the 9/11 attacks as "horrifying and destructive" and has expelled some suspected terrorists from Libyan territory.[35] Qadaffy has interceded with Muslim rebels in the Philippines to secure the release of Western hostages, and convinced the Taliban to release imprisoned Christian aid workers after the fall of Kabul in late 2001.[36]

Moreover, the Libyan leader was the first to pursue an international criminal complaint against Osama bin Laden after a Muslim group linked to al-Qaida was implicated in an assassination attempt against Qadaffy. This organization, the Libyan Islamic Fighting Group (LIFG) is listed by the U.S. government as a terrorist organization. Interestingly, the LIFG, according to a British intelligence officer named David Shayler, received funding from MI6 (Britain's CIA) for the assassination plot.[37] This came at a time when our onetime ally bin Laden had supposedly turned against us, but was still sending Islamic militant forces to fight our common enemies in the Bosnia and Kosovo wars.[38]

In October 2002 the British government issued a gag order to prevent further press stories on Shayler, who offered evidence concerning his allegations of payoffs to the al-Qaida-linked group.[39] By this time the British Foreign Office was floating trial balloons on Qadaffy as a "potential ally" in the war on terrorism, yet another in a series of dizzying about-faces.[40]

So when it comes to President Bush's insistence that the nations of the world are either with us or the terrorists, it remains to be seen which side Libya is on (or how many). But if the people of Libya, our official enemy, have suffered considerably from our government's machinations, some of our friends are even worse off, as the sad story of Lebanon illustrates.

Part II

ALLIED STATES

CHAPTER SIX

Lebanon

Like Paris with Craters

Once upon a time, the Lebanese capital of Beirut was known as "the Paris of the Middle East." It was a multicultural society, a popular tourist destination, and an intellectual and cultural crossroads. Today Beirut is a synonym for a disaster area. What happened is a textbook example of ostensible sovereignty trampled by self-interested neighbors, and another painfully clear window on the forces driving U.S. foreign policy.

Lebanon covers 4000 square miles, about as much as the landmass of Hawaii. During the Ottoman Empire, the Autonomous Province of Lebanon was roughly half that size. When the empire was carved up by the British and French following World War I, France took control of "Greater Lebanon"—though not without some resistance from the locals. During World War II, the French managed to unite the entire country against them by arresting the elected prime minister and his cabinet. Pressure from Britain and the U.S. led to Lebanese independence in late 1946.[1]

An earlier constitution, during French rule, had carefully divided the government among the dominant religious factions: the Maronite Christians and the Sunni and Shi'ite Muslims. An unwritten agreement established that the president would be a Maronite, the prime minister a Sunni, and the speaker of the parliament a Shi'ite. This rather neatly balanced off the major power groups while effectively disenfranchising minorities like the Orthodox Christians or the Druze Muslims. It also gave the Maronites more power than their population share might otherwise allow. U.S. policy has consistently opposed a more democratic arrangement because of Muslim opposition to our perceived "interests" in the region.[2]

From the beginning, the emerging Zionist movement in British-occupied Palestine looked for allies among the Maronite Christians of Lebanon. Once ensconced as the state of Israel, its leaders looked to cement ties with the Maronites based on common foes: first the Islamic parties, then Egyptian President Nasser and his pan-Arab movement, and finally the Palestinian diaspora. The problem with this strategy is that the Maronites had a limited political base to begin with; not even all of Lebanon's Christians supported them. As U.S. policy became increasingly synchronized with that of Israel, we made the same mistakes.[3]

In 1957, the U.S. provided covert election funding to the Lebanese president Camille Chamoun, a Maronite who had been elected five years earlier with the help of the CIA.[4] The rigged parliamentary elections resulted in a landslide win for Chamoun's party, with the opposition calling foul. Matters did not improve when he tried to use his new majority to amend the constitution in order to allow himself a new six-year term. Chamoun was popular with the Eisenhower administration for the same reason he outraged Arab nationalists: he had abrogated the country's traditional neutrality in foreign affairs by tilting towards the U.S. In gratitude for U.S. funding of his political career, Chamoun had endorsed the Eisenhower Doctrine, under which the U.S. claimed the right of unilateral intervention in the Middle East. Unsurprisingly, this didn't go over all that well with the

Lebanese public.[5]

Like the ethnic apportionment of the government, that policy of strictly avoiding foreign entanglements had helped keep Lebanon at peace since 1943. With both policies out of balance, that peace began to evaporate in 1958. Street demonstrations escalated into clashes with police and sporadic bombings. The assassination of an anti-government journalist provided the spark for armed insurrection, and a brief civil war ensued.[6] When a coup ousted a pro-Western regime in nearby Iraq, Chamoun requested that Eisenhower send in the Marines on his behalf. By that time he had already agreed not to seek a second term; he was simply worried about getting to the end of his first.[7]

The 20,000-strong contingent of Marines, accompanied by seventy warships, outnumbered all of Lebanon's armed forces. They left four months later with just one casualty (shot by a sniper) and without having fired a shot. The inactivity of the Lebanese defense forces was insured by a casual threat of the use of nuclear weapons.[8] The Lebanese were sullen and resentful at the U.S. presence, but the civil war petered out after the Chamber of Deputies chose Chamoun's successor, who took a more neutralist stance. The crisis was over, but the underlying ill will lingered on.

The contradictions papered over by Lebanon's ethnic balance of power were permanently knocked off kilter by the Six Day War of 1967. While Lebanon did not take part in the war launched by Israel (see chapter 9), the nearby Golan Heights were wrested from Syrian control. Meanwhile Palestinian refugees began to spill across the border; this flood increased in 1970 and 1971 when the Palestinian Liberation Organization (PLO) was ejected from Jordan, making a new home in southern Lebanon (see chapter 7).

Israel, backed by the U.S., was making raids across the frontier on Palestinian positions, and Syria was repositioning its forces in search of revenge.[9]

This time it was the Christians who were complaining that the Muslim parties had violated the neutrality pact, by siding with the PLO. Tensions rose between Palestinians and Israeli-backed Maronite militias, as arms flooded into the country. When full-scale civil war erupted in 1975, it would be another fifteen years before any sort of peace was restored; by that time, over 150,000 Lebanese citizens would lie dead.[10]

Israel, which had been bombing the border areas for several years, provided the Maronites with tanks and gunboats as well as air cover for attacks on PLO encampments.[11] The Phalange, a neo-fascist Maronite militia armed by Tel Aviv, destroyed Karantina, a largely Muslim neighborhood of Beirut, killing over a thousand civilians. In retaliation, PLO forces joined Muslim militias in attacking the Christian village of Damour, with three to four hundred killed and another thousand displaced.[12] Beirut was divided into Christian and Muslim sectors along the so-called "Green Line," and the central government virtually broke down.

The Lebanese civil war functioned as a proxy version of the Arab-Israeli conflict, or in Washington's eyes, of the Cold War. Perhaps for that reason, Secretary of State Henry Kissinger winked at Syria's 1976 invasion of Lebanon[13] which rescued the Maronites from defeat by the Palestinians (Syria's Hafez al-Assad mistrusted PLO chief Arafat and supported rival Palestinian factions). Operating on the principle that "the enemy of my enemy is my friend," U.S. policy wanted Palestinian resistance to its Israeli ally ended, even if Syria was more of a Soviet client than the PLO was (see chapter 3). But Assad soon turned around and started shelling the Maronites as well, and 25 years later there are still 40,000 Syrian troops in Lebanon.[14]

In 1978, the Israelis invaded Lebanon as well. Since the 1950s Israel had developed plans to break Lebanon apart and set up a client regime.[15] As Moshe Dayan put it, "the Israeli Army will enter Lebanon, will occupy the necessary territory, and will create a Christian regime which will ally itself with Israel. The territory from the Litani [River] southward will be totally annexed to Israel and everything will be all right."[16] This is more or less what happened, first in 1978, and then again, more forcefully, in 1982. But everything was not all right.

Incursions into Lebanon, by both the Israeli army and air force, were hardly unknown before 1978. But Prime Minister Menachem Begin was looking for a pretext for a full-fledged invasion; knowing this, the PLO largely refrained from responding to cross-border shelling.[17] When in March 1978, an Israeli bus was hijacked, even though the attackers had not come from Lebanese territory, it was the people of southern Lebanon who would pay the price. By the time UN "peacekeeping" forces arrived to replace the Israeli troops, some 2000 Lebanese civilians were killed and a quarter million rendered homeless.[18]

As the *Washington Post* reported, the 1978 invasion left "a broad path of death and destruction" with "hardly a town…left undamaged. Some have been all but flattened by air strikes and artillery shells."[19] Israeli bombers plunged all the way to the suburbs of Beirut, where PLO offices were located, "leveling restaurants, bakeries, service stations and houses for five hundred yards."[20] One Israeli general conceded that "we struck at the civilian population consciously, because they deserved it... [we] purposely attacked civilian targets even when Israeli settlements had not been struck."[21]

The first Israeli invasion was halted only when President Jimmy Carter, fearing a wider war with Syria, threatened to cut off arms and aid to Tel Aviv. But it was not lost on the survivors that U.S. arms and aid had made the destruction possible in the first place. Israel withdrew, while leaving a broad swath of southern Lebanon occupied by its proxy forces, the South Lebanon Army, headed by Major Saad Haddad, and staffed mainly by relatively well-paid mercenaries.[22]

Over the next four years, a tense three-way stalemate held between the Phalangists, the Muslim alliance (reinforced by the PLO), and the Syrian forces (along with whoever their current allies happened to be). Lebanon was informally carved up into nine different zones of influence, with the central government asserting authority in name only.[23] Given somewhat lower levels of violence, reconstruction began in parts of Beirut, and the status quo might have held if not for Israel's long-term plans to totally demolish the PLO. As Defense Minister Ariel Sharon (now Prime Minister) put it on the eve of the 1982 invasion, the intent was that "they will not be able to rebuild their military and political base." He also hoped that "a legitimate regime emerges in Lebanon, not a puppet government; that it signs a peace treaty with Israel; and that it becomes part of the free world."[24]

The "legitimate" government that Israel wanted most would be one headed by Bashir Gemayal, leader of the Phalange, the most extreme and violent of the Maronite factions. All of this sounded just fine to the U.S. government, or at least to those making the decisions: Secretary of State

Alexander Haig and President Ronald Reagan (others in the State Department warned against green-lighting Israel's invasion plans).[25] But cooler heads did not prevail, and when on June 3 a former Israeli ambassador was killed in London— not, of course, by any Lebanese—it was time once again for Lebanon to pay the price.[26] By this time Israel had signed the Camp David Accords establishing a cold peace with Egypt, freeing up the armed forces for redeployment to the north.

Estimates of civilian casualties from Israel's 1982 invasion range from 17,000 to 23,000 killed.[27] Hospitals were flooded with victims, but the hospitals too were destroyed, along with the headquarters of the Red Cross.[28] After pushing the Palestinians all the way to Beirut, the Israeli Army, wary of a ground assault for fear of losing public support back home, simply shelled the city for two and half months. In August, Israel began a daylong saturation bombing campaign of the city that has been compared to the firebombing of Dresden.[29] Once again, the Lebanese people were being bombarded with shells marked "made in the USA."

And once again, it was the USA that had to tell its local client that enough was enough. Yassir Arafat realized that the PLO could no longer remain in Beirut, and appealed to Washington to assist with an evacuation. The U.S., along with France and Italy, sent troops to move PLO forces out of Lebanon to new headquarters in Tunisia, then stayed on to help "maintain order."[30] The definition of order turned out to be the election of Gemayal, guaranteed by delegates from Israeli-occupied territory and copious amounts of bribe money.[31] It was, of course, a recipe for disaster, and the U.S. Marines were in the thick of it. Unlike their compatriots 26 years earlier, they did not leave without firing shots, nor without significant casualties.

On September 14, 1982, President-elect Gemayal was assassinated by a massive bomb at Phalangist party headquarters (he was soon succeeded by his brother Amin).[32] In response, the Israeli Defense Forces surrounded the Palestinian refugee camps at Sabra and Shatilla, and, under the direction of General Sharon, allowed the Phalange to march in for a two and a half day orgy of revenge killings. As the PLO fighters had already left the country, the victims, some two thousand of them, were mainly old men, women and children.[33] Eyewitnesses, including journalist Robert Fisk, report many babies killed as well (because, as one Christian militiaman explained, "they grow up into terrorists").[34] This was one of the single largest acts of terrorism in the entire bloody history of the Arab-Israeli conflict.

In support of the Amin Gemayal regime, U.S. warships off the coast of Beirut lobbed Volkswagen-sized shells into the surrounding hillsides, home to the increasingly enraged Muslim communities.[35] Not surprisingly, there was retaliation from the Lebanese side. The U.S. embassy was bombed twice, and the Marine barracks at the airport were completely destroyed by a car bomb, with 241 U.S. soldiers killed. Not long after, the U.S. decided it would be best to "redeploy" its forces far away from the Lebanese civil war.[36]

That war continued until 1990, however, with U.S. taxpayers indirectly funding the anti-Muslim forces through the multi-billion dollar annual subsidy to Israel. But the U.S. had not fired its final shot. That came in March of 1985, when CIA Director William Casey, seeking revenge for the bombing of the Marine barracks, sponsored a car bombing in downtown Beirut. According to journalist Bob Woodward, the intended target was Sheikh Fadlallah, whom the CIA believed to be responsible for the deaths of the U.S. soldiers.

But the Sheikh escaped unhurt. 85 innocent civilians killed by the massive blast were not so lucky, nor were the more than 200 injured.[37] Coincidentally or not, U.S. citizens continued to be taken hostage in Beirut throughout the 1980s.

The Israelis stayed on long after the civil war had ended, occupying southern Lebanon along with their proxy forces, battling interminably with Hezbollah guerillas until finally withdrawing in early 2000.[38] During the 22-year occupation, Israeli forces staged countless more small invasions and air raids, frequently targeting civilians, as when the UN base at Qana was destroyed in 1996. Over 100 civilians who had taken refuge there were killed.[39]

The people of Lebanon endured all these outrages as Washington continued to fund the perpetrators, and regularly worked to suppress condemnation of them at the UN. They watched as the U.S. punished Iraq for violating UN resolutions condemning its invasion of Kuwait, while UN resolution 425, calling on Israel to withdraw from Lebanon, was ignored.[40] Meanwhile, the Syrians remain in Lebanon, contrary to UN Resolution 520,[41] but as their help may yet be needed in our new war[42] (as it was against Iraq), that continues to be overlooked. As for the Lebanese, if they want to be protected from more powerful neighbors, they might do well to consider the example of Jordan.

CHAPTER SEVEN

Jordan

King of the Tightrope Artists

The history of U.S. intervention in Jordan is in large part the history of our relationship with the late King Hussein, who reigned from 1953 through 1999. The King started receiving suitcases of cash from the CIA in 1957 in exchange for his gossip and his cooperation.[1] The arrangement was leaked in 1977;[2] presumably the payments were simply wired to a Swiss bank thenceforth. Hussein was widely regarded as a feisty and heroic figure in the U.S. media, and an autocratic puppet in the Arab world.[3]

Hussein inherited the throne as a teenager after his grandfather, King Abdullah, was assassinated and his father was judged mentally incompetent. The royal family were not native to the Jordan River area; they came from the Arabian Peninsula. But the British had already installed the House of Sa'ud as their client regime there (see chapter 11), so the Hashemite dynasty were given Jordan as a consolation prize. Hussein's cousin Faisal was made King of Iraq until the Iraqis tossed him out in 1958 (see chapter 2).[4]

King Hussein might well have been overthrown himself that same year, but U.S. and British troops came to his rescue. Arab nationalism was on the rise, and the King was held in contempt as a decadent young playboy ruling over an impoverished country. He had already put down widespread rioting in 1955, and the CIA routinely warned him of coup and assassination plots. The Iraqi revolution of 1958—in which forces loyal to the pan-Arab nationalism of Egypt's president Nasser overthrew the monarchy—was greatly disturbing to the Western powers. President Eisenhower called the Iraqi revolution "the gravest threat since the Korean War."[5] Hussein was instructed to publicly proclaim his intention to march into Baghdad and reclaim the country for the Hashemite royal family. In reality, it was all he could do to hang onto his own throne.[6]

Two days after the anti-Western coup in Iraq, 6000 British paratroopers arrived in Jordan, while 20,000 U.S. Marines landed in neighboring Lebanon, another shaky client regime.[7] While Western military might kept the friendly governments in power, it did not end the grievances of the populations. King Hussein continued his autocratic rule, clamping down on the press, torturing opponents,[8] and dismissing 55 governments during his 46 years in power.[9] The majority of his subjects were Palestinians, some 800,000 of whom had fled their homelands after the creation of Israel in 1948.

Another 400,000 Palestinian refugees would arrive after the Six Day War in June 1967.[10] Hussein, as usual, played an ambiguous role, trying to balance the demands of his Western allies with the potential of a popular uprising against him. Like his grandfather before him, Hussein had always kept secret contacts and understandings with Israel. These were not always so secret, leading to considerable popular indignation in Jordan. King Abdullah had covertly assented to the founding of the Jewish state in the first place, and was preparing to recognize Israel when killed by a Palestinian nationalist.[11]

In early 1967, the Israeli army rolled across the border and ejected 5,000 Palestinians from their homes in the border town of Samu, which they then demolished. One U.S. diplomat ridiculed as a "fake claim" the Israeli justification that they were responding to attacks from Jordanian soil, saying, "all circumstances point to a carefully planned Israeli provocation."[12] More than 200 soldiers and civilians were killed. Jordanians were outraged that their king had done so little to protect them; he responded by cracking down on the Palestinians, jailing many of their leaders.

But Hussein also realized he could not survive without mollifying Arab anger, and so he traveled to Cairo to strike up a military alliance with Egypt and Syria. This balancing act might have worked if Israel had not been planning to launch a war against both those nations. In early June 1967, the CIA warned Hussein that the war was about to begin, that the Israelis were bound to win and that Jordan should stay out of it. If Hussein had to launch a token effort in keeping with his alliance, that would be understood, and Israel would pretty much leave him alone.[13]

Jordan's state-run radio had made Israel's job that much easier by taunting Egyptian President Nasser for "hiding behind" UN peacekeeping troops in the Sinai desert. Nasser asked the UN troops to withdraw, shortly before his air force was wiped out by the Israeli surprise attack. In keeping with his understanding with the CIA, the King of Jordan then launched pinprick attacks against the Israelis, whereupon his entire air force was also wiped out. That same day, he lost half his kingdom. The Israeli army occupied the entire West Bank, including the Jordanian-controlled Arab neighborhoods of East Jerusalem. That occupation continues to this day.[14]

The resulting influx of refugees made Palestinians 65% of the population in what was left of Jordan.[15] Anxious to retaliate, they launched regular attacks into the occupied territories, followed by predictable Israeli counterattacks. All of this made the King's balancing act even harder to carry off. The refugee camps were fertile recruiting ground for the Palestinian Liberation Organization (PLO) and other guerrilla groups, known collectively as the *fedayeen*. Hussein shared intelligence with the Israelis about these groups, and vacillated between providing training for the rebels and attempting to disarm various factions.[16]

Before long, the PLO constituted a virtual second government in parts of Jordan, and there were periodic clashes with the King's loyalist Bedouin army. There were several attempts at mediation, but many Palestinians called for overthrowing the monarchy. Though it was likely in his power to do so, PLO leader Yassir Arafat declined, explaining that he and his forces were guests in Jordanian territory.[17] Unfortunately, the King did not show similar reticence.

In September 1970, the situation escalated with calls for a general strike, and an airplane hijacking by one of Arafat's rivals, the PFLP. At this point, according to Henry Kissinger, the U.S. decided that "the hijacking should be used as a pretext to crush the *fedayeen*."[18] King Hussein imposed martial law and sent loyalist Bedouin forces against the Palestinians. A bloody civil war erupted, with a small Syrian force on the border attempting to aid the Palestinians, while the U.S. Sixth fleet and the Israeli Army prepared to aid the King if necessary. Hussein's tanks destroyed refugee camps while his planes dropped napalm. Curfew violators were shot on sight, and the corpses of rebel leaders were dragged through the streets as a warning to the general population.[19]

After ten days of fighting, the Syrians withdrew and a cease-fire agreement was signed between Arafat and Hussein.

Over the next year, King Hussein would use some $35 million in emergency military aid from the U.S. to completely crush the Palestinian presence in Jordan, sending the PLO into exile in Lebanon. And, as in so many other Middle East conflicts, the survivors could pick through the ruins of their villages to find shells marked "Made in the USA."[20] It is estimated that between 5000 and 20,000 civilians lost their lives in these raids.[21] Embittered Palestinians launched a radical new splinter group called "Black September" in commemoration of the crackdown.

Hussein had survived once again thanks to Western intervention, and he repaid the favor in 1973 when Egypt and Syria, frustrated by stalled negotiations, prepared to launch a new war to regain territories seized by Israel in 1967. The King secretly flew into Tel Aviv to warn the Israeli government, and passed similar warnings to Washington through the CIA. The Israelis chose not to believe the warning, though, and this time it was they who were surprised.[22]

King Hussein continued to survive by playing both sides against the middle, giving lip service to Palestinian aspirations and Arab nationalism where necessary, and providing services to his Western patrons where possible. Like most in the Arab world, he opposed the 1979 Camp David Accords between Egypt and Israel on the grounds that they failed to address the occupation and illegal settlement of the West Bank. Along with Saudi Arabia, he gave his blessing to Iraq's 1980 invasion of Iran, and developed increasing commercial ties with Baghdad.[23] This came back to haunt him when treaty obligations and survival instincts prevented him from endorsing the U.S. war against Iraq in 1991, as much of the Jordanian population was sympathetic to Baghdad.[24] Washington was quick to forgive, but the ongoing sanctions against Iraq have hurt the Jordanian economy.

The Palestinian Intifada against Israel, launched in 1987, also shook King Hussein's tightrope. Mindful of his restive population, the King renounced his claim to the West Bank, recognizing the call for an independent Palestinian state on his former territory. Ironically, this freed him up to sign his own peace treaty with Israel in 1994.[25] Like the Camp David Accords he had earlier criticized, this allowed the Israeli occupation to continue and freed their forces to concentrate on the Palestinians. It also earned the King billion-dollar loan forgiveness from Washington.[26]

Hussein was no doubt sincere in his wish for a regional settlement in which he could enjoy his monarchy in peace, but he was continually buffeted by forces beyond his control. The final years of his reign saw him negotiating a NAFTA-like free trade agreement with the U.S. He also imposed austerity plans backed by the World Bank and International Monetary Fund (IMF), which insist on privatizing government holdings, slashing funding for services like education and health care, and opening the economy to foreign investors. Consequently, Jordanians endured widespread poverty and unemployment. Riots arose from time to time at removals of food subsidies and similar measures, but ongoing military aid from the West kept the monarchy in place.[27]

As he was dying in 1999, the King performed one last service to the folks who signed his paychecks. In response to pressure from Washington, he removed his brother, Crown Prince Hassan, as heir to the throne. The CIA station in Amman had not been quiet about their unease with Hassan, and at a meeting with Bill Clinton, Hussein was finally persuaded to anoint his 36-year-old son Abdullah instead.[28] Presumably the new King was regarded as more malleable than his experienced uncle. The young heir, son of a British-born queen, was previously best known for a walk-on part in the second episode of "Star Trek: Voyager."[29] He also, upon assuming the throne, had to be given a crash course in Arabic as a second language.[30] Still, the U.S. showed its gratitude at King Hussein's funeral by announcing a $250 million aid package to help ease the transition of their new client.[31] He may need more than that; in early 2002, reports surfaced of grassroots organizing among Palestinian militants in Jordan. Expectations are that Abdullah will likely end up cracking down on the Palestinians as his father did in 1970.[32]

CHAPTER EIGHT

Egypt

Paying for Peace

In 1952, CIA officers in Cairo held a series of meetings with coup plotters in the Egyptian army, including Col. Gamal Abdel Nasser. The officers hoped to overthrow King Farouk, the corrupt and buffoonish puppet monarch backed by the British, while the U.S. hoped to replace Britain as the dominant foreign power in the region.[1] These overlapping interests insured that the coup took place in July of that year. Nasser, only 34, remained behind the scenes initially, with a General Neguib as the titular head of the new government. The younger man became prime minister in 1954 and assumed the presidency of Egypt in 1956 following a referendum.

Nasser's first priority, which dovetailed nicely with Washington's interests, was to get British troops removed from the Suez Canal, where they had been stationed since 1882.[2] As the canal no longer held much strategic value to Britain (after the loss of India), an agreement was reached in October 1954. For the first time in two and a half thousand years, Egypt was no longer under foreign occupation of any kind. This was a great catalyst for Nasser's growing reputation as a hero to Arab nationalists, fanned by his marathon radio broadcasts in colloquial Arabic.

Israel, however, viewed the presence of 80,000 British troops on the canal as a welcome buffer with Egypt. The Israeli secret service, the Mossad, sent agents to sabotage British installations and plant bombs in public buildings, hoping to scuttle the negotiations by blaming the terrorism on Egyptian nationalists.[3] This scheme was derailed when the agents were caught and exposed. France was also upset when, shortly after the British departure from Egypt, Algerian nationalists launched a revolt against French colonial rule; Paris was convinced (with help from the Mossad) that Nasser had encouraged them.[4] To counter Egyptian influence, France then began selling arms to Israel in defiance of a regional arms embargo. In February 1955 Israel, citing cross-border harassment by Palestinian refugees, attacked an Egyptian army outpost in Gaza, killing 40 soldiers and a number of civilians. Yet an Israeli historian has cited documentary evidence that Egypt was making a serious effort to keep the Gaza border calm.[5]

In fact, Israel had been planning an invasion of the Sinai Peninsula since at least 1953, according to the diaries of Prime Minister Moshe Sharett.[6] The Gaza attack precluded any hope of a peace agreement. At that point, as General Moshe Dayan put it, "one of these days a situation will be created which makes military action possible."[7]

Egypt's relations with Washington had begun to sour as Nasser refused to be bribed. U.S. antagonism was further aroused when he balked at buying arms with strings attached, and so turned to East Bloc sources. This in turn led Nasser to rely further on Soviet financing, and so the fear of a pro-Russian tilt became a self-fulfilling prophecy—the 1950s version of "If you ain't with us you're against us."[8]

In July 1956, Secretary of State Dulles reneged on a previous commitment to help Egypt build the Aswan Dam, and blocked international funding as well. In response, Nasser exercised his right to re-establish Egyptian sovereignty over the British-built Suez Canal—which was then closed to Israeli shipping. And in response to that, the British and the French made a secret deal with Israel to invade Egypt and seize back the canal. But this deal was made behind the backs of the Americans, and Israeli agents lied to their CIA counterparts about the impending invasion.[9]

On October 29, 1956, the Israelis used their French-supplied arsenal to launch a surprise attack on Egypt, seizing the Sinai. The plan was to falsely announce that Egypt had attacked Israel, after which Israeli troops would occupy the Sinai Peninsula all the way to the east bank of the Suez Canal. Then British and French troops would intervene to prevent a wider war, and hopefully, the whole thing would be so humiliating to Nasser that his people would rise up against him. Britain and France bombed Egyptian territory, and then sent troops to back up the Israelis.[10]

The Eisenhower Administration was outraged, not only by Israeli duplicity, but also by the Europeans' attempt to re-establish their influence in a region where the U.S. now wished to call the shots.[11] In order to counter that influence, the U.S. was even willing to cooperate briefly with the Soviets in condemning the Suez attacks in the UN. Stymied by a U.S. threat to withdraw aid, the Israelis reluctantly withdrew from the Sinai and Gaza, with UN monitors placed on the Egyptian border. Egypt regained control of the canal, subject to international guarantees of Israeli shipping in the Gulf of Aqaba.

Nasser emerged an even bigger hero than before, and began to talk of uniting the Arab world into one big federation. This set off alarm bells in Washington. Nasser's pan-Arabian dreams were short-lived, and amounted only to a brief federation with Syria, (which lasted until the next coup in that country undid the deal). The U.S. countered this alarming spurt of Arab unity by encouraging Jordan and Iraq to band together against the new United Arab Republic, rather than joining it. And no less than eight separate assassination plots were soon launched against Nasser, involving, at various times, America, Israel, Turkey, Saudi Arabia and Iraq.[12] These involved at least one CIA assassination plot in 1957. According to the memoirs of former CIA officer Wilbur Crane Eveland, the story goes that Eisenhower had mused that he wished the "Nasser problem" could be "eliminated"— which the CIA chief, Allen Dulles, took as an order to kill.[13] The plot never came to fruition, as Dulles ostensibly realized he had misinterpreted his boss. However, this account bears a marked similarity to other cover stories explaining away known CIA death plots,[14] so it should perhaps not be taken at face value. Britain's secret service MI6 also plotted with the Mossad to kill Nasser on several occasions.[15]

The Nasser problem continued, however, and in June 1967, 11 years after the Suez crisis, Israel tried the same trick again, this time successfully. The Israelis also had territorial designs on the West Bank and the Syrian territory of the Golan Heights, in order to secure control over the headwaters of the River Jordan and the aquifers of its basin. General Moshe Dayan later recounted how Israel had deliberately provoked firefights with Syrian forces. Israeli troops probed the Syrian frontier with tractors, then claimed that the inevitable Syrian reprisals constituted attacks on "peaceful farmers." This cat-and-mouse game intensified in the year leading up to the Six Day War.[16]

As tensions increased, the Soviets informed the Syrians that Israel was "massing troops" on its border, though only a single tank division had been sent several months before, following an earlier skirmish. But for its part, the Israeli government had threatened to invade Damascus if the Syrians did not suppress Palestinian raids. Nasser also called on the Syrians to do so, aware that neither he nor they had the power to prosecute a war with Israel. But as the putative leader of Arab nationalists, he was being goaded by the Syrians, Jordanians and Palestinians to do something about Israeli provocations, and to stop "hiding behind" UN troops.[17]

Eventually Nasser requested that UN forces depart from Gaza; instead the UN withdrew all its troops from the Sinai region. Egypt then moved two token divisions into the Sinai, far from adequate for any offensive action. In solidarity with Syria, Nasser then announced a blockade of ships bringing weapons to Israel through the Gulf of Aqaba. This was the pretext the Israelis required. Though only 5% of their imports came through Aqaba, Israelis told the world that Egypt's "economic stranglehold" threatened their very existence.[18]

Israel also announced at the time that the Arabs had struck first, though that claim too was later abandoned for the more credible formulation that the Israeli Defense Force (IDF) had launched a "pre-emptive strike", with the ostensible motivation being a massing of Egyptian troops. But as Israeli Chief of Staff Yitzhak Rabin admitted a year later, "I don't believe Nasser wanted war. The two divisions he sent into Sinai May 14 would not have been enough to unleash an offensive against Israel and we knew it." Or as one Israeli cabinet member put it, the "pre-emptive strike" story was "invented of whole cloth and exaggerated after the fact to justify the annexation of new Arab territories."[19]

Most of the Egyptian air force was destroyed on the ground and Israel seized the Sinai and Gaza, as well as the West Bank from Jordan and the Golan Heights from Syria. The latter three territories are occupied to this day. Many in the Israeli government had interpreted certain U.S. statements as giving a "green light" to their invasion plans; at the very least, they found "an absence of any exhortation to us to stay our hand." But U.S. support for the Israeli invasions went further than that; U.S. warplanes, painted with Israeli markings, helped with reconnaissance photography of Arab targets. President Johnson also moved the Sixth Fleet into the eastern Mediterranean, and secretly authorized shipments of spare parts to the Israeli military, while publicly calling for a regional arms embargo. After the war, the U.S. also vetoed a UN resolution calling for Israel to return to its previous borders.[20]

The Johnson Administration was so happy to see Israel strike a decisive blow at perceived "Soviet proxies" in the region that it was even willing to overlook an Israeli attack on the USS Liberty in the middle of the Six Day War. For years the attack on the U.S. ship, which killed 34 sailors, has been a mystery, the details covered up by both the U.S. and Israel. A recent book by author James Bamford posits that the American spy vessel had evidence that Israel had massacred Egyptian prisoners of war, and that the IDF destroyed the ship in order to cover up evidence of this war crime.[21]

The Six Day War ended in a cease-fire, which Nasser abrogated the following year, beginning intermittent skirmishes with Israel over the Sinai. The war significantly escalated tensions in the Middle East, leading to an accelerated arms race. As Nasser put it, "The problem now is that while the United States' objective is to pressure us to minimize our dealings with the Soviet Union, it will drive us in the opposite direction altogether. The U.S. leaves us no choice."[22] And indeed, though Israel had decisively defeated the Arabs, U.S. military assistance to Tel Aviv increased dramatically, as did East Bloc arms sales to Egypt. Nasser did show some interest in a land-for-peace swap[23]—indeed, he had explored peace negotiations with Israel in the 1950s before the provocative attack on Gaza[24]—but he died suddenly of a heart attack in September 1970.

He was succeeded by Anwar el-Sadat, who had been on the CIA payroll since 1960.[25] Despite this, the Nixon Administration was slow to work with Sadat, viewing Egypt through a Cold War prism. Sadat made a formal peace offer to Israel in February 1971, but Israel responded by expanding settlements in the occupied Sinai.[26] Secretary of State Henry Kissinger preferred to keep Egyptian-Israeli relations in a stalemate, hoping that the Russians would pressure Sadat into further compromise. Even after Sadat purged pro-Soviet elements from the Egyptian government, Kissinger couldn't be bothered. Sadat's intention, later realized, was to convert Egypt to a U.S. client state. He sent Soviet advisors home and intervened to prevent a communist takeover of Sudan. But frustrated by Washington's indifference to his lost sovereignty over the Sinai, Sadat launched a new war on Israel in 1973 with Syrian support.[27]

Both Jordan's King Hussein and Saudi King Fahd warned the Israelis in advance of the coming attack, but Tel Aviv refused to believe the Arab states were strong enough to pull it off.[28] This easily preventable war led to serious losses on the Israeli side, as Egypt regained control of the Suez Canal. At this point the U.S. suddenly became amenable to a negotiated settlement of the Israeli-Egyptian conflict, though Kissinger's ineffectual shuttle diplomacy produced few results for the remainder of his tenure.[29] This eventually led to Sadat's famous trip to Jerusalem and the Camp David Accords, sponsored by the Carter Administration.

Egyptian peace with Israel was bought with billions of dollars of U.S. taxpayer funds. Egypt became the second largest recipient of U.S. aid (after Israel), now totaling some $4 billion annually. Sadat bought peace by agreeing to vague promises that the Israelis would later negotiate peace with the Palestinians. In fact, the Israeli Knesset voted on "policy guidelines" stating that Israel had no intention of honoring these promises. The resolution stated that after a "transition period" agreed to at Camp David, Israel would "act to fulfill its rights to sovereignty over Judea, Samaria [their names for the West Bank] and the Gaza district." These "rights" were indeed fulfilled with increased repression and settlements in the West Bank. Israel also broke Camp David pledges regarding water rights, all of which engendered only weak protests from Sadat.[30]

For its part, Israel bought peace by returning (almost) all of the Sinai and removing Jewish settlements from those lands. Prime Minister Begin then exploited peace with Egypt (and later with Jordan) by using his freed-up forces to launch new strikes against Palestinian positions in Lebanon (see chapter 6).[31] And for its part, the U.S. used the Camp David talks to derail the international consensus in favor of a multilateral peace conference including Europe, the East Bloc and the Arab states. In this way, Washington alone remained in charge of any "peace process."[32]

The Camp David Accords were deeply unpopular both in Egypt and throughout the Arab world. Sadat also alienated his citizens through his economic policies, privatizing many state holdings and cutting food subsidies and other services in accord with World Bank and IMF advice. A hero in the West, he was widely despised at home. There was little public mourning when he was assassinated in 1982, in contrast to the millions who thronged the streets for Nasser's funeral. Sadat was killed by Islamic militants within his own elite guard units while he reviewed a military parade. According to author Douglas Valentine, the guards had been trained by CIA agent William Buckley.[33] Buckley himself sat in the stands during the assassination; also sitting nearby was Sadat's successor, Hosni Mubarak, who had the presence of mind to duck.[34]

Mubarak has ruled with the proverbial iron fist ever since. Egypt had been a police state under Nasser and Sadat, but human rights abuses reached new heights during the Mubarak regime. Mindful of Sadat's fate, he has cracked down on Islamists, moderates as well as radicals. This, of course, has had the effect of making the Islamic movement in Egypt ever more militant, in marked contrast to states like Yemen and Jordan where they are allowed to compete for parliamentary seats.[35] Many of Egypt's most radical Muslim fighters were trained by Western intelligence services for use in the anti-Soviet war in Afghanistan. The Egyptian arm of the Islamic Jihad has forged ties with Osama bin Laden's al-Qaida network, staging terror attacks against foreign tourists, as well as operating in the U.S.[36]

Egypt under Mubarak uses its billions in U.S. military aid to detain, beat and torture dissenters, opposition politicians and journalists; many have died in custody. Thousands of political prisoners and pro-democracy activists are held in overcrowded, disease-ridden prisons, without charges or trials. Press restrictions, including newspaper shutdowns, are widespread.[37] Arab nationalists view Egypt as a well-bribed client state of the U.S. and an obstacle to self-determination for its own people as well as its Palestinian neighbors. Nevertheless, the "Lion of Egypt" was re-elected to a fourth term in 1999 with just under 94 percent of the vote;[38] his party holds 97 percent of the legislative seats. He has never named a vice president.

But however much the people of Egypt chafe under Mubarak's regime, their plight pales beside the 54-year occupation suffered by the residents of Palestine.

CHAPTER NINE

Palestine

No Peace Without Justice

Even before the founding of the state of Israel, Theodore Herzl, founder of the Zionist movement, had written frankly of plans to "spirit the penniless [Palestinian] population across the border," while noting that the "removal of the poor must be carried out discreetly and circumspectly."[1] Chaim Weizmann, a future president of Israel, noted in 1917 that the British had told him that there was a population in Palestine of "a few hundred thousand Negroes, but that is a matter of no significance."[2]

In March 2002, after a decade spent ostensibly negotiating what would be a Palestinian state, the Israeli army invaded the territory in question, re-occupying the lands it had originally conquered in 1967. Tanks, missiles, warplanes and U.S.-built Apache helicopters assaulted every major Palestinian city, setting up roadblocks, cutting off water and electricity, blocking supplies of food and medical aid. Curfews were imposed, snipers were stationed, house-to-house searches conducted, and Palestinian schools, ministries, hospitals, broadcast facilities, were systematically looted, vandalized and destroyed.[3]

In the encampment of Jenin, home to thousands of Palestinian refugees (many of them expelled from their homes when Israel was founded in 1948), something horrible happened. In a report issued eight months later, Amnesty International accused Israel of war crimes, including "unlawful killings, torture and ill-treatment of prisoners, wanton destruction of hundreds of homes."[4] The Israeli Foreign Minister himself, Shimon Peres, initially described it as a "massacre." Military officers worried about the impact on Israel's image: "When the world sees the pictures of what we have done there, it will do us immense damage."[5]

So Israel set to work making sure that the world would not find out. It took about a week to crush all resistance within Jenin, but the camp remained sealed from outsiders for five more days; no journalists, no ambulances, no relatives could get in or out.[6] The Israelis initially estimated they had killed some 200 Palestinians; Dr. Wael Qadan, of the Palestinian Red Crescent Society, gave similar estimates.[7] Eyewitnesses (and amateur videos) noted bodies stacked in alleyways. But when the camp was reopened, they were nowhere to be seen. Many of the bodies had been removed to a "special cemetery" in the Jordan Valley, "to prevent the Palestinians from using the bodies for propaganda purposes." Many others were simply buried underneath their own homes, which Israeli bulldozers had reduced to rubble on top of them.[8] The Israeli paper *Haaretz* published numerous accounts of houses razed to the ground with helpless civilians still inside.[9]

But thereafter, the official line—repeated credulously in U.S. media—was that only 30 or 40 Palestinian fighters had been killed, and that no, repeat no "massacre" had taken place. Secretary of State Colin Powell, who was in Israel during the invasion, but never set foot in Jenin, said that "I have yet to see evidence of a massacre"—though "there was a great deal of destruction."[10] Curiously, despite Israel's best efforts, much of the world was shocked anyway. UN special envoy Terje Roed-Larsen declared, "We have expert people who have been in war zones and earthquakes and they say they have never seen anything like it. It is horrifying beyond belief."[11]

The UN was prepared to send an investigating team, but the Israelis simply refused to allow them access, preferring to negotiate the composition of the team. Then the U.S. stepped in and cut a deal to prevent any investigation, in return for the release of Palestinian leader Yassir Arafat. This was of little consequence to Israel; Arafat's lengthy house arrest was becoming another PR headache.[12] End of story.

The Israelis gradually withdrew from the West Bank cities, only to turn around and reoccupy them yet again a few weeks later—this time, perhaps, for good.[13] In July 2002, an Israeli tank was videotaped in Jenin firing into a crowd of Palestinian civilians, killing two children.[14] So whether or not a "massacre" did take place that April (either with bullets or bulldozers), it would not be inconsistent with Israel's historical methods and goals for the region.

Throughout the 20th century, the struggle over Palestine was marked by brutality and duplicity on both sides. But what concerns us here is the extent to which U.S. policy has helped to exacerbate that conflict. By backing extremists in Israel like Prime Minister Ariel Sharon, the U.S. has blocked solutions favored by most of the rest of the world—as well as by many Israelis (75 percent of the Israeli population said they were in favor of a negotiated Palestinian state; 85 percent say the large majority of settlements have to be given up).[15]

The dynamic created by aiding the Israelis predates the U.S./Israel relationship, and provides an important context for understanding how U.S. power has influenced the region and inflamed animosities. As in many other cases, the British

Empire left a huge mess behind when it pulled up its flag and went home. Britain had assumed control of Palestine after the collapse of the Ottoman Empire in World War I. In 1917 the Balfour Declaration promised a home in Palestine for the Jewish people, consistent with the demands of the Zionist movement of European Jews. At the same time Britain promised the inhabitants of Palestine an independent Arab state on the same land, and that Jewish immigration would not come at the expense of the "political and economic freedom of the Arab population."[16] So far, it hasn't worked out that way.

There were two main factions of the Zionist movement. The Labor Zionists, later the Labor Party, advocated a national home for the Jews in Palestine. The Revisionists, who later became the Likud Party, favored the use of force to create a Jewish state on the model of the biblical Kingdom of Israel. Other Zionists who called for peaceful cooperation with the Arabs were "maligned and scorned," according to Israeli author Benjamin Beit-Hallahmi.[17] As early as 1938, David Ben-Gurion, future founder of the state of Israel, anticipated a future partition of the territory: "After we become a strong force, as a result of the creation of a state, we shall abolish partition and expand into the whole of Palestine."[18]

Conflicts between the indigenous Jewish and Arab populations had been rare prior to the arrival of the Zionists, but became more frequent as Jewish immigration began to increase.[19] Jewish settlers from Europe began buying up large tracts of fertile farmland from absentee owners, evicting the "penniless population" who worked the land. Tension began to rise, leading to uprisings and violent incidents in the 1920s, and general strikes by Arabs in 1933 and '36, brutally suppressed by the British. Britain eventually promised the irate Palestinians to place limits on immigration, and in 1940 limits were placed on land purchases by foreigners in Arab areas. But these restrictions were widely ignored, and vast amounts of Arab land had been illegally purchased by the time the British pulled out.[20]

Jewish immigration to Palestine increased dramatically during and after World War II, as did Jewish militancy. Zionists assembled an army of some 60,000 men and also formed terrorist organizations to pressure the British on their demands for a Jewish state. Future Israeli prime minister Menachem Begin headed Irgun Zvai Leumi (IZL), which bombed Palestinian buses and marketplaces, killing hundreds of civilians. The Irgun also bombed the British embassy in Rome. Begin himself planned the bombing in 1946 of the King David Hotel in Jerusalem, killing 91.[21] Future prime minister Yitzhak Shamir led the Stern Gang, which assassinated the British minister for Middle East affairs in 1944 and the UN mediator for Palestine in 1948.[22] In 1941 the Stern Gang had even offered to collaborate with the Nazis if that would help oust the British from Palestine.[23]

The terrorism worked. In February 1947, the British Empire declared that it would withdraw from Palestine in mid-1948, leaving the problem of Palestinian/Jewish relations in the lap of the United Nations. As the most powerful nation in the UN, the United States became the leading advocate for a partition of Palestine. And as President Harry Truman said, "I do not have hundreds of thousands of Arabs among my constituents." Truman had personal misgivings about the Zionist movement. He pressed the British to allow more European Jews to immigrate to Palestine, but worried that a Zionist state could be destabilizing to the region. But Truman also had a sizeable constituency that was, as he put it, "anxious for the success of Zionism," and their support in the 1948 election was something he badly needed.[24]

In late 1947, the UN General Assembly voted narrowly for a partition plan. The U.S. role in its passage was pivotal. The U.S. pressured its territories and allies, threatening war-torn France with a total aid cutoff.[25] At the same time, the U.S. and other supporters of the partition were limiting their own immigration of European Jews, in effect forcing even more Jewish refugees into Palestine.[26]

Even with the increased migration to Palestine during and immediately following World War II, at the time of the partition, Jewish residents made up less than one-third of the population and owned less than 10% of the land. The partition plan gave them 56% of the territory of Palestine. Much of the best arable land ended up in the Jewish portion. In exchange, the Arab state was to be awarded an annual subsidy. The cities of Jerusalem and Bethlehem were to be international territory, while it was envisaged that the two states would share a common currency as well as joint postal, telephone and transportation services. But there was no plan to implement these key aspects; they were left to be resolved by the forces on the ground.[27]

The UN partition was unacceptable to the Palestinians, then constituting a two-thirds majority, since they were being denied their right to self-determination. Unbeknownst to them, however, King Abdullah of Jordan had made a secret deal with David Ben-Gurion to prevent the emergence of any Palestinian state by seizing the West Bank.[28]

Palestinians were at a military disadvantage. The Jewish forces were already well armed by 1948, and continued to import weapons from Eastern Europe as well as from private citizens in the U.S.[29] The Palestinians had no such organized forces, and were dependent on neighboring Arab states. As the date for British withdrawal drew nearer, Jewish forces mounted dozens of military operations, while Arab armies (mainly from Jordan, Egypt and Syria) infiltrated into the Palestinian portion and along the borders. Both sides prepared for all-out war. The Israelis have always claimed that they were attacked first by the Arab armies. But as Ben-Gurion later stated, "until the British left, no Jewish settlement, however remote, was entered or seized by the Arabs."[30]

Ben-Gurion declared the formation of the state of Israel on May 14, 1948, one day ahead of the British departure. The joint Arab forces then formally entered into a state of war in order to secure the Palestinian portion. But by that point the Jewish army had already occupied many key cities, whether they were part of the Jewish portion or not.[31] Violence between the two sides had already spun out of control. A month earlier, on April 9, Irgun paramilitaries had entered the village of Deir Yassin and executed more than two hundred men, women and children, and then mutilated many of the bodies. In reprisal, Arabs attacked a Jewish convoy, killing 77 civilians. These were, of course, neither the first nor the last such incidents.[32]

To give a sense of the balance of terror, virtually all of the fighting took place in the Arab portion of Palestine. The official Zionist history of the war shows that of the thirteen major offensives staged by Jewish forces prior to independence, eight were in Palestinian territory.[33] The Jordanian army in particular was under orders not to enter the Jewish portion. And as Israeli historian Uri Milstein put it, nearly every skirmish between Israeli and Arab forces "ended in a massacre of Arabs."[34]

In the end, no Palestinian state was established; the West Bank and East Jerusalem were claimed by Jordan, while

Egypt occupied the Gaza Strip, and Israel took the rest. By the end of the 1948-49 war, over 700,000 Palestinians were expelled from their homeland or fled in terror.[35]

Israeli media had long claimed that the Arabs left in response to pleas from neighboring states broadcast via radio. But internal Israeli documents show that more than 75% of the refugees fled because of Israeli military actions, including psychological operations to instill fear, as well as direct expulsions (what we now call "ethnic cleansing"). More than 50,000 Palestinians were expelled from the towns of Lydda and Ramle alone.[36] As the these facts have come to light, the claim that the migration was voluntary and due to persuasion over the radio has been largely abandoned in Israel, though it is still widely repeated in the U.S.

When it was over, Israel controlled not 56% of the land (as originally allotted by the UN partition plan) but 78% of it.[37] At least 55% of the Palestinian population had fled or been forced from Palestine, and were living in squalid refugee camps.[38] To prevent the return of the inhabitants, some 350 Arab villages had been depopulated and either partially or completely demolished.[39] Implicitly endorsing these events, the United States immediately recognized the state of Israel—within eleven minutes of its founding.[40]

The U.S. did not become Israel's number one military patron until the 1967 war (replacing France). But after Israel's founding, Ben-Gurion immediately set up a liaison between the Israeli intelligence service Mossad and the fledgling CIA—and blackmailed one prominent CIA officer, the infamous James Jesus Angleton, into serving as an Israeli mole.[41] Eventually the Mossad became a sort of proxy force for the CIA in places where congressional opposition or budgetary restraints prevented our own involvement, such as in South Africa and Guatemala during the Reagan years. But as a self-interested proxy, Israeli intelligence often created as many problems for the U.S. as it solved—most notably in the Mossad's links to the Iran-Contra scandal of the 1980s. (Israeli middlemen helped transport U.S. arms to the Khomeini regime in Iran and helped Reagan to circumvent Congressional restrictions on aid to Nicaraguan rebels. While Israeli profited financially from its role, the scandals blew up in Reagan's face.)[42] Today, Israel is among our closest allies, forming a strategic alliance with Turkey to help project U.S. power in the region (see chapter 10).

But relations were not always so warm, especially in the early days. While Truman was guardedly pro-Israel, his successor Dwight Eisenhower's administration was noticeably cool to the new state at first. The turning point in the relationship came with the Suez crisis of 1956. While Egyptian President Nasser had quietly let it be known that he was prepared to negotiate a peace treaty with Israel,[43] the Israelis were more interested in getting rid of him. He represented what they had most feared: the rise of a charismatic Arab leader to replace the easily bribed monarchies set up by the British and French. Ben-Gurion said, for instance, "I always feared that a personality might rise such as arose among the Arab rulers in the seventh century or like [Kemal Ataturk] who rose in Turkey after its defeat in the First World War. He raised their spirits, changed their character, and turned them into a fighting nation. There was and still is a danger that Nasser is this man."[44] The Mossad began filtering disinformation on Nasser to the Europeans and the U.S., and set off bombs in U.S. and British offices in Cairo, hoping to blame the Egyptians and poison their international relationships. The Israelis had also, as an act of provocation, attacked the

Egyptian-held city of Gaza in 1955, killing 37.[45]

After Nasser nationalized the Suez Canal, Britain and France made a secret deal with Israel to invade Egypt and take it back. Their joint forces captured the Sinai Peninsula and the Gaza Strip from Egypt in a surprise attack. But Washington was not in on the secret plan, and was alarmed by this European influence in this region so rich with oil and strategic importance. To counteract the European powers, the U.S. intervened on Egypt's behalf by pressuring the Israelis to withdraw. That withdrawal marked the end, once and for all, of the role played by Britain and France as colonial powers in the Middle East.[46]

From that point on, despite the U.S. having sided with Egypt over the Canal, Nasser was seen more and more as an enemy, and the strategic alliance with Israel was established. President Eisenhower came to share Israel's fear of "radical Arab nationalism," especially as it might lead to the disruption of the neighboring oil-rich monarchies. And Mossad assistance proved valuable when the U.S. sent troops to intervene in Jordan and Lebanon. By 1958 CIA Director Allen Dulles called Israel's intelligence service "the only one on which we can count."[47]

Emboldened by their growing alliance with the U.S., the Israelis immediately began planning to re-conquer the Sinai,[48] which came to fruition 11 years after the Suez crisis.

While the Egyptian border was secured, the frontiers with Jordan, Syria and Lebanon had been in contention ever since the armistice of 1949 (to this day the state of Israel has never officially declared its borders). Palestinian refugees resisted the appropriation of their homelands with cross-border raids into Israel. Massive retaliation from the Israeli Defense Forces (IDF) inevitably followed. Often, the IDF did not wait for the Palestinians to attack before retaliating. According to Palestinian writer Edward Said, these regular skirmishes led to the deaths of at least ten times as many Arab civilians as compared to Israelis.[49] In 1964 the Palestinian Liberation Organization (PLO) was founded with the intention of reclaiming the Palestinian homeland. Several factions vied for control of the PLO; Yassir Arafat, the head of Fatah, assumed overall command by 1969.[50]

By the time of Arafat's ascent, the Six Day War of June 1967 (see chapter 8) had destroyed not only the air forces of Egypt, Jordan and Syria, but also their credibility as champions for the Palestinian cause. Israel had re-conquered the Sinai along with the Gaza Strip, seized the Golan Heights, and occupied the West Bank, including the entire city of Jerusalem.

The situation for the Palestinians within Israel had been dire since the country's 1948 inception. Treated as second-class citizens, the Palestinians' homes, lands and businesses were confiscated or destroyed; their olive orchards were uprooted; they were restricted from purchasing land and barred from military service; display of the Palestinian flag was forbidden; even the gathering of herbs for traditional recipes was restricted. Palestinian villages paid taxes, but received virtually no services from the government.[51] With the illegal 1967 conquests that (except for the Sinai) remain in place 35 years later, a million more Palestinians were placed under direct military occupation.

After the war, the U.S. and Israel assisted Jordan in its own crackdown against the PLO, killing thousands of civilians (see chapter 7). Unsurprisingly, this led to the emergence of more militant factions. Extremist Palestinian splinter groups began hijacking airplanes and staging other acts of terrorism in order to draw attention to their cause. Among

the most infamous of these were the massacre of Israeli ath-
letes at the 1972 Olympics and the mass shootings of passen-
gers at the Rome and Vienna airports, carried out by the
Black September movement as revenge for the massacres in
Jordan.[52] While these atrocities did indeed draw attention,
they set the Palestinian cause back by at least a generation.
It would be nearly 20 years before either Israel or the U.S.
would openly negotiate with the PLO. "Palestinian" became
synonymous with "terrorist," a shift in perception that con-
veniently minimized and obliterated from memory Israel's
own acts of terror.

In conjunction with the terrorist assassinations by the
Stern and Irgun groups mentioned earlier, Israel had in fact
invented airplane hijacking back in 1954, and had used bus
bombings and car bombs in order to establish their state.[53]
The IDF uses the bombing of vehicles and assassination on a
regular basis to this day.[54]

In any conflict involving terror, reprisal, and counter-
reprisal, it is often hard to sort out which party bears the
greater responsibility for the casualties. But Israel's deliberate
provocation is a conscious strategy, not a response to terrorism. The Israeli war hero General Moshe Dayan explained
quite frankly that "[Israel] may—no, it *must* invent dangers,
and to do this it must adapt the strategy of provocation and
revenge."[55] This strategy was used quite effectively in the
wars of 1948, 1956, 1967 and 1982, as well as in both of the
Palestinian *Intifada* uprisings. Israeli terror had (and has)
killed far more Palestinians than vice versa. The Israeli
human rights group B'Tselem has reported that between
1987 and 2000, more than 1500 Palestinian civilians were
killed by Israelis, as opposed to 270 Israeli civilians killed by
Palestinians.[56] But in a major propaganda victory for the

Israelis, it was the PLO that carried the stigma.[57]

The PLO was chased from Jordan into Lebanon, and later into Tunisia (see chapter 6). In the meantime, after Nasser died suddenly of cardiac arrest in 1971, his successor, Anwar Sadat, also let it be known that he was interested in signing a peace treaty with Israel. Like Nasser, he was initially ignored; Egypt had to fight another war with Israel in 1973 before those efforts were taken seriously (see chapter 8). At Camp David in 1978, Sadat signed a separate peace to get back the Sinai, and left the Palestinians to their own devices. This "peace process" freed Israeli forces to focus with greater intensity on the West Bank and Lebanon. Sadat's peace efforts also exacerbated a schism within the Palestinian movement between those who also sought a negotiated settlement and those committed to military action.

Sadat was not the only one who tried to negotiate peace with Israel; nor was he the only one who faced indifference and hostility from the U.S. in trying to do so. UN Resolution 242 was passed in November 1967. It called for Israel to withdraw from territories gained by force, and emphasized the right of both peoples to live in secure and recognized boundaries. But from the beginning, both the U.S. and Israel rejected 242, and the Nixon Administration actively worked to subvert it.[58] In 1974 Yassir Arafat addressed the United Nations, the first head of a liberation movement to do so. He said, "I come to you with an olive branch and a freedom fighter's gun; do not let the olive branch fall from my hand." He initially proposed a one-state solution: a united, secular Palestine as a democratic homeland to Christians, Jews and Muslims on the entire territory of the divided Palestinian homeland, including Israel.

Soon after, the PLO was granted observer status at the UN, and the General Assembly passed UN Resolution 3236, "reaffirming the inalienable rights of the Palestinian people, including the right to self-determination." In 1976, the UN called for a Palestinian state in the West Bank and Gaza, but the resolution was vetoed by the U.S. By 1978, Arafat had accepted the two-state solution, and agreed to renounce the use of violence in order to enlarge the Palestinian portion, though he said he hoped to do so through negotiation. And in 1982 a PLO spokesman stated that "the PLO has formally conceded to Israel, in the most unequivocal manner, the right to exist on a reciprocal basis."[59] But by that point Israel was gearing up to destroy both the PLO and Arafat himself.

According to Israeli media, the 1982 invasion of Lebanon (see chapter 6) was necessary as a response to Palestinian cross-border attacks. But according to Israeli statistics, the total number of Israelis killed by such attacks was 106—over the previous 15 years. The IDF killed more civilians than that in the very first day of the invasion.[60] As the Israeli Chief of Staff put it (in reference to a previous Lebanese incursion), "we struck the civilian population consciously, because they deserved it."[61] In fact, the acquisition of Lebanese territory shared something in common with Israel's annexations of the Sinai and the West Bank. Contrary to assertions that they were in response to terror, the conquests had been planned many years before, as part of the "Greater Israel" project.[62] With the Likud Party in power for the first time, Israel's revisionists also saw the chance to fulfill long-cherished dreams of installing a friendly Christian regime in Beirut.[63]

The justification Israel used to invade Lebanon stands as clear evidence that it sought to create a greater Israel and was not as a response to terrorism. To avoid giving Israel any excuse to invade, the PLO had been rigorously adhering to a cease-fire in northern Lebanon.[64] When a rival Palestinian faction—one not even based in Lebanon—made an attempt on the life of the Israeli ambassador in London, Prime Minister Begin seized on this as a pretext for the long-planned invasion. Begin turned Defense Minister Ariel Sharon loose on the Palestinians and their allies.

This context makes clear that it was not so much Palestinian violence that required an Israeli military attack. Rather, it was their insistence on a negotiated two-state solution—anathema to the Israeli government.

Begin had announced a brutal aim for the invasion: to expel the Palestinians from a 25-mile security zone north of the border. But Israeli forces went far beyond this, pushing all the way to Beirut. Occupying half the city, Israel bombed indiscriminately for nine weeks. In the end, Israel had killed at least 17,000 civilians,[65] in the process so inflaming world opinion that the U.S. agreed to help evacuate the PLO from Beirut to Tunis.

With the PLO leadership in exile, the situation for millions of Palestinian refugees remaining in the West Bank, Gaza and Lebanon worsened as they had even less protection from the actions of the Israeli occupation forces. Under the Likud Party, Israel stepped up the pressure by dramatically increasing the number and size of its illegal settlements on the occupied territories. In defiance of international law, Labor governments had established the infrastructure for Israelis to consolidate control over the West Bank and Gaza beginning in 1967. But they had proceeded gradually. In 1972, there were 1500 Israeli settlers in the West Bank; by the time Begin refused President Carter's request to freeze settlement activity in 1977, that number had increased to 7,000.[66]

In 1977, Ariel Sharon, then Minister of Agriculture, published a blueprint for a "demographic transformation" of the West Bank, envisioning a majority of 2 million Jews on the seized lands by the end of the 20th century. By 1983, just six years later, the settler population of the West Bank alone had quadrupled to nearly 30,000. Other Israeli settlements were established in Gaza and the Golan Heights, and tens of thousands of Israelis were encouraged to move into and around the Arab neighborhoods of East Jerusalem. Generous subsidies from the government helped to fuel the migrations, and many of the new communities were built on land previously occupied by demolished Palestinian homes or farms—or villages. Many were fitted with swimming pools and lush lawns, appropriating scarce desert water resources. The impoverished Palestinians in surrounding villages were forbidden to dig new wells.[67]

Palestinians began to chafe more and more under the misery of the occupation and its daily humiliations. They continued to have their homes demolished and confiscated; were subject to routine harassment at border checkpoints when crossing into Israel for menial jobs; suffered continuing expulsions into Jordan—often, wives and children were deported across the Jordanian border on short notice while the men were away at work.[68] Military authorities quashed any show of Palestinian nationalism and incarcerated men and boys in squalid prisons where torture was not only commonplace, but also actually legal according to the Israeli Supreme Court.[69] Israeli settlers and soldiers literally got away with murder, including killing children. Those who beat and killed Palestinians often received no more than slaps on the wrist like fines and probation.[70]

As Palestinian rage in the occupied territories intensified, the exile of the PLO left a power vacuum, which was increasingly filled by radical Islamic groups. Ironically, the

Israelis had initially sponsored Muslim groups like Hamas to weaken the authority of the PLO[71] (Funding rival groups who share a common aim antithetical to the funder may seem odd. But it is in fact standard practice, in the hopes that a more vigorous rivalry between the funded groups will turn their focus on each other with mutually destructive effects. But often it is the funder who gets it in the end. For example, as seen in chapter 13, the U.S. was funding Islamic militants in Afghanistan from 1979 through 1995—with devastating consequences).

In 1978, seeking to counter Arafat's influence and prevent the success of his peace initiatives, the governing Likud Party registered a religious organization led by Sheikh Ahmad Yassin. The Sheikh not only opposed Arafat's secular rule, but also opposed the land-for-peace negotiations sought by the PLO. Israel funded Yassin's organization, which set up mosques, schools and clinics in the occupied territories. The Israelis also set up a system of "Village Leagues," used to recruit and bribe Palestinian collaborators and informers. Yassin used funding—and Israeli-trained Palestinian fighters—from the Leagues to set up a military wing of his movement, which he named Hamas. During the 1990s it grew into a rival power to counter Arafat's PLO, but not in the way Israel had hoped.[72]

A measure of how out of touch the PLO leadership was with frustration in the Occupied Territories came in December 1987. An Israeli truck killed four Palestinians, and Gaza and the West Bank erupted into a spontaneous uprising that was as much a surprise to the PLO as it was to Israel. It became known as the Intifada, and would last, in varying degrees of intensity, until 1993.[73]

At first much of the resistance was non-violent, including strikes, demonstrations, tax resistance, boycotts of Israeli products and institutions, and the establishment of Palestinian schools and other alternative institutions.[74] Much of this was put down with force by the Israeli authorities. The outburst of anger had also begun with rock-throwing youths, who were shot down with live ammunition.[75] When this led to a public relations crisis for Israel in the court of world opinion, orders went out to simply "break the bones" of the protestors. Surprisingly, the beating of unarmed demonstrators was also not too popular.[76] But within the first few years, the uprising was more or less crushed by Israeli military power.

In the first 17 months of the Intifada, 424 Palestinians were killed, and 17 Israelis.[77] The Mossad also infiltrated Palestinian groups and executed Intifada organizers.[78] The IDF responded to the uprising with mass arrests, and curfews for which violators were shot on sight. Schools and universities were closed, and in the most egregious example of collective punishment (long held illegal under international law), Palestinian workers were prevented from commuting to their jobs in Israel, with unemployment reaching 30 to 50%.[79]

In the midst of the Intifada, the plight of Palestinians worsened. Many of the Gulf monarchies rebuked the PLO for its support of Iraq in the Gulf War by cutting off financial aid to the organization. The monarchies also meted out another collective punishment by expelling hundreds of thousands of Palestinian workers.

Finally, as Israel had hoped, the Islamic groups were at odds with the PLO (many of whose leaders were Christians). Mutual recriminations had undermined Palestinian unity. In many ways the Intifada was also a Palestinian civil war—250 were killed by their own countrymen.[80] Yet the Israeli/ Palestinian conflict was primary: Palestinians killed 405

Israelis while the Israelis killed over 1,400.[81]

By 1993, the Palestinians were severely weakened, both politically and economically. But Israel had also seen damage to its international reputation, and the U.S. had promised many of the Arab states to push for some movement on the Palestinian question as a condition of their involvement in the Gulf War coalition. In 1988, Arafat had proclaimed a Palestinian declaration of independence—though he was still in Tunisia with no state to rule—and had agreed to recognize Israel's right to exist (This was a concession of 78% of what was once Palestine).[82] A peace conference was held in Madrid in 1991, which led to secret negotiations between Israel and the PLO in Oslo, Norway. In September 1993, Prime Minister Yitzhak Rabin and PLO Chairman Arafat signed the Oslo Accords, shaking hands on the White House lawn.

The agreement established a declaration of principles for talks leading to a final settlement, with many of the terms on borders, refugees and Jerusalem left intentionally vague. It also created a Palestinian Authority (PA), initially based in Gaza and Jericho, to which Arafat was easily elected President. The accords also declared Israel to be responsible for the "overall security," but also established a Palestinian police force, which was trained by the CIA.[83]

The PLO agreed to this ambiguous and flawed arrangement because they felt they had no choice, but the peace process was popular with a majority of Palestinians as it seemed to be predicated on the promise of a Palestinian state. Many Palestinians, though, opposed the Oslo Accords from the beginning. Some saw them as an opportunity for Israel to set up a Bantustan-style occupation, like that of South Africa. Exiled writer Edward Said characterized any state Arafat might conceivably set up as "the largest jail in the world," and predicted an eventual second Intifada.[84]

Though a timetable was drawn up for eventual Israeli withdrawal from West Bank towns and cities, the PA never ended up fully controlling more than 17% of the territory.[85] A deadline of September 2000 was set for a final agreement, but that deadline was never met.

Extremists and rejectionists on both sides undermined any hopes for peace. In 1994, a crazed Israeli settler massacred 30 Muslims at a mosque in Hebron. Right-wing Israelis launched a campaign of vilification against Rabin, culminating in his assassination by a Jewish fanatic in 1995.[86] Under his successors, both Labor and Likud, the pace of settlements and land appropriations continued to increase. West Bank settlements alone had reached over 100,000 settlers by the end of the Intifada; over the eight years of the Oslo process, they doubled to more than 200,000.[87] Israel now controls 85% of the water supply in the Jordan Valley.[88]

Palestinian rejectionists were also empowered by events which followed the agreement. The Palestinian poverty rate doubled in the Oslo years, and general despair continued to increase (along with the number of Israeli settlements. Hamas and Islamic Jihad launched a series of suicide bombings beginning in 1995, and began to gain more recruits among young Palestinians who saw no hope for the future. This in turn led to the 1996 election of Likud Prime Minister Benjamin Netanyahu, who openly disdained the Oslo process and dragged his feet on implementing its agreements.[89] Final status negotiations scheduled to begin in 1996 took place only after Netanyahu had been replaced by Ehud Barak in 1999.

But Barak opened the Camp David summit by breaking another promise of West Bank force withdrawal, and laid down a series of positions from which he said he would not budge.[90] Under the circumstances, Arafat was reluctant to attend at all, but agreed under the condition that he not be blamed as a scapegoat if the talks should fail. That turned out to be yet another in a series of broken promises, as President Clinton publicly blamed Arafat for the failure to reach an agreement.

One of the enduring myths of the continuing crisis is that Barak offered Arafat "95% of the West Bank," but that the latter rejected it, preferring to return to armed conflict. In fact, a look at the maps of Barak's initial offer show that Israel was actually seeking to retain nearly 40% of the West Bank in one form or another—including the most desirable land.[91] In May 2000, he called for a "temporary" security zone along the Jordan Valley, amounting to 14% of the territory. Another 25%, incorporating 90% of the illegal settlers, would be annexed permanently, while the remaining islands of Palestinian sovereignty would be criss-crossed by a network of "Jewish-only" highways connecting the settlements.[92] Though this "generous" offer was later modified somewhat, no Palestinian leader could agree to anything like it and expect to retain his job.

And, in fact, the Camp David summit sponsored by President Clinton in July 2000 did collapse without an agreement, but the Palestinians did not walk away from the process. They continued to send negotiating teams to Taba, Egypt, working ever closer to an agreement, even after the eruption of the second Intifada in September 2000.[93] But by January 2001, both Clinton and Barak were lame duck leaders. Ariel Sharon had helped to spark the renewed violence by marching to the holy Islamic site of the Temple Mount with 1000 armed policemen. Once again Palestinian rock-throwers were met with lethal force, and Sharon exploited the ongoing tragedy to win election as Prime Minister.[94] The newly inaugurated President Bush refused to send a U.S. delegation, and Israel—not the Palestinians—withdrew from the negotiations.[95] In fact, the Bush camp advised the Israelis *during Clinton's Camp David talks* that they should be prepared to walk out of the negotiations—four months before the U.S. presidential election.[96]

Sharon came to power in early 2001, promising Israel "security"—but has instead delivered just the opposite.[97] Refusing all calls for a settlement freeze as the precondition for a cease-fire, he established dozens of new settlements in the West Bank.[98] Whenever there was a lull in the violence, Israel assassinated an Islamic leader, virtually ensuring another retaliation.[99] The levels of violence on both sides were considerably higher than in the first uprising, as the grisly suicide bombings increased in both number and intensity. When one of them killed 20 Israelis at a Passover celebration in March 2002, Sharon's IDF forces invaded the West Bank, re-establishing the occupation and working to destroy all vestiges of the Palestinian Authority.[100] Just as with earlier incursions, the reoccupation of the West Bank had been planned well in advance, during the summer of 2000, while peace talks were still ongoing.[101] Ironically, this renewed warfare came just as the Arab League issued an unprecedented joint offer to recognize Israel, in return for a withdrawal to the 1967 borders.[102]

As with his incursion into Lebanon 20 years earlier, Sharon stands accused of complicity in war crimes, including summary executions, use of human shields,[103] and the aforementioned bloodbath at the Jenin refugee camp.[104] Finally, after 15 months of looking the other way, the Bush

Administration turned its attention to the ongoing carnage, under pressure from both Arab and European allies. Vice President Dick Cheney was sent to Arab capitals to drum up support for an attack on Iraq, and was told in no uncertain terms that no such support would be forthcoming without progress on the Palestinian issue. Subsequently (and belatedly) Secretary of State Colin Powell was sent to the region to try to arrange a cease-fire as Sharon defied the president's call to withdraw.[105]

Powell tried (in vain) to arrange an international conference to address the crisis, and prospects for the ultimate success of the "peace process" are dim[106]—particularly since President Bush called on the Palestinians to replace both their leader and their system of government before any further negotiations.[107] Both the U.S. and Israel are too powerful to be thwarted, and the Bush Administration seems sympathetic to Sharon's "Greater Israel" fantasies.[108] Israel will eventually relinquish only enough territory to mollify America's so-called "moderate Arab allies," which is unlikely to defuse the newly heightened levels of hatred on both sides. A 2002 poll[109] found 46 percent of Israelis in favor of simply expelling the Palestinians from the West Bank altogether—and it appears that their prime minister may be planning to do just that.[110] In November 2002 the Labor Party pulled out of the governing coalition with Sharon's Likud. He then formed a new government allied with far-right parties, while calling for new elections in January 2003. In the meantime, the IDF began work in June 2002 on a 200-mile "Berlin Wall" that will eventually encircle most of the occupied territories.[111]

The strategy behind these moves was laid out many years before by the late Israeli General Moshe Dayan. He argued that the Palestinians should be told "that we have no solution, that you shall continue to live like dogs, and who-ever wants to can leave—and we will see where this process leads...."[112]

The greatest tragedy here is that so much of this was avoidable. An international conference held thirty years ago would have reflected the consensus of most of the world, as expressed in UN Resolution 242, which called for Israeli withdrawal from the occupied territories. Israel's ongoing rejection of these terms has been made possible by U.S. aid, which currently runs at some $5 billion a year.[113] Over the history of the state of Israel that has amounted to nearly $100 billion in military and economic aid, the vast bulk of it after 1967, when Israel—the region's only nuclear power—had proved capable of handily defeating the combined forces of all its adversaries.[114] The real threat to Israeli civilians (as well as to U.S. citizens at home and abroad), comes from the ongoing delusion on the part of both countries' rulers that Israel can occupy territory at will and still expect to negoti-ate peace.

It may serve U.S. interests for Israel to be our proxy, a sand-covered aircraft carrier in a sea of hostile Arab states, as it helps to keep the Arabs divided and squabbling. But it doesn't necessarily serve the interests of the Israeli people, who are subject to reprisals for this brutal and cynical strate-gy. Just as useful to U.S. interests is another well-armed ally that is arguably even more brutal than Israel in the treatment of despised minorities: Turkey.

CHAPTER TEN

Turkey

Military Rules

As the only NATO member in the Middle East, Turkey serves as a political bridge between the Islamic world and the West, as well as a literal bridge between Europe and Asia. Writer Anne Applebaum, of *Slate*, has lauded the regime in Ankara as a "secular, democratically elected government" with "an advanced market economy."[1] That may be the conventional wisdom, but its market economy hasn't kept Turkey from becoming an economic basket case in need of a massive bailout. And while its government may be more democratic than that of, say, neighboring Syria, the Turkish military has been one of the most impressive human rights abusers of the past decade.

The modern Turkish state arose from the ashes of the old Ottoman Empire at the end of World War I.[2] At its peak, the empire had ruled much of the Middle East, along with northern Africa and the Balkans. After allying itself with Germany in the war, the empire was beaten and broken up— with Britain and France, as well as various neighbors, moving in to divvy up the spoils. But in 1920 a charismatic officer named Mustafa Kemal reorganized the armed forces and reclaimed the Turkish homeland—along with a few other homelands. Communities of Greeks, Kurds, and Armenians were brutally cleansed from the new state; the latter group suffered the genocide of 1.5 million victims at Turkish hands, during and after World War I.[3]

Kemal also sought to align Turkey with the West, renaming himself Atatürk and remaking the nation in his image. He banned the Arabic alphabet, the veil and the fez, along with polygamy and other Islamic practices. Resistance to these sweeping changes was harshly repressed. Yet Atatürk also had significant success in modernizing the economy and attacking corruption. After his death in 1938, his revolution largely remained in place.[4]

Turkey stayed neutral during World War II, but allied itself with the U.S. against the USSR during the Cold War, joining NATO in 1951. Washington was so pleased to have an ally on the border with the Soviet Union that it promptly installed nuclear missiles, listening posts and radar facilities.[5] To this day the U.S. maintains several bases in Turkey. Incirlik air base, the largest, has served as a staging ground for the war in Afghanistan, and would be vital to any war in Iraq. The U.S. also helped to set up a network of right-wing paramilitary groups like the notorious Grey Wolves, responsible for death-squad activity and assassinations since 1949— and discreetly allied to the CIA.[6] As we shall see, these proxy forces have proved useful in suppressing the Turkish left and intervening in elections.

Postwar Turkey moved towards multiparty democracy, but there have been regular military takeovers and purges throughout the years whenever the generals didn't like the election results. The ruling Republican People's Party was unseated in 1950 by the Democratic Party, which, despite its name, steadily clamped down on the opposition. But the military coup leaders of 1960 objected not so much to the misnamed Democrats' abrogation of democracy, but their economic mismanagement. The generals banned the Democratic Party, put hundreds of its leaders on trial, hanged a few, and rewrote the constitution. As the country returned to electoral politics in 1961, coup leader Col. Alparslan Türkes reinvented himself as a civilian politician, and later became head of the ultra-right National Action Party (NAP).[7]

Turks became increasingly polarized into right and left wing camps throughout the 60s, as anti-American sentiment began to rise over the situations in Palestine (see chapter 9) and Vietnam. Col. Türkes organized training camps for urban guerrilla warfare, and after the next coup in 1971, things began to get ugly. The Grey Wolves killed thousands of leftist students, journalists, activists and officials in a series of bombings, kidnappings and shootings. They operated with the assistance of the government's Special Warfare Department, itself headquartered on a U.S. military base.[8] During the height of this violence, CIA officer Dewey Clarridge, later famous in the Iran-Contra Scandal, was the Agency's top man in Turkey. Both the Wolves and the NAP were also allied with the CIA's global fascist organization the World Anti-Communist League—a neat fit for Col. Türkes, who had been an enthusiastic supporter of Hitler.[9] Turkish fascists were also allied with organized crime elements, and financed their arms purchases by facilitating heroin shipments from Afghanistan into Europe.[10]

All of this skullduggery by our proxies served to safeguard the crucial U.S. military bases on the Soviet border, by making sure no popularly elected government might try to establish a more neutralist policy. The warm relationship with Washington served Ankara well in its ongoing rivalry with fellow NATO member Greece. In the 70s the Greek regime was a mirror image of the Turkish fascists: a military government run by right-wing gangsters, backed by the CIA. The U.S. backed fascists in Greece for much the same reasons as in Turkey (and elsewhere): to crush leftists, and make sure the government was headed by the sorts of people we could do business with. Both governments had their eye on the strategically valuable island republic of Cyprus, then 82 percent Greek and 18 percent Turkish. The democratically elected president, Archbishop Makarios, was seen by both sides as an impediment to the work of their Mafia operations. U.S. foreign policy, as overseen by Henry Kissinger, was also disdainful of Makarios, since as an elected leader he would not be as easy to deal with as the military governments in Athens and Ankara. Washington let it be known that it didn't matter too much which side took him out—though it was generally understood that this might result in a war with the other side.[11]

So, with a wink from Kissinger, Greece staged a "coup" in Cyprus in July 1974, using regular Greek forces from the mainland. Turkey responded to the Greek invasion with two of its own, eventually seizing 40 percent of the island and setting up a Berlin Wall to seal off its territory. Thousands of civilians were killed and some 200,000 refugees were sent fleeing. A later inquiry by the European Commission on Human Rights found that Turkey had tortured and executed prisoners, deliberately killed civilians, herded residents into mass detention camps, and raped and looted with impunity.[12] Like Israel, Turkey then proceeded to illegally import settlers into its occupied territories.[13] The partition of Cyprus continues to this day, surviving a series of failed peace initiatives.

While the invasion led to an arms embargo against Ankara, it was wildly popular with the Turkish public. But even this surge in national pride could not erase the deep divisions in Turkish politics, and violence surrounded the elections of the late 70s. By 1979 this led to widespread imposition of martial law, and finally to a third coup, with CIA blessings, in 1980. The CIA-backed Counterguerrilla

Organization within the Turkish military provided weapons to paramilitary groups like the Grey Wolves. The Wolves, in turn, provided much of the street violence that served as a justification for the military takeover. The day after the coup, the CIA station chief in Ankara sent a simple message back home: "Our boys have done it!"[14] This earned him a congratulatory phone call from President Jimmy Carter.[15] The coup was followed by widespread purges, thousands of arrests, scores of executions, dismissal of hundreds of mayors and other officials, and yet another new constitution.

After three years of military rule, Turgot Özal was elected prime minister in 1983, leading the Reagan Administration to ease the arms embargo. Since that time, the U.S. has sold Turkey some $12 billion in military equipment.[16] Until 1999, Turkey was the third-largest recipient of U.S. aid, behind Israel and Egypt (it's now fourth, just behind Columbia).[17] The U.S. is determined to retain Turkey as a key client state in the region, since even after the fall of the USSR, its proximity to the Middle East and Central Asia makes it a valuable asset. The well-trained Turkish military has also provided troops to assist U.S. operations in Somalia, Korea, Serbia and Afghanistan.[18] All of the friendly assistance from Washington has of course been invaluable to Ankara in its ongoing project of ethnically cleansing its Kurdish population.

The 12-15 million Kurds constitute nearly one-fifth of the population of Turkey, but the use of their language in schools, courts, broadcasts or (until 1991) publications has been strictly forbidden.[19] Following World War I the Kurds had appealed to the allied powers for the establishment of a free Kurdistan. But their population ended up being divided amongst Turkey, Syria, Iran, and Iraq. Turkey alone took sovereignty over half of the Kurdish homeland, and in the 1920s killed some 15,000 Kurds who objected to this arrangement.[20] There have been periodic resurgences of Kurdish nationalism ever since, similarly quashed. In response to the imposition of "sheer state terror" in Turkish Kurdistan following the 1980 coup, the Kurdish People's Party (PKK) launched a guerrilla war in 1984.[21] From an original force of 200 fighters, the PKK grew to over 10,000 by 1992, with 50,000 local militias and some 375,000 active supporters.[22]

The reason for this rapid growth was the predictably bloody response of the Turkish military, which inspired PKK support from many Kurds who might otherwise have disdained its Marxist leanings and brutal tactics. Since 1984, Turkey has killed some 30,000 Kurds, scattered some 2 million refugees,[23] and depopulated more than 3000 villages. Turkish forces have used napalm, poison gas and other chemical weapons against the Kurds[24]—and 80% of the weapons have come from the U.S.[25] A program of assassinations has been carried out against Kurdish journalists, intellectuals and politicians, and thousands more have been imprisoned.[26]

The 1991 Persian Gulf War was a particular boon to Turkey's campaign. U.S. planes regularly bombed Iraq from Incirlik airbase, and in return Uncle Sam was willing to look the other way as the Kurds were crushed—not that he was looking all that carefully to begin with. In the wake of the Gulf War, the U.S. had encouraged Iraqi Kurds to rebel against Baghdad. But when Saddam's forces overwhelmed them, the U.S. did nothing to help the Kurds (see chapter 2). The resulting PR disaster led Washington to proclaim a "no-fly zone" in northern Iraq to protect the Kurds. Apparently, though, Washington only wants to protect Kurds from Iraqi planes. Turkey has regularly flown into Iraq, using U.S.-built

F-16s, to bomb Kurdish forces and refugees. Likewise, the Turkish army crosses over into "protected" Iraqi Kurdistan with impunity.[27]

Turkey also tried a carrot and stick approach, allowing Kurdish parties to participate in elections. But the government could not resist arresting their representatives for such crimes as speaking the Kurdish language in the legislature, or spreading "anti-state" propaganda.[28] Eventually the Kurdish People's Labor Party was again banned. The growing strength of the PKK, meanwhile, led Turkey to initiate major anti-insurgency campaigns in 1993 and 1996, with massive support from Washington. In 1994 alone, Turkey used U.S. helicopters and warplanes to wipe out 137 Kurdish villages, along with the forests surrounding them. And as Human Rights Watch complained, "The U.S. poured sophisticated weapons into Turkey every year, becoming complicit in a scorched earth campaign that violates the fundamental tenets of international law."[29]

This havoc led to the decimation of Kurdish civil society and eventually to the weakening of the PKK and the capture of its leader, Abdullah Ocalan, with critical intelligence from the CIA leading to his capture.[30] Kurdish resistance continues, though, and will either be suppressed or defused, lest it endanger the impending Baku-Ceyhan oil pipeline from Azerbaijan (see chapter 14). The proposed route travels directly through Kurdish territory, and will provide badly needed income to the ailing Turkish economy.[31]

Owing nearly $10 billion, Turkey is the world's largest debtor to the International Monetary Fund.[32] Turkish assistance to U.S. war campaigns in Afghanistan (and Georgia) led Washington to cancel some $5 billion of Ankara's military debt, and to influence the IMF for a massive $19 billion bailout.[33] Still, the IMF's typical austerity requirements, including clampdowns on labor rights and social spending, are unlikely to improve matters. The Turkish economy has been on the ropes for years, suffering from both high inflation and rising unemployment, with the national currency losing half its value in little more than a year. Still, this has not stopped Turkey from seeking still more military purchases, including an $4.5 billion purchase of 145 attack helicopters from U.S. defense contractor Bell Textron.[34]

Turkey's strategic value to the U.S. is its ace in the hole. When, in 2000, the U.S. Congress considered a non-binding resolution recognizing the 1915 Armenian genocide, Turkey made noises about closing Incirlik, and the measure was quickly dropped at President Clinton's suggestion.[35] Ankara has also formed a military alliance with Israel, beginning in 1996, with joint training and arms manufacturing agreements, as well as extensive cooperation between their intelligence services.[36] This has led to widespread resentment by Islamic partisans in Turkey, whose forces were on the rise in the 90s following years of enforced secularism imposed by Atatürk. These forces were strong enough to win major electoral victories, prompting the Turkish military to intervene once again in the late 90s to prevent Islamic parties from forming a government.[37]

More recently, though, in April 2002, the Turkish foreign minister forged an unprecedented joint venture with his Greek counterpart to visit Yassir Arafat, then under house arrest in the Israeli-occupied West Bank.[38] It was an effort to show that old enemies can sometimes cooperate. But the effort was not entirely altruistic. Turkey has an interest in settling the Cyprus conflict, since the Greek portion of the island will be granted membership in the European Union by

2004, with or without a peace deal. Turkey has been seeking
EU membership since 1964, but has been repeatedly rebuffed
due to its sordid human rights record.[39] It remains to be seen
whether that economic goal will prove more important to
Ankara than its military role as Uncle Sam's junior partner
in the region. By mid-2002, differences over concessions to
the EU had led the governing coalition to the brink of collapse, just as U.S. officials courted Turkey's support for another war on Iraq.[40]

In November 2002, the Islamic-oriented Justice and
Development (AK) party swept Turkish elections in a landslide. The ruling party of Prime Minister Ecevit received
approximately one percent of the vote as opposed to 34 percent for AK. The party's leader, Recep Erdogan, has been
banned from holding any seat in parliament (due to "inciting
religious hatred"), but made known his intention to form a
new government. His party pledged to respect secularism and
enact economic reforms to please the EU, but is also opposed
to any U.S. war on Iraq. This sets up a potential showdown
with Ankara's military leaders, who have made no secret of
their distaste for Erdogan and his party.[41]

Meanwhile, for another example of the type of friendly
regime we like to cut deals with, the example of Saudi Arabia
can be instructive.

CHAPTER ELEVEN

Saudi Arabia

The Family that Reigns Together

The nature of the U.S. relationship with Saudi Arabia proves that we have not learned our lessons after making similar messes in Iran and Iraq. The U.S. has always wanted a surrogate power to police the Persian Gulf, in order to safeguard the enormous oil reserves. To that end, we blindly armed the Shah of Iran, averting our eyes from his repression, until he was overthrown and his arsenal fell into the hands of a virulently anti-American regime (see chapter 1). To counter that threat, we blindly armed Saddam Hussein, averting our eyes from his repression, until he became too powerful and we had to fight a major war to destroy his arsenal, turning a generation of Iraqis against us in the process (see chapter 2).

Today, to counter the threat of Iraq, we have blindly armed the Saudi royal family, averting our eyes from their repression, which has created a generation of anti-American militants bound and determined to overthrow the corrupt regime propped up by our support. Nor do the Saudis seem to have learned much from the example of the Shah. By suppressing advocates of democracy as well as socialism, they leave dissidents no other avenue but the Islamic movement. All other religions are outlawed, and the state religion is the extreme puritanical sect of Islam known as Wahhabism, which the regime has sponsored the world over.[1]

Among the results of that sponsorship are Osama bin Laden and his al-Qaida network, who show no compunction about biting the hand that feeds them. The Saudis, as the Shah did, have attempted to pay off the religious movements in their country with what amounts to protection money,[2] while simultaneously enraging them with their personal corruption and gluttony—as well as what are perceived as anti-Islamic policies. Some influential Muslim fundamentalists have issued a *fatwa* (decree) against the royal family for allowing foreign troops on Islam's holiest soil[3] (where they have stayed since the Gulf War). But the Saudis could hardly do otherwise—that's why they were installed into power in the first place.

The name Saudi Arabia means that it literally belongs to that one family, the House of Sa'ud. They rose up out of the Riyadh area in the 18th century, hitching their wagon to the emerging Wahhabi movement. From the beginning, they showed a ruthless streak, massacring the village of Taif in 1802 on their way to looting the holy cities of Mecca and Medina.[4] It took 17 years for forces of the Ottoman Empire to crush the Saudi uprising. In 1902, they were at it again, when Abdul Aziz ibn Saud attacked and occupied the fortress at Riyadh, killing the Ottoman governor.[5]

About this time, the British were looking for local proxy forces to help counter Ottoman influence, and found that their agenda neatly coincided with Ibn Saud's. The British were especially keen to have access to intelligence from Mecca and Medina, from which non-Muslims were excluded. Just to hedge their bets, Britain backed both ibn Saud and a local rival, Sharif Hussain, promising each of them control over the Arabian peninsula once the Ottoman Empire was broken up. The Saudis managed to consolidate power during World War I, and signed a secret friendship treaty in 1915, which effectively installed the Saudi monarchy into power. Ibn Saud assumed control over the holy cities in 1933.[6]

That same year Saudi Arabia granted an oil concession to the U.S. company Socal, which grew into the jointly owned Arab-American Oil Company (Aramco). Following World War II, the Americans generally assumed control over most of Britain's imperial possessions in the Middle East (though not without some friction). The new relationship, guaranteeing Saudi security in return for oil rights, was cemented in the waning years of the war by a meeting between FDR and Ibn Saud.[7] A U.S. airbase was built at Dhahran, a source of indignation to Arab nationalists to this day (to save face, the base was later nationalized by the Saudis, who promptly hired the same Americans to run it for them).

Neither the Americans nor the British were deterred by Ibn Saud's habit of laughingly beating his servants with a large stick in front of his visitors. Nor was the relationship impeded by the family tradition—celebrated to this day—of lopping off hands, feet and heads in public squares for various infractions. The first Saudi king seeded his dynasty with more than forty sons from upwards of 100 wives, concubines and slaves. Today the Saudi royal family numbers an estimated 5000 males, with 30 to 40 more born every month, each granted a half million dollar annual stipend at birth to get started in the world[8] (Saudi princesses receive no such stipend, but rely on the generosity of their fathers and husbands).

Sons of ibn Saud rule the peninsula, and palace intrigue in the House of Sa'ud is of epic proportions. The eldest son Saud ruled from his father's death in 1953, until handing over power to Faisal in 1964. Faisal was assassinated by a nephew in 1975, and his successor Khalid was king in name only due to ill health. Crown Prince Fahd was the real power behind the throne until taking over formally in 1982, but now he too has been felled by illness, and a bitter succession struggle is under way. Pro- and anti-American forces are vying for control, with many, of course, playing both sides of the fence.[9]

Crown Prince Abdullah, 77, is nominally in charge. Abdullah is a pious Muslim, unlike many of his siblings, and is not too deferential to American wishes, though he will of course be happy to continue selling us oil. On the other hand, he is in favor of closer security ties with Iran, is enraged by U.S. policy towards Palestine, and recognizes that greater profits could be made by selling oil to South Asian markets. Abdullah has also made some efforts to crack down on the pervasive corruption in the royal family, a campaign that has earned him many enemies. It's said that King Fahd, who cannot recognize even his closest friends, is being kept alive only to prevent Abdullah from formally assuming the throne.[10]

The level of corruption in the House of Sa'ud is staggering. While they impose strict Wahhabi law on their subjects, with public beatings for alcohol consumption and amputations for thievery, the thousands of princes have siphoned off billions of dollars from the public treasury, wining and dining all over Europe and America, building lavish palaces and gambling away their stipends. A minor scandal ensued in Washington when some of the Saudi entourage's slaves tried to escape from a hotel suite by jumping out of windows. Meanwhile the standard of living for ordinary Saudi citizens has fallen dramatically over the past two decades, while annual budget deficits are soaring from the family's high living and the extraordinary level of military spending.[11]

After the Iranian revolution in 1979, which was followed soon after by an Islamic uprising in Mecca, the Saudi military budget began to expand dramatically. Growing mil-

itary ties with the U.S. were politically dicey for both countries. Pro-Israel members of the U.S. Congress were opposed
to major weapons sales to the Saudis, while King Fahd had to
placate the anti-Western faction led by Crown Prince
Abdullah throughout the 80s. So a covert relationship was
established that included privatized military training, oral
agreements rather than written treaties, and breaking arms
deals into smaller packages which would escape congressional review. The Saudis felt they could accommodate occasion-
al U.S. military deployments but no permanent basing of
U.S. troops.[12]

To that end, Saudi Arabia spent nearly $200 billion
from 1979 to 1989 on a network of secret military bases,
which were characterized as a "freeze-dried" U.S. presence:
just add personnel. The King Khalid Military City, just south
of the Kuwaiti border, was expanded from a small outpost to
a $6 billion megacomplex, complete with air-conditioned
underground bunkers, and a nearby port, built from scratch,
which instantly became one of the largest in the region. The
Arabian Peninsula was divided into five sections, each with
a state-of-the-art command and control center, all of them
tied into Riyadh by digital satellite links.[13]

This unprecedented secret arrangement (by contrast,
the CIA's entire ten-year war against the Soviets in
Afghanistan cost only $6 billion) dramatically increased the
stakes for both sides. The Saudis now required U.S. assistance to operate all their high-tech equipment, while the
U.S. became more committed to the House of Sa'ud than
ever, lest the network fall into hostile hands. Thus when
Saddam Hussein invaded Kuwait in August 1990, the first
Bush Administration was adamant that the freeze-dried army
be reconstituted.[14]

King Fahd was ambivalent; he felt that Saddam's com-

plaints against the Kuwaitis—of price-fixing and oil theft—
were not without merit (see chapter 2), and that perhaps a
face-saving agreement could be negotiated. But President
Bush wanted war, not negotiations; his administration
regarded a peaceful resolution as "the nightmare scenario."[15]
Defense Secretary Dick Cheney was sent to Riyadh with
satellite photos, which showed hundreds of thousands of
Iraqi troops massing on the Kuwaiti-Saudi border. But com-
mercially available satellite photos obtained by reporters
showed no such deployment.[16] That information, however,
came too late and was little noticed. By that time Fahd had,
against his better judgement, invited U.S. troops into Saudi
Arabia. Within months there were over 500,000 Americans
on Saudi soil, preparing to do battle against Iraq.

Ten years later, there are still up to 13,000 U.S. military
personnel and staff in Saudi Arabia,[17] as a more or less permanent deployment (the Pentagon says it expects to be
engaged in the Persian Gulf for the next 30 to 50 years).
Along with the soldiers are some 30,000 civilian personnel
working for U.S. companies.[18] These commitments have
caused some difficulties for both countries, as we have seen.
The Islamic opposition sees U.S. troops, not surprisingly, as
there, in part, to prop up the House of Sa'ud. So in an endless feedback loop, the U.S. military presence makes the
royal family even less legitimate in the eyes of Muslim critics—which, of course, makes the deployment to protect the
royals that much more necessary from the U.S. standpoint.

Saudi Arabia is not only our principal oil supplier in the
region but the keystone of a security arrangement involving
the smaller Gulf sheikdoms, including Kuwait, Bahrain,
Oman, Qatar and the United Arab Emirates.[19] U.S. companies have nearly $5 billion in investments in Saudi Arabia;

the royal family's investments in the U.S. are estimated in the hundreds of billions—perhaps half a trillion.[20] The U.S. is also the regime's principal arms supplier, with more than $40 billion in purchases from Riyadh during the 1990s.[21] Torture equipment has also been supplied by both U.S. and British companies, and according to Amnesty International, it is widely used against dissidents.[22]

In order to placate Islamists, the regime has set up a chain of Wahhabi religious schools both at home and worldwide, and anti-Western rhetoric is commonplace. Schools set up in northern Pakistan trained the students who became the Taliban regime—which could not have come to power without Saudi assistance.[23] Some 10,000 Saudi citizens are veterans of the U.S.-backed war against the Russians in Afghanistan during the 80s—and many are now opposing both the U.S. and the Saudi government. They are getting considerable assistance from wealthy Saudi citizens—including some within the royal family itself.[24]

The Saudi government initially refused to freeze the assets of al-Qaida or assist U.S. investigators in following the money.[25] According to the *Boston Herald*, banks controlled by bin Laden have "well-established ties to a prince in Saudi Arabia's royal family, several billionaire Saudi bankers, and the governments of Kuwait and Dubai."[26] Likewise, the Saudi-funded International Islamic Relief Organization (IIRO), a Muslim charity, has given more than $60 million to the Taliban regime. The IIRO has also supported separatist guerrillas in the Philippines through bin Laden's brother-in-law, who headed the Manilla branch.[27]

Prince Turkl al Faisal was forced to step down as chief of intelligence after the 9/11 attacks, due to his extensive links with the Taliban government and reputed sympathies for bin

Laden.[28] U.S. investigators are privately furious over Saudi foot-dragging in helping to investigate the backgrounds of the Saudi nationals involved in the hijackings. This mirrors earlier terrorist incidents on Saudi soil against U.S. targets. When, in 1995, five Americans were killed by a car bomb, immigrant workers who had "confessed" to the crimes were executed before U.S. agents could interrogate them.[29]

The same thing happened a year later when the Khobar Towers apartments in Dhahran were bombed, killing 19 U.S. soldiers. Investigations eventually showed that Iran may have been responsible, but Saudi authorities let the trail go cold, fearful that U.S. action against Iran might stir up their own Islamic radicals.[30] The split in the royal family reflects a debate within Saudi society on how much Western influence to accept, with those in favor generally the ones who are making a handsome living off their Western ties. Among the opposition, the argument was over whether to strike at the Saudi government, or its U.S. sponsor. The latter camp seems to have won that argument (at least for now), and the royal family apparently views this as a welcome reprieve. In their view, anti-Western agitation serves as a safety valve, letting off steam that would otherwise be directed at the government.[31] Needless to say, this is not a picture of a healthy alliance.

As a result, our national security has been endangered by powerful Americans who are making a handsome living off their Saudi ties. Among them, unfortunately, are the current President of the United States and his father, the former president. The elder Bush is a senior advisor to the Carlyle Group, an investment bank whose major shareholders included the bin Laden family of Saudi Arabia (at least until the 9/11 attacks made their participation an embarrassment, after which they quietly cashed out).[32] The younger Bush has also served on the board of a Carlyle subsidiary, and received a loan from a bin Laden family representative to start his first oil company, Arbusto Energy.[33] Many of the current president's closest backers have ties to the wealthy and influential Saudi businessman Khalid bin Mahfouz, known as a backer of Osama bin Laden (as well as his brother-in-law).[34] Vice President Cheney's old firm, Halliburton Co., has hundreds of millions of dollars in Saudi contracts, and numerous other Bush family friends and colleagues do extensive business with the Kingdom.[35]

As if all that were not disturbing enough, BBC investigator Greg Palast has reported that after taking office, the second Bush Administration told the FBI and military intelligence to "back off" from investigations of bin Laden's relatives.[36] The administration also quashed investigations into the Islamic charity WAMY, which links both to al-Qaida and to key GOP strategist Grover Norquist.[37] And shortly after 9/11, when all commercial air traffic in the U.S. was grounded, members of the bin Laden family were flown out of the U.S.—without being questioned by the FBI—reportedly at the behest of the president's father.[38] FBI agent John O'Neill, the government's top al-Qaida hunter, resigned in protest over the cover-up of the corrupt U.S.-Saudi connections. O'Neill told French journalists that the main obstacles to investigating Islamic terrorism were "U.S. corporate interests and the role played by Saudi Arabia in it."[39]

So on the one hand you have a cadre of government, military and corporate officials in both countries, all in bed together and making themselves wealthy at the expense of Saudi and U.S. citizens. On the other hand, the House of Sa'ud is split between those who wink at and those who fund terror attacks on Western targets—and neither government wants to look too closely at that situation for fear of upsetting the "alliance."[40] It's not too hard to imagine Saudi Arabia erupting into civil war, with our hundreds of billions of dollars in military equipment falling into the hands of the faction that loathes us for supporting the tyrants in Riyadh. And if that happens, we will once again be facing enemies we made for ourselves.

But Saudi Arabia is not the only place where that could happen, or even the most dangerous. The consequences of our shortsightedness could be even more serious in the case of another valued ally that just happens to be a sponsor of terrorism: Pakistan.

Part III

FRONTLINE STATES

CHAPTER TWELVE

Pakistan

Fair Weather Allies

From the point of view of Pakistanis, the U.S. has been a fair-weather friend, showering them with military and financial aid when their help was needed, otherwise ignoring or sanctioning them.[1] Obviously the world's largest superpower has a multiplicity of interests. The problem is that, arguably, it's the periods of friendship which have hurt Pakistan the most; the most radical and militant Islamic groups have been strengthened far beyond what their level of popular support would otherwise allow.

Islam is the reason Pakistan separated from India in the first place. Prior to the British occupation of the Indian sub-continent, the area now known as Pakistan had been a patchwork of small states and principalities. When the British left in 1947, they divided their vast dominion into predominantly Hindu and Muslim areas, creating East and West Pakistan on either side of the state of India.[2] This appeased the demands of the largest Islamic party, the All-Muslim League, who were then in conflict with Jawaharlal Nehru (later India's first prime minister). The problem is that there was no neat way of slicing up the turf, as the communities were intermingled. Many of the local politicians were given the power to decide to which country their region would belong, regardless of the view of the inhabitants. Border disputes were ultimately settled by the chair of the British boundary commission.

The partition was massively painful for both sides; from four to eleven million Hindus and Muslims moved from one state to the other,[3] while hundreds of thousands (some say millions)[4] were slaughtered by militants on either side. Among the messes left by the British Empire was the situation in Kashmir, in which several million Muslims ended up in Indian territory. Periodic wars, skirmishes and guerrilla activity have continued ever since, and both nuclear-armed states vow they will never relinquish their claim to the turf. In 2001, more people were killed every week in Kashmir than in the Israeli-occupied West Bank.[5]

The other legacy of the British is the Durand Line, which forms the border between Afghanistan and Pakistan. It was drawn to help weaken the rebellious Pashtun tribes, by dividing them between the two territories. Today, while Pashtuns are the majority ethnic group in Afghanistan, more of them live in northern Pakistan. Many have never accepted the Durand Line and call instead for an independent Pashtunistan. Even today, while Pakistan has repeatedly suppressed Pashtun nationalism, the province retains a semi-autonomous status and a porous border with the Afghan north.[6]

Pakistan has alternated between relatively weak civilian governments and military juntas, but the military has always been the main power in the country. U.S. military aid began in 1954, with Pakistan joining regional NATO-like alliances SEATO and the Baghdad Pact. That same year a "constitutional coup" took place when Pakistan's fractious Constituent Assembly was dissolved. A new assembly was elected not by the general population but by provincial leaders, who established a constitution two years later. But general elections were never held before General Ayub Khan took over in a 1958 military coup.

Under Ayub Khan the constitution was suspended, regional and national parliaments were dissolved, and martial law was imposed for four years. In 1962, a new constitution was written and Ayub the dictator became Ayub the president. That same year, during a border dispute between China and India, the U.S. 7th Fleet, complete with aircraft carriers and nuclear submarines, began patrolling the Indian Ocean as a show of force. Even if this was a message directed at the Chinese, it made the Indians nervous. A few years later the U.S. set up a military base on the Indian Ocean island of Diego Garcia, helpfully cleared of its original inhabitants by their British landlords.[8] The Diego Garcia base (later used in the Afghan and Gulf War campaigns) was armed with missiles in range of the Indian subcontinent. Many in India felt that Washington might not have been so bold if New Delhi were a nuclear power as well.[9] This helped to set in motion India's push to build a nuclear bomb, and Pakistan's in response.

In 1965, India and Pakistan went to war over Kashmir but neither side could make much headway and it ended in a stalemate and a cease-fire negotiated by the USSR. Opposition to Ayub Khan's rule grew following the war debacle despite (or because of) strict press censorship and his control of key politicians in the parliament. By 1969, this opposition had grown to the point of rioting in the streets and the breakdown of local authority, particularly in the East. Ayub Khan passed his power over to General Yahya Khan (no relation; "Khan" is an honorary title), who once again imposed martial law.[10]

Disaffection in Bengali-speaking East Pakistan over distant rule by the Urdu-speaking West had been simmering for years. In the 1970 elections, Bengalis voted as a unified bloc, gaining a parliamentary majority, which they intended to use in rectifying past grievances. Yahya was caught by surprise and reacted by putting off the convening of the assembly and arresting a key Bengali leader. Not surprisingly, this caused the situation in the East to escalate, resulting in the 1971 declaration of independence by Bangladesh.[11]

With the tacit approval of the Nixon Administration, Yahya Khan used his U.S.-made arsenal to brutally crack down on the independence movement. Thousands were slaughtered in the first few days. By the time it was over, ten million Bengalis had fled into India, and an estimated 1.5 million were killed. The secessionists also killed some 150,000 non-Bengalis in the East before independence was achieved.[12]

Yahya Khan's genocide against the Bengalis was carefully planned and took place after a lengthy and well-organized military buildup of West Pakistan forces in the East—with U.S.-supplied weapons, of course. The regime in Islamabad (West Pakistan's custom-built capital) planned the systematic assassination of political and cultural leaders in Bangladesh, and an indiscriminate campaign of mass murder and ethnic cleansing, which is exactly what occurred beginning on March 25, 1971.[13] The U.S. State Department had recommended a few weeks earlier that America use its influence to dissuade Yahya from the use of force. This suggestion was rejected by Henry Kissinger. His boss President Nixon regarded Yahya warmly, and had been using him for back-channel communications in forging a new relationship with China. Kissinger's deputy Winston Lord explained, "We had to demonstrate to China that we respect a mutual friend." What was demonstrated instead, as author Christopher Hitchens put it, was that "a perceived need to mollify China outweighed even the most minimal concern for human life elsewhere."[14]

Despite clear intelligence regarding Islamabad's intentions, no warnings were passed to Bangladesh. As Kissinger put it, Nixon "doesn't want to do anything…. He does not favor a very active policy." This "passivity" extended to the policy on arms sales as well. The rest of the world expressed horror over the months-long orgy of violence in Bangladesh, but the Nixon Administration kept silent, following the president's order not to "squeeze Yahya at this time." Finally world opinion led the U.S. to announce a ban on further arms sales, but the key word was "further." While the slaughter continued, shiploads of U.S. arms continued to sail into Pakistani ports for another nine months, until the entire $15 million of previously-ordered weapons had been delivered. According to the Nixon Administration, cutting off arms shipments would have been "an unwarranted intrusion into an essentially internal problem."[15]

The war finally ended when India intervened on behalf of the Bengalis to stop the bloodbath and the refugee flow on its eastern border. In response, the U.S. sent nuclear warships into the Bay of Bengal for another show of force. This led, in turn, to India's first nuclear test and an arms race on the subcontinent.[16]

Condemnation of Yahya Khan both inside and outside of Pakistan led to his downfall. Upon his resignation, Zulfiqar Ali Bhutto, who had led opposition to Ayub, became president. Bhutto tilted Pakistani politics in a populist direction, founding the Pakistani People's Party (PPP) under the slogan of "food, clothing and shelter."[17]

Bhutto pursued an independent foreign policy, maintaining friendly relations with U.S. allies like the Shah of

Iran and U.S. enemies like Salvador Allende of Chile. In 1975 he began military support of Islamic rebels in Afghanistan, worried that the Daoud regime was too friendly with the USSR[18]—and also that Daoud had designs on Pashtun lands in northern Pakistan.[19] Many of the Islamic militants nurtured by Pakistan, including Massoud, Hekmatyar and Rabbani, would go on to be leaders of the U.S.-backed Afghan war against the USSR (see chapter 13).[20]

The U.S. had reason to be both pleased and displeased with Bhutto, but one factor may have tipped the equation towards the latter: the "Islamic Bomb." It was Bhutto who coined the term, and extracted money from oil-rich Gulf sheikhs in order to counter India's first nuclear test in 1974.[21] Still, if Bhutto's Pakistan had been a favored ally like Israel or South Africa, it's doubtful that the nuclear program would have been an issue.

In his memoirs, Henry Kissinger calls Bhutto a "steady friend of the United States" who acted with "panache and wisdom" but who eventually "destroyed himself by seeking a popular mandate too rapidly" (whatever that means).[22] In his 1979 memoirs, "If I Am Assassinated," Bhutto paints a slightly different picture. He says that Kissinger threatened him, warning that he should "either give up the idea of a nuclear bomb or we will make of you a horrible example for the entire Islamic world."[23] This was no idle threat, nor was the title of Bhutto's book mere self-aggrandizement; it was written from death row, where he was later executed.

After the PPP won the 1977 elections with a huge majority, Bhutto was overthrown in a military coup. Two years later, despite protests by Jimmy Carter, Leonid Brezhnev and Pope John Paul II, he was put to death after a rigged show trial. Bhutto had antagonized his country's economic elites through his reform agenda, and the military elites through his growing authoritarianism.[24] Some have charged that the CIA backed the coup led by General Zia al-Huq.[25] Officially, the U.S. deplored Bhutto's execution and imposed sanctions in 1978 for the nuclear program. But behind the scenes, President Carter's national security advisor Zbigniew Brzezinski made the decision in 1979 to funnel U.S. aid to Islamic guerrillas in Afghanistan (eight months before the Soviet invasion), using Zia's regime as a secret conduit.[26]

From that point on, Zia's fortunes were on the rise. Bhutto may have been Pakistan's most popular leader, and Zia its most hated; he presided over the longest period of martial law in its history. But Zia had friends where it counts: in Washington. During his eleven years in power, ties between the CIA and its Pakistani counterpart, the ISI, became much stronger. Some six billion dollars in aid to the Afghan rebels, or *mujahedin*, was funneled through the ISI.[27]

In the process, the most ruthless elements of the movement were strengthened, and the Pakistan-Afghan border became the home to most of the world's heroin production.[28] CIA support for the *mujahedin* helped to strengthen conservative forces and weaken the left, both in Pakistan and in Afghanistan.[29] It also helped bolster Zia's program of Islamization. Pakistan's Islamic parties had never won a significant share of the vote in free elections, but Zia's 11-year dictatorship dramatically increased their influence.[30]

When the war against the Soviet presence in Afghanistan was over, the U.S. cash pipeline was shut down; Washington let Islamabad continue to serve as its regional proxy, with more latitude but fewer resources. Afghanistan was left in a state of anarchy, poverty and misery, and continued to be engulfed in civil war. The effects of this spilled across the border into Pakistan, and the culture of drugs, guns and religious extremism affected much of the border areas. While there had been almost no heroin addicts in Pakistan before the war, afterwards there were some four million—thanks to the ISI-backed heroin labs which helped fund the Afghan war effort.[31] There were also more than two million Afghan refugees on Pakistani soil. All of this thanks to the CIA's love affair with General Zia, who had by that time outlived his usefulness.

Zia was killed in a plane crash in 1988, which few regarded as an accident.[32] Elections later that year brought Bhutto's daughter Benazir Bhutto to power. She made efforts to mend fences with the omnipresent military, and moved away from her father's economic populism by agreeing to austerity plans recommended by the IMF and World Bank, which, of course, only weakened her popular support.[33] But Bhutto was deposed after less than two years in office following disputes with military leaders over internal security in the Sindh and Punjab provinces.[34]

During the 1990s, Pakistan experienced a spate of political crises, with four elected governments in a row cut short by the military, culminating in the coup of 1999.[35] Nawaz Sharif succeeded Benazir Bhutto until he too was deposed by the military in 1993. Then Bhutto was returned to power following elections held by a caretaker government. In 1996, Bhutto was again deposed, following corruption allegations against her husband (he remains in jail and Bhutto is in exile). Subsequently, Sharif returned to power for three more years.[36] Finally, in 1999, the military again resumed control after the second Sharif regime had lost all credibility. When he tried to dismiss the head of the army, General Pervez Musharraf, the latter took over in a bloodless coup.[37] Musharraf declared a national emergency, suspended the constitution, and broadly curtailed civil and political rights.[38]

In fact, the military and the ISI had been the most powerful elements in Pakistan all along. Bhutto complained that she had been left in the dark about many elements of the nuclear weapons program even when she was supposedly the head of government. Despite the 1978 sanctions, the U.S. never made much fuss about the Islamic Bomb as long as Zia's help was needed against the Soviets. But in 1990, the sanctions were strengthened, to the point that the U.S. refused to deliver F-16 aircraft for which Pakistan had already paid $600 million. While Bhutto was able to negotiate delivery of some military hardware, to this day neither the money nor the planes have gone to Pakistan.[39]

During Benazir Bhutto's second government, the ISI began funding the Taliban movement,[40] which had grown among war orphans educated in Saudi-financed religious schools in the border region (most had no other choice for schooling since IMF austerity had helped to decimate public schools in Pakistan).[41] The Pakistani trucking mafia was tired of the ongoing civil war in Afghanistan, which required endless tolls paid to various warlords. The Clinton Administration was also looking for stability in Afghanistan in order to facilitate a pipeline agreement connecting Pakistan and Turkmenistan, favored by the U.S. oil company Unocal.[42] The overlapping agendas of the ISI, the Saudis, the U.S. and various economic entities helped to bring the Taliban to power in Kabul in 1995. But the Taliban proved to be unreliable allies.[43]

When the U.S. decided to go to war against the Taliban

regime in 2001, Pakistan's help was required once again. But Musharraf's military government was stuck between a rock and a hard place. The ISI continued to be one of the main sponsors of the Taliban,[44] and assisting in an attack on Afghanistan would enrage Islamist forces both within the military and in civil society as well. But Washington would not take no for an answer.[45] After a few days' hesitation, Musharraf agreed to host U.S. forces for the war. He was rewarded with billions of dollars in loan forgiveness.[46] But the long-term effects of the war may further destabilize Pakistan.

Millions more refugees poured across the Afghan border, including unknown numbers of Taliban and al-Qaida fighters. Pakistan's hated enemies the Northern Alliance are in control of most of Afghanistan, and Musharraf has little to show for his support of the U.S. Over the past decade the poverty rate in Pakistan has doubled, from 17.2% to 35%.[47]

Press reports have indicated that members of the ISI and Pakistani nuclear scientists have been supportive of the al-Qaida network.[48] In fact, one ISI official was forced out after it was learned he had funneled cash to Mohammed Atta, reputed leader of the 9/11 hijackers.[49] Al-Qaida fighters have also assisted Pakistan in the ongoing jihad against Indian sovereignty in Kashmir.[50]

Though Musharraf has attempted to purge Islamist elements in his government and in the streets, he must also mollify them; it's unclear whether he will be able remain in control. In December 2001, after ISI-linked terrorists attacked the Indian parliament, the two nations were brought nearly to the brink of nuclear war.[51] Soon after, the *Wall Street Journal's* correspondent Daniel Pearl was abducted and murdered by a group also linked to the ISI—as well as to al-Qaida.[52]

In May 2002, U.S. forces officially brought the war across Pakistan's borders, something that had been previously denied in deference to Musharraf's political dilemma.[53] This did not stop him from claiming a 98% mandate in a rigged "referendum" granting him another five years in power,[54] but the heavy-handedness of the ploy suggests he's not a secure as he claims. Eager to remain useful to his patrons, Musharraf was also quick to sign on to the revived Afghan pipeline deal with that country's interim leader Hamid Karzai.[55]

In an effort to present a democratic façade, Musharraf pledged that a newly-elected legislature would take over the governing of country. But the elections did not go as planned. Despite the military's best efforts, the new Musharraf-backed party, the PMLQ, failed to win a majority. Instead, an alliance of six Islamic parties did unexpectedly well, taking over the provinces bordering Afghanistan and preventing any one party from forming a majority. The alliance, called the MMA, did far better than any Islamic party had in previous elections.[56] Observers said this was in part a result of anger towards the U.S.-backed war along the Afghan border and Musharraf's alliance with Washington.[57]

Ironically, Musharraf helped create a political vacuum by banning former prime ministers Bhutto and Sharif from participating in the elections.[58] From exile, the two of them joined forces and steered their PPP into an alliance with the MMA. The two groups held little in common besides antipathy to the military dictator. Bhutto's party supports better relations with the U.S. and cooperation with international financial institutions. In contrast, the leader of the MMA, Fazlur Rehman, is an admirer of bin Laden and the Taliban and once called for a "holy war" against George W. Bush.[59] But together, the coalition claimed enough parliamentary seats to form a new government. Unsurprisingly, Musharraf used his new constitutional powers (which the opposition parties had promised to nullify), and decided to "postpone the national assembly's inaugural session." With a straight face, the general claimed to be taking this step "in the best interests of democracy."[60] When the parliament reconvened a week later, Musharraf had managed to cobble together a majority for a prime minister loyal to him.[61]

This move is unlikely to permanently defuse the crisis. As one Pakistani professor predicted, "There will be a lot of confrontation."[62] At the very least, MMA support in the border provinces is likely to complicate the U.S.-led war effort. In a worst-case scenario, these deep-seated antipathies could fester into civil war. Both the military and the opposition face the dilemma between either pushing the other too hard, or backing off and strengthening the other side's hand.

But once Pakistan's help is no longer needed, the question of the Islamic Bomb may again complicate relations with Washington. The U.S. has shown it is certainly not averse to "regime change" when it so desires, but the political pressures rocking General Musharraf would not disappear under any successor. The billions of dollars with which the CIA nurtured Islamic radicalism in Pakistan may come back to haunt us more than once. As the history of this and other chapters shows, we have nurtured radical Islamic forces to pursue foreign policy goals in Saudi Arabia, Afghanistan, Iran, Pakistan...all the while financing those who impose economic hardship on their populations, for example in Jordan, Pakistan and Egypt. Is it any surprise when these very forces—which increasingly are the only means for protesting our policies—come back to attack us?

With that in mind, let's take a look at the history of Afghanistan.

CHAPTER THIRTEEN

Afghanistan

Proxy Wars, Proxy Victims

The history of Afghanistan and the U.S. involvement in it provide a stark example of the costs of using countries as pawns and of elevating control of resources such as oil over human rights. The consequences, as we suddenly learned on September 11, have hit home.

The root of the terror inflicted on Afghanistan can be traced back to its very identity as a nation: its borders represent a clumsy imposition of colonial administration by the British Empire. Like those of so many other colonial remnants, its arbitrary boundaries are a recipe for tribal and ethnic conflict. About a dozen major ethnolinguistic groups have been forced under the umbrella called Afghanistan. Some are of Persian descent, like the Tajiks in the northeast and the Pashtuns in the southeast, who also spread across northwestern Pakistan. In the northwest are Turkic tribes, like the Uzbeks bordering Uzbekistan and the Turkmens of neighboring Turkmenistan. Then there are the Baluchs in the southwest, who are part of the theoretical country known as Baluchistan, which would also take up chunks of eastern Iran and western Pakistan if it were allowed to exist.[1] Diversity can be a strength to any nation, but such advantage doesn't accrue when mandated by the whim of an empire—nor when communities are intentionally divided by borders.

Wherever you draw the borders, this turf has been the stomping ground of imperial armies since the time of

Alexander the Great—who was the last to successfully conquer it, in 329 BC. The British and Russian empires fought several wars there in the 19th and early 20th centuries. It was known as the "great game," a struggle to counter each other's influence over various resources and land routes between Europe and Asia. But the locals weren't keen on being occupied and repeatedly humbled the infidels. Afghanistan achieved full independence in 1919.[2]

Not all empires are created equal, and U.S. support for the fanatical Islamic guerrillas known as the *mujahedin* was, ostensibly, a benevolent response to the Soviet invasion of Afghanistan in 1979. How could the world's greatest democracy have stood by and not thwarted Soviet imperial ambitions? It's a compelling appeal to principle. But one fact gets in the way of our lofty image of the U.S. as crusader for freedom: our intervention predated the Soviets' move and was designed with two objectives in mind: provoke the Soviets to invade,[3] and squelch a popular move toward socialism.

What propelled the U.S. to suppress the very values we claim to promote throughout the world? Our sometime allies in Pakistan began funding mujahedin rebels in 1975, hoping to destabilize the secular Afghan regime of Daoud Khan, who had overthrown the monarchy in 1973 (King Zahir had likewise replaced Daoud's earlier government in 1963). Daoud suppressed the rebellion, with the help of the neighboring Shah of Iran, who had his own troubles with Islamic fundamentalists. But weakening the Muslim factions inadvertently helped to strengthen Afghan socialists. After crushing the Muslims, Daoud sought to purge the left as well, but they took over in a popular coup in 1978.[4] Afghanistan, as one of the poorest countries on the planet, was fertile ground for a Marxist appeal.

This caught the attention of the United States, who saw

the new government of Noor Mohammed Taraki as a domino to be pushed back in the wake of our setbacks in Vietnam. When the Shah of Iran was overthrown in early 1979, the balance of power in the region became severely unbalanced. A 1979 State Department memo strips away any pretense of being a force for freedom in the region: "The United States' larger interest would be served by the demise of the Taraki-Amin regime, *despite whatever setbacks this might mean for future social and economic reforms in Afghanistan*"[5] (emphasis added). U.S. efforts marked the beginning of Afghanistan's descent into hell.

Taraki had embarked on a program of land reform, including suppression of opium cultivation by fundamentalists, who had used the revenues to fund further insurrections. The mujahedin were also outraged by the new government's emphasis on women's rights.[6] Far from being alarmed by this threat to human rights and stability, U.S. National Security Advisor Zbigniew Brzezinski saw the fury of the Islamic rebels as "an opportunity of giving to the USSR its Vietnam War."[7] Brzezinski advised President Carter that the new Afghan regime was part of the Soviet plan to dominate South Asia. This despite the fact that the State Department had found no Soviet complicity in the 1978 coup,[8] and that the Russians were, in fact, advising Taraki to slow down the pace of reforms in the interest of stability.[9] Nonetheless, Brzezinski advised Carter to authorize aid to the mujahedin, noting, correctly as it turned out, that "this aid was going to induce a Soviet military intervention."[10]

Brzezinski's advice, and the orders of a President who would subsequently retire to teach Sunday school, were designed to and succeeded in setting in motion a war. A war that created five and a half million refugees, half a million injured, and left a million dead. About half of Afghanistan's pre-war population of 12-15 million were maimed, made homeless, or killed; more than half the villages were destroyed.[11] The country has been at war ever since.

Brzezinski is unrepentant and crystal clear about U.S. priorities. "Regret what?" he asked an interviewer years later. "That secret operation was an excellent idea. It had the effect of drawing the Russians into the Afghan trap and you want me to regret it?"[12]

U.S. funding of renewed the Islamic insurgencies, combined with funding by Pakistan and Saudi Arabia, created problems for Taraki, who traveled to Moscow in September 1979 for advice. On his return, he was arrested and executed by his deputy, Hafizullah Amin. Amin, who was meeting regularly with U.S. embassy officials, had been educated in the U.S.[13] U.S. officials, meanwhile, were in turn meeting with the Pakistani-backed Islamic rebels.[14] The Soviets, not surprisingly, viewed U.S. interventions in the area as part of Washington's plan to dominate South Asia. Alarmed by the possibility of a fundamentalist regime on their borders, the USSR invaded in December 1979 and set up the puppet government of Babrak Kamal.[15]

Afghanistan's fate as the latest pawn in the Cold War was sealed. If the underlying intent of U.S. actions had been to nurture freedom and democracy in the country, a natural step would have been to aid Afghan moderates; at that point there were still constitutional reformers and secular nationalists who had not yet been purged by Islamists and Marxists.[16] There was even a pacifist movement in the Pashtun areas, led by Abdul Gaffar Khan, the "Islamic Gandhi."[17] No dice: the plan to "bleed" the Soviets was paramount. Pakistan's ISI was used as middleman to recruit the most fanatical Islamic warriors (of the seven Islamic groups backed by the CIA, nearly half of all funds went to the nastiest, headed by Gulbuddin Hekmatyar, a bloodthirsty medieval theocrat).[18] The hope was to destabilize not only the regime in Kabul, but also the predominantly Muslim border republics of the USSR.[19] The recruiting met with great success: 35,000 Muslims from all over the world came to join the jihad against the atheistic Soviets.[20]

One of the volunteers was a young Saudi millionaire named Osama bin Laden. Bin Laden was recruited by the CIA in Istanbul in 1979. A civil engineer, he was initially responsible for logistics, but soon became the main financial intermediary for U.S. and Saudi funding. Working closely with the Agency and his friend Prince Turkl, the Saudi intelligence chief, he helped to recruit other radical Muslims throughout the Arab world, and proved to be a talented fundraiser for the cause. Bin Laden also worked closely with the fanatical warlord Hekmatyar, the CIA's favorite, in raising funds through opium trafficking.[21] While distributing resources to the seven Islamic resistance groups, bin Laden also developed close ties with some of the fundamentalist Afghans who later formed the Taliban, helping to set up a network of schools along the Pakistani border to train young Muslim boys for the jihad.[22]

The Soviets matched the rebels' fury with near-genocidal intensity, and seemed to be winning the war until 1986, when CIA Director William Casey authorized the sale of U.S.-made Stinger anti-aircraft missiles to the rebels.[23] The mujahedin, who had already shot down a civilian airliner in 1984, began inflicting greater losses on the Soviets. The USSR withdrew its troops in 1989, after losing nearly 15,000 soldiers. The day after the last Soviet troops departed,

Mikhail Gorbachev proposed a cease-fire, to be followed by UN-supervised elections. The Soviet-backed Afghan leader, Najibullah, offered to step down prior to elections, or to form a coalition government with moderate Islamists to prevent the rise of extremists. But the U.S. and its Islamic proxies would have none of it, preferring instead to press on to total victory.[24]

So Afghanistan's agony didn't end with the Soviet withdrawal. Having accomplished its aim of bleeding the USSR, the U.S. turned its back while Pakistan and Saudi Arabia continued to back the most radical Islamic factions, and the country descended into endless civil war. The mujahedin took Kabul in 1992, but fighting continued as the guerrilla leader Hekmatyar reduced what was left of Kabul to rubble in a series of rocket attacks. Some 50,000 more Afghan civilians were killed during this period.[25] Hekmatyar took over in 1994, but was himself attacked by the Taliban—an extremist Islamic sect influenced by Wahhabism, the state religion of Saudi Arabia and the other Gulf monarchies.

The Clinton Administration made U.S. foreign policies clear again when it supported the flow of military and financial aid from the Saudis and Pakistanis to the Taliban from 1994-96. Despite Taliban fanaticism, the U.S. initially welcomed their takeover of Afghanistan in 1996. Again the interests were monetary: the U.S. hoped the Taliban could impose enough stability on Afghanistan to allow construction of a natural gas pipeline from the energy-rich countries to the north. The costs to the civilian population were high: the Taliban installed a ruthless theocracy, with religious police beating suspects in the streets for even minor offenses. Women were not permitted to attend school or take jobs, and could not appear in public unless shrouded from head to toe. Meanwhile, fighting continued with northern tribes armed by Russia, India and Iran. Relations with Washington deteriorated after Osama bin Laden returned to Afghanistan in 1997 and began attacking U.S. targets, a matter to be discussed below later. Sanctions were imposed on Kabul in 1999.[26]

But hopes for the pipeline continued. John Maresca of Unocal testified before Congress in 1998, noting that construction could not, of course, not begin until a more satisfactory government took power in Kabul. Still, he explained that the route from the energy reserves of the Caspian Sea, running through Afghanistan down to the Pakistani coast, was "the best option with the fewest technical difficulties. It is the shortest route to the sea and has relatively favorable terrain for a pipeline." Maresca added, "there is considerable international and regional interest in this pipeline."[27]

Once the Bush Administration took office in 2001, a warming trend in U.S.-Taliban relations began anew. Secretary of State Colin Powell was said to have disapproved of the thaw but was overruled by CIA interests in the administration.[28] Kabul sent envoys to meet with old allies from the Reagan/Bush years at CIA headquarters. Afghanistan's unofficial U.S. ambassador Laili Helms, niece-in-law of former CIA Director Richard Helms, arranged the meetings.[29] Following these meetings, the U.S. tilted against the anti-Taliban forces of the Northern Alliance still fighting on the Turkmen and Tajik borders.[30] Increased food aid went to help the Afghans, struggling with a four-year drought, and Bush Administration officials also sent $43 million in drug war funds, lauding the Taliban's efforts to suppress opium exports.[31] At least $125 million went from Washington to Kabul in 2001, making the U.S. the largest source of funds to what George W. Bush later called the regime of "evildoers."[32]

All that good feeling ended on September 11, of course,

because as it turns out the mujahedin had been doing a lot more than simply fighting amongst themselves after the Russians left. Just as Brzezinski and Casey had hoped, they had brought their jihad to the southern republics of the Soviet Union, even after there was no more Soviet Union left to destabilize. Rebellions in Kazakhstan, Uzbekistan, Kyrgyzstan, Turkmenistan and Tajikistan continue to simmer more than a dozen years later (see chapter 14). Islamic forces linked to bin Laden and the Taliban have also helped pin down the Russians in Chechnya, the Chinese in Xinjiang, and the Indians in Kashmir.[33] Bin Laden's jihad has also served U.S. interests in the Balkans, fighting on the side of NATO-backed Muslim forces in Bosnia, Kosovo and Macedonia.[34]

At the same time, bin Laden and other former mujahedin have actively worked against U.S. interests by attacking client regimes in Egypt, Jordan and Saudi Arabia. The Saudi-born bin Laden returned to his homeland in 1990, disillusioned with Afghan infighting. He founded a charitable organization for Arab veterans of the Afghan war and survivors of those killed. When Iraqi leader Saddam Hussein's secular regime invaded the Emirate of Kuwait, bin Laden offered to help set up a new Islamic army to assist his fellow Wahhabis. Instead, to his eternal outrage, the Saudi royal family brought in half a million American troops.[35]

Even worse, to the Islamic radicals, was that after the end of the Gulf War, some U.S. troops remained on Saudi soil, home to some of Islam's holiest sites. Alarmed by his calls for the overthrow of the royal family, the Saudis revoked bin Laden's citizenship and expelled him in 1994—though many influential Saudis continued to support him (see chapter 11). Disgusted by the corruption of the U.S. client states and their acquiescence in Israel's occupation of other holy sites in Jerusalem, bin Laden and other ex-mujahedin declared a jihad against America. Alliances between the various Islamic paramilitary groups and with states in the region are difficult to sort out, but bin Laden and groups alleged to be "linked" to him are suspected in a number of attacks against U.S. installations. These include a car bombing in Riyadh, the destruction of the Khobar Towers housing U.S. troops in Saudi Arabia, bombings of U.S. embassies in Tanzania and Kenya, and the suicide attack on the USS Cole in Yemen.[36]

But as the second Bush Administration tilted towards the Taliban, bringing bin Laden to justice seemed to be less of a priority than rekindling the dormant pipeline deals. The CIA, eager to work with old mujahedin pals from the drug smuggling and arms trafficking days, argued that the threat from bin Laden was "overblown."[37] So further meetings followed the Taliban envoys' trip to Washington, but the negotiations did not go well. The U.S. demanded that transit rights be granted to Western companies, that the mullahs share power with deposed King Zahir Shah, and that bin Laden be handed over.[38] There were factions of the Taliban willing to extradite bin Laden to an international court, provided they were shown evidence against him.[39] The U.S. refused this utterly reasonable request, both before and after 9/11, on the grounds that such information would compromise security sources.

For their part, the Taliban were insulted at being ordered to share power with a monarch deposed in 1973, who they believed to be corrupt. As for the pipeline, they had a better offer from an Argentine firm, which offered to build terminals and other infrastructure in Afghanistan instead of just bypassing it on the way to the Pakistani coast.[40] Apparently the U.S. felt the Taliban should be satisfied with the cash influx from the pipeline transit rights. If not, the alternative was spelled out: "Either you accept our offer of a carpet of gold or we will bury you under a carpet of bombs."[41] Pakistani diplomat Niaz Naik was told in mid-July 2001, at a UN conference on Afghanistan, that the U.S. was planning military action against the Taliban to begin no later than October. While the Taliban had refused to attend, the Pakistanis duly passed this war threat along to them.[42] By this point reports on the planned military action had also appeared in the periodicals *India Reacts* and *Jane's International Security*.[43] Military plans for an attack on Afghanistan reached President Bush's desk on September 9, 2001.[44]

So while none of the 9/11 suicide attackers came from Afghanistan, the Afghan people paid the price—for living on a strategic piece of turf, if nothing else. After 22 years of war, war was waged again with renewed intensity. After a punishing drought and the resulting famine, international aid agencies reluctantly withdrew in advance of the pending U.S. attack, putting millions of lives at risk.[45] While the U.S. made war on the Taliban and tilted back to the Northern Alliance, civilians died by the thousands in allied bombing raids[46] or in squalid refugee camps.[47] While the Taliban were deposed and al-Qaida dispersed, their leaders remained free.[48] The Afghan people were freer than under the Taliban, but were still ruled by brutal warlords with appalling human rights records—many of whom had shelled Kabul into ruins a decade earlier.[49] And the rekindled civil war had no end in sight.

As head of the interim government in Kabul, the U.S. installed Hamid Karzai, who had previously worked as a consultant for none other than Unocal. (The U.S. also sent another Unocal consultant, Zalmay Khalilzad, as the

President's special envoy).[50] Not surprisingly, the Karzai
regime revived the pipeline deal so strenuously desired by
Washington, signing an agreement with Pakistan and
Turkmenistan in May 2002.[51]

To support Karzai, the U.S. continues to make war on
uncooperative warlords, including the resurgent Gulbuddin
Hekmatyar.[52] Afghan civilians continue to be caught in the
crossfire; one soldier told his hometown paper, "We were told
there were no friendly forces. If there was anybody there,
they were the enemy. We were told specifically that if there
were women and children to kill them."[53] In July 2002, the
U.S. waged a two-hour assault on a wedding party after mis-
taking celebratory gunfire for anti-aircraft attacks. Scores
were killed, mostly women and children.[54] And in case you
think the Afghans have suffered everything but a plague of
locusts, think again: the locusts arrived in April 2002.[55]
Right after the earthquake.[56]

By providing thousands of fanatics with weapons and
cash beyond their wildest dreams, then giving them ample
reason to hate America, our Afghan policies have demonstra-
bly harmed our national security. Our current sojourn in
Afghanistan is likely to do the same, providing plenty of new
recruits for the terrorist forces. Even the British, our closest
allies, felt compelled to protest the "blundering" of our
"march-in-shooting" raids in Pashtun territory, which, they
said, "will just backfire and increase sympathy for al-Qaida."[57]

In pursuit of cheap energy and taxpayer-subsidized profits for a few oil companies, our nation is likely to be engaged
in Afghanistan for many years to come. But Afghanistan isn't
even the real prize; as we shall see, its main strategic value is
that it provides transport routes from the energy-rich countries surrounding the Caspian Sea—notably Turkmenistan,

Uzbekistan and Kazakhstan.

It's important to note that some critics have belittled the notion that energy policy has had anything to do with our ongoing war in Afghanistan. Widely cited is an article by Ken Silverstein in the *American Prospect*,[58] which dismisses anyone who entertains the idea that oil is central to our policy in Afghanistan. The piece equates this point with the idea that the Bush Administration had foreknowledge of the 9/11 attacks—but these are two separate matters. You don't have to believe that Bush had prior knowledge of 9/11 to understand that oil and gas were a significant prize in the mix of our invasion of Afghanistan.

Silverstein quotes a few oil experts who find the idea of a Trans-Afghan Pipeline "utterly ridiculous"—despite the fact that it was pursued by both the Clinton and Bush II administrations. And as noted above, the pipeline deal was revived as soon as the Karzai regime took over in Kabul. Silverstein holds that this deal is irrelevant, though, without the financial backing to make it happen. But just as his article appeared in the summer of 2002, the Asian Development Bank stepped in with financing.[59]

Nothing in Silverstein's article refutes—or attempts to refute—the evidence above that the U.S. was planning a war in Afghanistan well before the attacks of September 11, 2001. Those war plans were sent to the president, not just kept on a shelf until needed—and that occurred in the context of the U.S. having made threats of war against Afghanistan during the summer of 2001, and having indicated to allies the intention of following through on those threats.

At first glance, Silverstein's other arguments may appear valid. But further excavation of key facts shows just how important Afghanistan is to the oil picture—and our strategy of world domination.

- **"We didn't care about Afghanistan, we cared about bin Laden."** If so, we had a funny way of showing it. As soon as the Bush Administration took the White House, they reversed Clinton's policy of not negotiating with the Taliban. Several rounds of talks were held and from all accounts, bin Laden was not our main interest.[60] According to *Washington Post* reporter Barton Gellman, Bush also reversed Clinton's aggressive policy of targeting bin Laden. The Bush Administration had our special "get bin Laden" forces in Uzbekistan stand down. They also canceled the cruise missiles stationed on submarines off the Pakistani coast, which were on permanent stand-by to launch if bin Laden's coordinates could be ascertained.[61] And, according to BBC reporter Greg Palast, the Bush Administration also put pressure on the FBI to lay off investigating the bin Laden family.[62] Finally, as is well known, bin Laden's relatives were flown out of the U.S. in a chartered jet at a time when all U.S. airliners were grounded.[63] If we cared so much about bin Laden, we might have spent a bit of time interrogating those who knew him.

    Recall Niaz Naik, the Pakistani diplomat who witnessed U.S. threats against Afghanistan in July 2001. He told the BBC after the 9/11 attacks (but before the war began in October) that "it was doubtful that Washington would drop its plan even if bin Laden were to be surrendered immediately by the Taliban."[64]

    But most damaging to this thesis is the flat out statement, made after 9/11, from General Tommy Franks, commander of U.S. forces in Afghanistan, that apprehending Osama bin Laden was not his mission.[65] Journalist Seymour Hersh provides corroborating evidence, describing how U.S. forces held back while al-

Qaida fighters were airlifted out of Afghanistan by the Pakistanis.[66] But while al-Qaida has scattered, our troops remain in Afghanistan to this day, and by all appearances, they are going to be there for a long time to come.[67] Furthermore, as General Franks suggests, it may be necessary to expand the war into neighboring countries[68]—specifically, those in the oil-rich Caspian region. Franks would of course not suggest that we plan to stay around the Caspian in order to be the pipeline police. What he says, in classic bureaucratese, is that we will "do the work that all of us recognize needs to be done. It won't be finished until it's all done [i.e., pursuing al-Qaida/Taliban terrorists]." The beauty of this, from the Pentagon's standpoint, is that anybody who opposes our presence can be labeled al-Qaida and/or Taliban, just as anyone who resisted U.S. interventions during the Cold War had to be a communist.

Silverstein's article in no way concedes that the oilmen in the Bush Administration had any interest in the region's resources, despite the extensive focus on same in Vice-President Cheney's energy plan, issued earlier that year. Obviously, following the 9/11 attacks, the U.S. cared a great deal about Osama bin Laden, and would have pursued al-Qaida forces even if they were holed up in a resource-poor corner of the world. But it's just as obvious that the U.S. cares a great deal about controlling strategic resources, and had long been interested in Afghanistan for that reason—even when bin Laden was living in Sudan (see chapter 4).

- **Many who have written about the Trans-Afghan Pipeline don't understand that the original Unocal deal was for gas, not oil, and that Unocal now says it**

wants nothing to do with it. Perhaps. But Unocal's denial may just be for public consumption, as it has suffered frequent criticism for its alliances with abusive regimes.[69] Industry insiders say they expect Unocal to come back on board. A separate oil pipeline deal is also in the works, and Unocal has pointedly failed to contradict reports that it has an interest in this project.[70]

- **Afghanistan itself is a resource-poor "desert waste with a few fly-ridden bazaars, a fair number of feuding tribes and a lot of miserably poor people," says Silverstein, quoting from *The Wall Street Journal's* Peter Kann (in 1973)—thus it is hardly worth fighting over.** Yet Afghanistan has gas reserves of about 5 trillion cubic feet, about half that of its neighbor Turkmenistan. And according to the State Department, Afghanistan has "a wealth of natural resources," including coal, copper, lead, zinc, iron ore and precious and semiprecious stones.[71] But even without any mineral wealth, Afghanistan's turf is strategically located just south of the more valuable countries of the Caspian region. The war in Afghanistan has allowed the U.S. to set up more than a dozen new military bases in and around that region.[72] And as noted in this book's introduction, projecting military might in a strategic area can be critical to controlling the flow of oil and gas; having bases even in a country with little mineral worth itself could be an important asset (see chapter 14).

- **The Trans-Afghan Pipeline was so risky from the start that it can't possibly be part of the U.S. objective there, and the country is even less stable than it was under the Taliban.** Here Silverstein raises a host of objections to the Afghan pipeline: extremely expensive, financing questionable, unstable leadership, violent clashes along the route, more attractive options elsewhere, and seeming indifference from major industry players. The objections have merit. But all these indicators that prove such a project is not feasible or worthy of the effort would have applied equally to the Baku-Ceyhan pipeline, now under construction. Critics such as Andrew Kilgore argued[73] that the line from corrupt Azerbaijan, through unstable Georgia, over mountainous eastern Turkey with its ongoing ethnic tensions, would never be built. Yet construction has begun, due to the sheer force of will of the U.S. government (see chapter 14).

Returning to Afghanistan, the risks are indeed obvious. But it's clear from the Baku-Ceyhan example that assessments of whether risk deters such construction may well be wrong. What counts in understanding U.S. and corporate motives isn't a guess about relative risk; it's what those parties are actually doing. In the case of Afghanistan, risk didn't stop the U.S. government from backing the pipeline. Silverstein points out that the Clinton Administration changed its focus from building a pipeline to responding to al-Qaida after the bombings of our African embassies. But the U.S. has backed and abandoned many players in Afghanistan, including Rabbani, Hekmatyar, and the Taliban, in an effort to find a reliable client like Hamid Karzai.[74] What is critical in assessing enthusiasm for a pipeline—and more crucially the role of oil in U.S. plans—is the fact that even after the African bombings and that of the USS Cole, the Bush Administration went back to the Taliban to try and strike a deal and revive the project.[75]

- **The U.S. won't benefit from Caspian energy reserves, which will be marketed in Europe, Russia and Asia.** U.S. companies like Bechtel, GE, Chevron, Halliburton and Unocal would not be active in the Caspian if they didn't think they could benefit from it. And in fact, pending completion of the Baku-Ceyhan pipeline, Caspian oil could (potentially) be shipped to American shores, through the Mediterranean Sea. But obviously if Russia and Europe are buying more Caspian oil it frees up other sources for the U.S. market. More importantly, Silverstein throughout acts as if the motivation for interventions in Central Asia is the *purchase* of oil when in fact it's the *control* of oil that matters more. Anybody will sell you oil, because they need the money as much as you need the energy. But the more client regimes you have to help affect pricing decisions, the more control you have. America gets the majority of its oil supply from outside the Middle East, but that doesn't stop us from expending considerable blood and treasure there in an effort to maintain control. The Saudis and other client regimes can be counted on to open up the taps in order to lower prices in a crisis, or restrict production when prices get to be too low. And while we ourselves are not overly dependent on Middle East oil—though we will be in another decade or two—the Europeans and the Japanese are. So whatever control we can maintain gives us strategic and political leverage against our allies, helping to keep them dependent on us.[76]

- **Now that Russia is being more cooperative, a pipeline south from the Caspian makes less sense.** But what Silverstein also fails to note is that although there is a glut of sources in Russia to serve its own and European markets, Asian markets are and will be more profitable, as demand skyrockets in India, China, and smaller states.[77] Even Baku-Ceyhan doesn't help with that; only the Trans-Afghan lines get oil and gas to those markets. Likewise, as reserves all over the planet begin to run out, untapped oilfields will become that much more profitable, and the U.S. wants to be sure its firms get a big piece of that pie. Moreover, while Russia has become more cooperative, it could again become less so. Moscow has proven to be an unreliable partner, not always paying what it promised, and using its pipeline monopoly to extract political leverage (see chapter 14). The dangers of putting all the eggs in one basket are by now apparent; an Afghan pipeline alleviates this risk.

- **The leader of Turkmenistan is an unstable megalomaniac, which makes Western companies reluctant to invest in a pipeline running from that country into Afghanistan.** Such companies have, of course, shown little hesitation to work with far more unstable characters if they thought there was a profit to be made— Muamar Qadaffy, for instance, or Saddam Hussein before the invasion of Kuwait. And such personality problems in Turkmenistan's leader haven't prevented the Russians from dealing with the country, as Silverstein demonstrates. Why should that be true for the U.S.? In any event, as discussed in the next chapter (and not in Silverstein's piece) there seems to be a budding effort to effect a regime change in Turkmenistan. Such a change would render this particular objection about Turkmenistan's leadership moot.

CHAPTER FOURTEEN

Caspian Region

Previews of Coming Attractions

As much as 3 to 5 trillion dollars worth of oil and gas may lie beneath the area surrounding the Caspian Sea—reserves second only to those in the Persian Gulf region.[1] This makes the eight former Soviet republics surrounding the Caspian some of the most strategic turf on the planet. As Dick Cheney put it in 1998 (when he was in the oil pipeline business), "I can't think of a time when we've had a region emerge as suddenly to become as strategically significant as the Caspian."[2] But since the Caspian is landlocked, getting all that energy to paying customers requires building pipelines across some pretty dicey territory.[3]

One way out is to the Pakistani coast through Afghanistan, where progress was stalled until the Taliban could be removed from power (see chapter 13).[4] An easier path would be south from the Caspian through Iran—but that nation has been declared to be part of an "axis of evil," and so is off limits without a regime change.[5] Another proposed route goes through Georgia—where U.S. troops arrived in the spring of 2002—to Turkey, where we spend billions of dollars helping the regime to ethnically cleanse Kurds who just happen to live on top of the proposed pipeline route (see chapter 10).[6] Yet another route is planned in order to bypass the Bosphorus, because that Turkish strait is too narrow and busy for modern supertankers.[7] Instead they would ship oil across the Black Sea and unload the black gold into a new pipeline running into Europe from Burgas, Bulgaria—where the U.S. has established another new military base.[8] The other end is in Albania, host to U.S. forces who intervened in 1999 to help return neighboring Kosovo to Albanian control.[9]

While the Kosovo war and its aftermath helped NATO consolidate its influence over virtually all of southeastern Europe, the Afghan war and its aftermath have helped the U.S. to set up at least 13 new military bases in the Caspian region (that we know of).[10] This puts us in prime position to take part in what are likely to be some of the most interesting wars of the next ten or twenty years.

It was the turn-of-the-century wise guy Ambrose Bierce who said "War is God's way of teaching geography to Americans."[11] And as America made war in Afghanistan, we started to learn of unfamiliar names on the map to the north, nations that didn't even exist ten years ago. Turkmenistan, Uzbekistan and Tajikistan abut the Afghan border—and in some sense overlap it, as Uzbeks and Tajiks make up much of the Northern Alliance. Kyrgyzstan (also known as the Kyrgyz Republic) is intertwined with the borders of Uzbekistan and Tajikistan like three crossed fingers. And to the north of these four countries is giant Kazakhstan, bigger than the other four "Stans" combined.

These five are all former Soviet republics, taken by surprise and thrust into nationhood on the breakup of the USSR in 1991. So too are three smaller nations to the west, across the Caspian Sea: Azerbaijan, Armenia and Georgia. To their north, two other territories are fighting to break free of what's left of the Soviet Union; both Chechnya and Dagestan are fighting guerrilla wars with Russia, with the active assistance of Osama bin Laden's al-Qaida network.[12] Islamist militants are active in most of the other countries as well.[13]

While most Americans hadn't been paying much attention to this part of the world, our government certainly wasn't ignoring it.[14] It's been one of the planet's great prizes for a long time. The Russian and British empires struggled for control of it. Part of the reason Hitler invaded the USSR was to seek control over the Caspian's oil reserves. And Moscow's ownership of its Central Asian republics proved to be one of its most valuable resources. So, unsurprisingly, the Caspian has been the target of long-term strategic planning from the U.S. government as well. Back in the 1970s, when Zbigniew Brzezinski started backing militant Islamic groups in Afghanistan (see chapter 13), the hope was not only to provoke a Soviet invasion there, but to use radical Islamism to destabilize the five Stans, in hopes of breaking them off from Russia.[15] Once again, radical Islam—that enemy so fervently hated by the U.S. today—was used and built up by the United States to serve our own ends. Eventually Brzezinski's wish came true, but ten years after the demise of the USSR, the Stans are still destabilized.

More recently, in 1997, the U.S. tried to pull together a junior-league NATO in the area, known as GUUAM[16] (for Georgia, Ukraine, Uzbekistan, Azerbaijan and Moldova, which includes two other ex-republics nestled into Eastern Europe). The Pentagon had even gone as far as running some war games and joint maneuvers in the region, and had been conducting joint covert operations with Uzbek intelligence.[17]

But prior to September 11, 2001, it looked as though GUUAM was starting to drift apart. In June, Uzbekistan had joined Kyrgyzstan, Tajikistan and Kazakhstan in a security alliance with Russia and China.[18] This restlessness came in part from the need to jockey for position in the coming bonanza of oil wealth. The U.S. has tried to promote pipeline routes that would not go through either Russia or Iran, as a way of weakening their influence and increasing our own. We had conceived of GUUAM as a counterweight to Russian power in the region, but our pipeline politics alienated Ukraine, which stood to benefit more from a Russian pipeline than a Turkish one. Then Uzbekistan, hedging its bets, apparently decided it might be wise to stay on Russia's good side as well. Kazakhstan, the biggest prize in terms of oil wealth, had just about finished building a joint pipeline venture with Russia (which bypassed the latter's troubled Chechnya conflict)—so they weren't too keen on angering Moscow.[19]

Prior to September 2001, the situation in Afghanistan looked like an endless stalemate between the Taliban and the Northern Alliance—who were backed, not coincidentally, by Russia and Iran.[20] The entire balance of power changed after 9/11, as U.S. military forces began to move into the region, striking deals with regional players, and taking over former Soviet military bases—particularly in Uzbekistan, Kyrgyzstan and Tajikistan. Thus we have begun a new version of the great game—Rudyard Kipling's term for the struggle for influence in Central Asia between Russia and Britain in the 19th century. Each of the eight former Soviet Republics becomes a strategically important piece on the chessboard, whether or not that particular country is rich with resources. Not only the oil itself but leverage over its world price is important, and even the weaker states can be useful in the search for control. Keep in mind that Kazakhstan, Turkmenistan and Azerbaijan are the real prizes; the other pieces are crucial to the extent that they can help capture these three.

The U.S. is certain to be engaged in the region for many years to come.[21] In some areas the U.S. hand is weaker. But in others, support for ruthless violators of human rights (who also back our interests) follows a familiar pattern—where the U.S. backs those who serve our needs, whatever the costs. So we seem poised to repeat some of the same disasters we've created in the Middle East: bribing despots, rigging elections, fomenting coups, and putting all our chips on corrupt, brutal, autocratic regimes, thereby earning the enmity of their peoples. Thus it may behoove us to take a few notes while God gives us another geography lesson.

Armenia

Even before the breakup of the USSR, Armenia had been fighting with neighboring Azerbaijan over the disputed territory of Nagorno-Karabakh. It turns out the Soviets weren't much better at drawing maps than the British Empire was. The borders of the old Soviet republics placed a large community of predominantly Orthodox Christians of Armenian descent within the largely Muslim state of Azerbaijan.[22]

When both states achieved independence in 1991, full-scale war broke out as the ethnic Armenians in Karabakh sought independence from Azerbaijan. A cease-fire in 1994 left the Armenians in control of the area, as well as about 20% of Azerbaijan proper.[23] A stalemate has ensued ever since, with various peace plans being rejected by one side or the other. The Bush Administration made the conflict one of its top foreign policy priorities upon taking office, since stability in the region is essential to the proposed Baku-Ceyhan pipeline.[24]

Both sides have been hurt economically by the lack of a resolution, with Azerbaijan having slapped an energy embargo on Armenia. This has led the latter into greater reliance

on both Russia and Iran.[25] While Russia has supplied arms to
the Armenians, Azerbaijan has called for a NATO peacekeeping force. With both Azerbaijan and neighboring
Georgia looking to join NATO, Armenia has been one of
Moscow's closest allies among the former republics.

In 1999 five gunmen stormed the Armenian parliament
in the capital city of Yerevan and killed eight of the nation's
most prominent political leaders.[26] Among these were the
prime minister, the speaker of the parliament, and the heads
of two of the largest parties. As with any violent change of
government, various theories have attempted to explain the
matter.[27] The leader of the assassins claims that they never
intended to kill anybody, only to hold them hostage for political leverage, but that they panicked and began shooting. He
says their motive was opposition to policies leading Armenia
towards economic collapse.[28] The reality of that collapse is
undeniable; some 20% of the population have fled, and of
the remainder, 45% live below the official poverty line. One
government official claims the real figure is more like 80%.[29]

Whatever the motivations, the main beneficiary of the
killings was President Robert Kocharian, since nearly every
other powerful politician in the country had been eliminated. The president immediately installed his brother as prime
minister, and ruled out the question of a larger plot.[30]
Nevertheless, a military investigation later arrested (and
then released) one of Kocharian's aides.[31] Kocharian himself
is a former president of the Nagorno-Karabakh region. While
he has not yet achieved a settlement with Azerbaijan, one
month after the shootings he endorsed the idea of a regional
alliance which would include both Turkey and the U.S., and
would require the removal of Russian troops from Armenia.
If that happens, it would help to decrease Russian influence

and boost that of the U.S., which is already allied with Georgia and Azerbaijan. In March 2001, talks were held in Yerevan on expanding Armenia's cooperation with NATO forces operating in the region.[32] U.S. military assistance has increased, and the U.S. ambassador has been quoted as saying that the two countries would soon "accelerate" the coordination of military projects.[33]

Azerbaijan

In contrast to Armenia, Azerbaijan is home to abundant oil and gas reserves, making it is one of the main economic prizes in the region.[34] Unfortunately, the Azeris are ruled by a crude autocrat named Heydar Aliyev, a former KGB official. He took power in a 1993 coup allegedly bankrolled by British Petroleum and Amoco (UK and U.S. companies who have since merged).[35]

The 1991-94 war with Armenia did not go well for Azerbaijan. In addition to losing Nagorno-Karabakh and surrounding environs, the regime in Baku was placed under sanctions for its energy blockade of Yerevan.[36] But the Aliyev regime has attempted to make itself indispensable to Western energy companies.[37] As one official put it, "we are surrounded by Russia and Iran, two big states with big armies. It makes sense to seek alliances elsewhere."[38] Aliyev doubtless also hopes that being useful to NATO makes Azerbaijan more attractive to Western oil companies—and vice versa.

Thus, as one opposition website puts it, "Azerbaijan's leaders are wined and dined on oil company expense accounts, while 600,000 Azeris still live in the most horrendous conditions, in makeshift housing outside of Baku and throughout western Azerbaijan."[39] Baku is a boomtown, and the biggest game in town is the Baku-Ceyhan pipeline deal.

It makes no sense economically, since other routes would be much cheaper to build. It only makes sense politically, as a way of forging ties with NATO member Turkey (see chapter 10) while shutting Russia and Iran out of the action.[40]

The expense of Baku-Ceyhan is complicated not only by political instability along its route, but by the fact that Azerbaijan may not turn out to have quite as much oil as previously believed. There may yet be a good amount of oil, but not enough to justify the enormous cost of the pipeline. So recently, Kazakhstan has been persuaded to consider a pipeline across the floor of the Caspian Sea, to link its richer resources into the new system—which only makes things more complicated.[41]

After the 9/11 attacks on America, Baku was quick to offer assistance, both in terms of the use of its territory as well as intelligence sharing.[42] But the new reality of regional geopolitics also dramatized the balancing act Azerbaijan must play. With Russia joining in the anti-terrorist coalition, President Putin has pretty much been guaranteed a free hand in dealing with the conflict in Chechnya. Both Azerbaijan and Georgia share borders with Russia. From the north has come a stream of refugees, which Russia claims also include Chechen terrorists who then use Azeri and Georgian territory to launch cross-border raids. From the south come Islamic militants, including those linked to the al-Qaida network, to join their Muslim brothers in the fight against Russia.[43] In both directions, the arms and drug trades flow more or less unabated.

Under the circumstances, Baku cannot afford to alienate Moscow too much, and has renewed the lease on an old Soviet radar station. An existing pipeline runs north to Novorossysk, Russia, and revenue from that could be cut off at Moscow's discretion. Then, too, in the current climate, Putin would not risk much in the way of international censure if he chose to attack suspected terrorists across the Azeri border.[44]

But in May 2002, Azerbaijan signed a series of agreements forging closer ties with U.S. allies Turkey and Georgia, while Armenia announced closer military cooperation with the U.S., to which Moscow could only grumble.[45] Despite the lack of a Nagorno-Karabakh settlement, the U.S. relaxed sanctions and gave both Azerbaijan and Armenia $4 million in military aid apiece.[46] The U.S. also took a tough stance regarding an ongoing series of border disputes between Azerbaijan and Iran, saying "we will not stand idly by," if such incidents continue.[47]

At the same time there are the beginnings of a succession struggle in Baku as the 77-year-old Aliyev indicates he would like to install his son in power upon retirement.[48] Opposition groups boycotted an August 2002 referendum in which Aliyev attempted to change the constitution. The proposals would alter the methods by which the president and parliament are elected, and critics charged that the election was rigged.[49] Tensions erupted into violence a few months later, as police stormed the headquarters of one of the opposition parties, seizing documents and smashing furniture.[50] Stability in Azerbaijan may be elusive for some time to come.

Georgia

Eduard Shevardnadze is hailed by many in the West as an exemplar of democracy, for having led his country out of the Soviet era into closer ties with the West.[51] In keeping with many other U.S. allies, he is known in his native Georgia for electoral manipulations, press restrictions, religious repression, the torture of opposition leaders, and widespread corruption.[52]

Shevardnadze had previously ruled Georgia from 1972

to 1985 as Communist Party chief in the old USSR. He presided over the suppression of the Georgian language as well as torture of political opponents. Later he served as Soviet Foreign Minister but resigned in 1990 in anticipation of the impending coup attempt against Gorbachev. In 1989, in the waning days of the Soviet Union, longtime Georgian dissident Zviad Gamsakhurdia was elected president of the Georgian Republic following widespread revulsion over a massacre of demonstrators by Soviet authorities.[53]

Gamsakhurdia was overwhelmingly re-elected in 1991, but was soon overthrown in a coup after the dissolution of the USSR. While no one has ever proven Shevardnadze's involvement with the coup, the leaders quickly installed him as president. In turn, he placed them in high positions in his government, despite their having fired upon unarmed supporters of the popular Gamsakhurdia. The new government in Tbilisi was immediately recognized by Germany, which began sending the first of many packages of economic and military aid from the West.[54]

The newly independent state of Georgia soon faced no fewer than three separatist movements. The ethnic Ossetian community found itself on both sides of the Russian border, and the South Ossetians began agitating for reunion with the North, one way or another. The Adzhariya region claimed a semi-autonomous status, and pretty much ignores whatever goes on in Tbilisi. And with covert aid from Russia, the Muslim territory of Abkhazia staged an insurrection, which dislodged it from Georgian control. It is now host to Russian peacekeeping troops.[55]

The Russian/Georgian border is subject to many of the same forces as in neighboring Azerbaijan: the rugged mountains are ideal for smuggling arms, drugs and humans. Guerrilla forces from Chechnya have taken refuge in

Georgian territory, and operate with near-complete impunity. While Georgian authorities fear the Chechen fighters in the border region, they may have also worked together against the Russian-backed Abkhazian rebels.[56] Shevardnadze has called for NATO intervention to help him subdue the breakaway regions, and was a vocal proponent of NATO's war against Yugoslavia.[57] NATO was happy to provide military aid and stage joint exercises, but was reluctant to get involved. Still, one NATO official did say, without going into specifics, that someday the conflicts in the Transcaucausus might be settled by resort to the "Yugoslav model."[58]

All of this has made Moscow more than a little bit annoyed with Tbilisi. The two countries have continually traded charges against one another for harboring terrorists. Nevertheless the Russians did not actively oppose Shevardnadze's inevitable re-election in 2000, as they were reluctant to rock the boat with the West, and chose to wait for better opportunities. Despite the dramatic decline in living standards under Shevardnadze's reign, he was handily re-elected, thanks to his control of the media. German Chancellor Schroeder and CIA Director George Tenet arrived shortly before the election to give their blessings, along with further aid packages. Georgia is central to the proposed Baku-Ceyhan pipeline, known to the oil industry as BTC, for Baku-Tbilisi-Ceyhan. President Bill Clinton called the project "the most important achievement at the end of the twentieth century."[59]

Nevertheless, it may be well into the twenty-first century before the achievement is realized.[60] During the election campaign Georgia's already poor human rights record deteriorated still further. Throughout 2001 the country had begun to descend into chaos, pulled in too many directions by the civil wars, rampant corruption, and drug trafficking.[61] Politicians have begun jockeying for position to succeed Shevardnadze.[62] Georgia, as the West's most ardent ally among the ex-Soviet republics, responded to the 9/11 attacks by offering its territory and whatever help it could provide.[63] At the same time, the armed conflict in Abkhazia heated up again, after a UN helicopter was shot down in October 2001, killing all nine aboard. Attempts at negotiations have so far proved fruitless.[64] That same month, following government raids on a Tbilisi TV station and resulting street demonstrations, President Shevardnadze sacked his entire cabinet.[65]

And then, just as the entire country seemed on the verge of collapse, the U.S. announced it was sending troops into Georgia, ostensibly to help capture a few dozen al-Qaida terrorists operating in the Pankisi Gorge.[66] Most observers found this to be a thinly veiled excuse to counter Russian influence[67] and safeguard the construction of Baku-Ceyhan.[68] Shortly after, Georgia forged even closer ties with Azerbaijan and Turkey, while NATO held war games in the area in June 2002.[69]

But relations with Russia continued to worsen, with Moscow threatening repeatedly to invade the Pankisi Gorge in hot pursuit of Chechen "bandits."[70] Russian hostility to Shevardnadze is longstanding, and rumors surfaced that Moscow was looking for a free hand in Georgia as its price for supporting a U.S. invasion of Iraq.[71] But Washington, reluctant to abandon its foothold in the Caucasus, proposed instead a "trilateral" security arrangement with Moscow and Tbilisi.[72] While this may paper over the problem in the short term, Georgia is likely to be a regional hot spot for the forseeable future.

Kazakhstan

When the Soviet Union collapsed in 1991, Kazakhstan suddenly found itself to be a nuclear power and owner of one of the planet's only spaceports.[73] It also found itself sitting on top of the planet's largest untapped oil reserves.[74] The space-port is leased out for satellite launches, and while the nuclear weapons were willingly dismantled, the years of bomb tests have left a legacy of birth defects and higher cancer rates.[75] As for the oil, it hasn't been enough to lift most Kazakhs out of abject poverty—yet.

As with other ex-Soviet Republics, power in Almaty (then the capital) devolved to the local Communist Party boss, in this case President Nursultan Nazarbayev, whose devotion to human rights is scant improvement over that of the Russians. Arrest and torture of political opponents, along with restrictions on religious and press freedoms, remain commonplace.[76]

Like the other ex-republics, Kazakhstan is simultane-ously motivated both to stay on Moscow's good side and to seek alternative alliances. Thus Nazarbayev has looked for deals with Iran, though U.S. oil companies are barred from assisting in any such endeavors.[77] He has also agreed to study a pipeline link across the Caspian to Azerbaijan, and remains open to linking up with pipelines in Turkmenistan—which could then proceed south through Afghanistan, if a stable government ever takes hold there.[78]

But compared with other Central Asian states, ties with Russia are much stronger. 35 percent of the population is eth-nic Russian, rising to 70 percent in Almaty.[79] Most of the oil resources lie in the rich Tengiz oilfields along the Russian bor-der. In October 2001, the new Tengiz-Novorossysk pipeline, built with both Russian and American assistance, finally began pumping Kazakh oil to Western markets.[80] Unless sanctions against Iran are lifted, trustworthy partners in Afghanistan take hold, or expensive Turkish links are constructed, Moscow maintains control over the Kazakh lifeline.[81]

If other outside powers wished to destabilize the regime in Astana (the new capital) in hopes of gaining control of its vast potential wealth, it would not be hard to do. The population is half-Christian and half-Muslim, and Islamic guerrilla movements to the south have made Nazarbayev exceedingly nervous.[82] So far, no incursions have been made into Kazakh territory, but in the wake of 9/11, the regime has tightened security along the borders with Kyrgyzstan and Uzbekistan.[83] Astana expelled hundreds of ethnic Kyrgyz, Uzbeks and Tajiks, along with longtime Afghan refugees.[84] Meanwhile, Kazakhstan was initially more reluctant than its southern neighbors to make military facilities available to U.S. forces for the war in Afghanistan, but in July 2002 agreed to let U.S. warplanes make emergency landings at Almaty's airport. The Bush Administration has also budgeted $5 million for refurbishing a Kazakh airbase in order to establish "a U.S.-interoperable air base along the oil-rich Caspian."[85]

At the same time, internal politics have gotten more contentious.[86] Nazarbayev sacked a number of cabinet ministers after they helped form a mildly reformist group called the Democratic Choice of Kazakhstan.[87] Looking towards future prosperity, economic elites are looking for a wider voice in the country's affairs, but Nazarbayev has shown little interest in sharing power with anyone beyond his relatives, who control major media and other resources.[88] Whatever the political future of Kazakhstan, decisions made there will doubtless be of central importance to both the regional and the world economy. Indeed, before joining the Bush Administration, both Vice President Dick Cheney and National Security Adviser Condoleezza Rice served as Kazakhstan experts for their respective oil companies (Halliburton and Chevron).[89] These ties may yet prove embarrassing due to investigations from two federal grand juries into corruption scandals involving Kazakh pipeline deals.[90]

Kyrgyzstan

Until recently, Kyrgyzstan had been known as an "island of democracy" among the nations of Central Asia. But in 2000, President Askar Akayev cracked down on dissidents and journalists, and the rights of ethnic and religious minorities came under attack.[91] Akayev backed down from imposing a constitutional power grab in 2001, but Kyrgyzstan's future remains clouded.[92] In March 2002, he jailed an opposition leader for what he called a "coup attempt," then freed him after violent street protests.[93] Two months later, Akayev accepted the resignations of the entire Kyrgysz government, which he conceded may do little to quell the ongoing tensions.[94]

Like the other ex-Soviet Republics in Central Asia, Kyrgyzstan was plunged into widespread poverty upon the breakup of the USSR, with state assets grabbed by a wealthy elite at fire sale prices.[95] Unlike the others, it doesn't have many prospects for improvement. The Kyrgyz Republic has little in the way of resources worth exploiting—which is perhaps one reason why the political climate was stable for the first decade.[96] But the government in Bishkek is being buffeted by forces outside its control.[97]

To the east is mighty China, currently battling an Islamic insurgency in the bordering Uighur province.[98] To the north is Kazakhstan, recently given to expelling its Kyrgyz residents.[99] To the south is continuing unrest in Afghanistan, also spilling over into neighboring Tajikistan, which contributed forces to the Northern Alliance. And to the west is Uzbekistan. Larger and stronger than its Kyrgyz and Tajik neighbors, the Uzbek regime is bent on regional domination, and perhaps on territorial expansion.[100]

Uzbekistan is involved in an ongoing internal conflict with the Islamic Movement of Uzbekistan (IMU), which has been supported by both the Taliban and al-Qaida.[101] Both Uzbek and IMU forces have operated with impunity in Tajikistan and Kyrgyzstan, and each country faces Islamic insurgents of its own as well. Uzbekistan has not hesitated to conduct bombing runs across borders, resulting in many civilian casualties.[102] The three countries also share one large geographic feature: the fertile Ferghana Valley. The valley is overcrowded and suffers from high unemployment and widespread poverty as well as religious and ethnic strife. Security along the winding borders of the three states has been tightened in recent years, creating new opportunities for smugglers as well.[103]

Uzbekistan may be tempted to seize the entire area, ostensibly in order to crack down on the IMU.[104] But the valley also contains one of Kyrgyzstan's few tangible assets: the Popan Reservoir, which brings needed revenue to Bishkek since it generates far more hydroelectric power than is needed domestically. But the dam at Popan is in an earthquake zone and is in dire need of maintenance. Negotiations with neighboring countries on sharing the costs of repair have bogged down. The dam is also a tempting target for terrorists.[105]

On top of all this, the IMU has increased recruiting near the Kyrgyz capital, and has skirmished with state forces

in the border regions. Bishkek has also cracked down on the
Hizb-ut-Tarir, which is a political, not military organization,
though with much the same agenda as the IMU: providing
an outlet for the grievances of fundamentalist Muslims in the
Ferghana region.[106] Kyrgyzstan has entered into a Russian/
Chinese security arrangement called the Collected Forces of
Quick Deployment (CFQD), which includes neighboring
Tajikistan and Kazakhstan as well as former Soviet Republics
Belarus and Armenia.[107] Uzbekistan has sometimes cooper-
ated but belongs to the more pro-NATO alliance GUUAM.
But with or without the Uzbeks, CFQD has so far been
unable to suppress the IMU insurgency.

With the coming of U.S. forces to the region,
Kyrgyzstan, like Uzbekistan and Tajikistan, is gaining needed
revenue by leasing old Soviet military bases.[108] And the U.S.
has increased military aid to the country, while removing
restrictions on weapons sales.[109] What remains to be seen is
whether the U.S. will stay on to help defend Kyrgyz forces—
or perhaps our own—from increased Islamic militancy. A
U.S. Congress member touring the beefed-up new bases told
reporters that our troops would remain in Kyrgyzstan "as long
as it takes to wipe out international terrorism," but pointedly denied that we planned to stay there "forever."[110]

Tajikistan

Of the five Stans of Central Asia, Tajikistan is the poorest and the least stable. In fact, out of 206 countries surveyed
by the World Bank, Tajikistan ranked 197th.[111] The per
capita annual income is about $180,[112] and unemployment is
at 30%, with 83% of the population living in poverty.[113] In
the first five years after leaving the USSR, Tajikistan suffered
a 60% drop in GDP.[114]

Tajikistan is ethnically diverse, with the Tajiks themselves making up about 65% of the population.[115] They are of course spread about surrounding states as well. Tajiks are related to Iranians, and speak the same language, Farsi. With Iranian support, the Islamic Party of the Resurrection (IPR) took control of Tajikistan in 1992. Later that same year, a rural insurrection chased them out of power and into Afghanistan. At the same time, President Emomali Rakhmonov came to power in Dushanbe, the capital.[116] And then all hell broke loose, as Tajikistan descended into five years of civil war.

According to Belgian reporter Jef Bossuyt, the IPR returned, "now sponsored by Pakistan, in neat American uniforms, with stingers, night vision equipment, Motorola radio stations, and jeeps." This is consistent with journalist Ahmed Rashid's revelation that the CIA, Pakistan's ISI and Britain's MI6 had recruited Islamic militants to attack Tajikistan beginning in 1987.[117] By 1997, there were 50,000 dead in Tajikistan, 150,000 injured, and half a million refugees.[118] The civil war tore the country apart, and at the same time, the Afghan civil war to the south (see chapter 13) made Tajikistan a stomping ground for heroin traffickers, a variety of foreign paramilitaries, and waves of desperate refugees.[119]

A truce was reached in 1997 and a coalition government was formed, with Rakhmonov conceding a third of cabinet posts to the Muslim opposition.[120] 75,000 Russian "peacekeeping" troops were dispatched to patrol the border with Afghanistan, in the process helping to funnel arms and equipment to the Northern Alliance.[121] Dushanbe exerts little control over the interior of Tajikistan, where warlords, clan leaders and gangsters compete for influence. Rakhmonov attempted to consolidate power by dominating the presidential election in 2000 and the parliamentary elections of 2001.[122] International observers witnessed numerous electoral irregularities and, thereafter, fighting broke out once again. There have been assassinations, car bombings and shootings in Dushanbe, and state security forces operate with unrestrained violence.[123]

Meanwhile, tensions with neighboring Uzbekistan have intensified, with no commercial air traffic allowed between the two countries.[124] Kazakhstan has cut off the Dushanbe-Moscow rail line used by hundreds of thousands of Tajiks to travel to Russia as migrant laborers. More than 8500 Tajik immigrants in Kazakhstan are being detained and many have been deported.[125] Tajikistan has no oil resources, a crumbling infrastructure, and is suffering from the same drought that has brought Afghanistan to the brink of famine.[126]

In the midst of all this chaos and despair, U.S. troops are operating out of several old Soviet bases,[127] and Tajikistan has joined NATO's so-called "Partnership for Peace."[128] The American presence is hardly likely to soothe Islamic militants, and guerrillas from both Uzbekistan and Afghanistan may be regrouping on Tajik territory.[129] It's hard to believe, but the situation in Tajikistan could potentially get even worse unless a major effort is made to bring some stability to its suffering people.

Turkmenistan

"President for Life" Saparmurad Niyazov has ruled Turkmenistan with an iron fist, forging an increasingly bizarre cult of personality which some have compared to that of Josef Stalin.[130] Domestically, he brooks no opposition, and even the trappings of democracy have been largely discarded. Beatings and torture of dissenters are commonplace, and religious and press freedoms are suppressed.[131] In foreign affairs, Niyazov has tried to keep Turkmenistan as neutral as possible, joining neither the U.S.-backed GUUAM alliance nor the Russians' CFQD.[132] Unlike his neighbors, he has offered no appreciable assistance to the U.S. war effort—at least not publicly.[133] Niyazov did maintain friendly relations with the Taliban, though, and has forged some economic links with China.[134]

Turkmenistan is ethnically homogenous, and the Turkmens mainly practice a milder form of Islam known as Sufism. The country has more or less escaped the turmoil that has engulfed many of its neighbors, with relatively little activity by militant groups. But in contrast to Tajikistan, where thousands of Russian troops guard the border, Turkmenistan has a much more porous frontier with Afghanistan. As a result, the drug trade has flowed freely, and fighters from the south could easily escape into Turkmen territory disguised as refugees.[135]

Turkmenistan is strategically located in two ways. First, it's one of the five states bordering the Caspian Sea, and as such has a voice in any agreements on offshore drilling or pipeline routes.[136] Second, its abundant natural gas reserves and proximity to Afghanistan brought Ashgabat into a pipeline plan to traverse the Afghan plateau through to Pakistan's coast. The U.S. and Pakistan initially supported the Taliban in the first place, in hopes they could bring stability to the country, allowing the pipeline deal to proceed (see chapters 12 and 13). Turkmenistan signed an agreement with the American oil company Unocal in 1997, but it fell apart soon after, due to the situation in Afghanistan.[137] Some say it was because the Taliban had imposed a little too much "stability," while others hint it was because they were demanding too large a cut of the revenue.[138]

Unocal made it clear that it would not proceed with its pipeline plans as long as the Taliban ruled Afghanistan.[139] Back channel meetings did take place throughout the Taliban years, but as soon as they were removed from power, the old pipeline deal was put back on the fast track.[140]

But even with a friendlier regime in Kabul, it's not clear that Niyazov is still regarded as a reliable partner. His human rights record is hardly unique, but can be used as an excuse to depose him if need be. Niyazov's neutrality has not won him any friends, and his increasingly mercurial personality and heavy-handed rule have interfered with regional negotiations on energy resources. None of the Central Asian countries has seen a (permanent) regime change since they achieved independence in 1991, and there is widespread speculation that Niyazov could be the first to go.[141]

In November 2001, a former Turkmen government official launched a scathing verbal attack against Niyazov. Boris Shikhmuradov, speaking from a Moscow hospital where he had checked in for unspecified reasons, called for the Turkmen people to "find an exit from a historical dead end."[142] Shortly thereafter, he formed an exile group called the Turkmenistan Popular Democratic Movement and began seeking international support for deposing Niyazov.[143] In reaction to Shikmuradov's plotting, President Niyazov abruptly sacked his security chief and purged other high officials in September 2002.[144] Niyazov narrowly escaped an assassination attempt in November 2002 when gunmen fired on his limousine.[145] Given the immense resources controlled by this one man, if he insists on remaining President for Life, his life may not last much longer.

Uzbekistan

In a region that has never been noted for its fealty to human rights, the sorry record of Uzbekistan is perhaps the worst.[146] At the same time, Tashkent has become one of America's most important allies in the Afghan war.[147] According to Zbigniew Brzezinski, "The key to controlling Eurasia is controlling the Central Asian republics. And the key to controlling the Central Asian republics is Uzbekistan."[148]

When agreement was reached in October 2001 for military cooperation, it was revealed that U.S. special forces had been operating in Uzbekistan since 1996, though both sides had always denied it.[149] In that period, Washington had sold at least $4 million in weapons and provided military training at the rate of over a half million dollars annually.[150] As the *Washington Post* reported, "The ultimate size of the U.S. military presence remains unclear, but every indication suggests that it will grow, and remain in place for months or even years."[151]

Press restrictions in Tashkent have been an added bonus. One U.S. Air Force official exulted at being able to operate in a country where "We can put our aircraft where CNN can't film them taking off." An Uzbek government spokesmen confirmed that silence on the details of the deployments were "not because Uzbekistan is a closed country. That is what the Pentagon wants as well."[152]

Tashkent will be rewarded not only by a free pass from Washington on its human rights abuses, but U.S. support for a lifting of international loan restrictions arising therefrom. Thus, the more than 7000 political prisoners can expect to remain in the Uzbek gulag for some time to come.[153] President Islam Karimov, having played his cards right, is likely to emerge as one of the biggest winners of the U.S. intervention in Central Asia.

Despite his first name, Karimov is no friend of Muslims. Many have been arrested and tortured even without any links to the guerrilla movement Islamic Movement of Uzbekistan (IMU). Anyone practicing their religion outside state control is subject to jail terms of up to 20 years for "anti-constitutional activity." Many devout Muslims are incarcerated after having drugs or bullets planted on them by security forces. Christians are routinely repressed as well.[154]

Once the "faith violators" have entered the prison system, Uzbekistan's harsh police state on the outside looks like paradise by comparison. According to Human Rights Watch, many prisoners are tortured to death. Confessions are extracted by threats against family members. Rape of male and female inmates is common. Bribes are required for adequate food supplies. Prayers are punished with beatings and solitary confinement. Medical treatment is virtually nonexistent, and many have died after long struggles with untreated cancers and other illnesses.[155]

President Karimov was handily re-elected in January 2000, pulling in 92% of the vote. This is perhaps not unusual when one considers that there are no opposition parties and no independent media.[156]

Uzbekistan has been one of the main supporters of the Northern Alliance, with Uzbek General Rashid Dostum leading forces in the capture of several key cities (and presiding over ghastly slaughters of defeated soldiers).[157] It's ironic that Karimov would oppose the Taliban, since his regime is virtually a mirror image. Under the Taliban, beatings in the street were routine for clean-shaven men and unveiled women; under Karimov, bearded men and veiled women are beaten.[158]

Unsurprisingly, the Muslim opposition to this brutal

regime has grown stronger—and increasingly more violent—no matter how harshly it is repressed.[159] Now that Washington has openly thrown in its lot with Karimov, we can be expected to stay on to help him combat the Islamic menace within and beyond his borders.[160]

Those borders may yet expand as well. Tashkent covets the resources of the Ferghana Valley, an agricultural bread-basket which it shares with Tajikistan and Kyrgyzstan. There are also natural gas fields just across the Turkmen border which would be absurdly easy to seize.[161] Neighboring states have grown weaker while Karimov has grown ever stronger with covert assistance from the U.S. The Uzbek government's counter-insurgency campaign against the IMU is both the cause of increased violence across its borders and the potential excuse for incursions into neighboring territory. Meanwhile U.S. support for Karimov's dictatorship may only serve to further polarize the region.[162] Rent from U.S. bases is enriching the regime further—as well as helping to bail out Dick Cheney's old company, Halliburton, which rebuilds and supplies the bases.[163]

Karimov traveled to Washington in March 2002 to sign an agreement on "Strategic Partnership and Cooperation" with the U.S., which both sides have so far kept secret—though the U.S. made it clear it now took a "grave concern" over any threats to Uzbekistan's security.[164] Though he is little known in the West, President Karimov has the potential to someday be as famous as other staunch U.S. allies from decades past—friends like Saddam Hussein, the Saudi royal family, and the Shah of Iran.[165]

Afterword

Ending the Killings Abroad—And Avoiding New Ones at Home

As astonishing as the crimes detailed in this book may be, they exclude what the U.S. has done in Africa, Latin America, Southeast Asia and elsewhere. A handy review of our interventions in the Middle East and Central Asia is in order. Over the past fifty years, the United States has:

- Sponsored assassination attempts against the leaders of Iran (Mossadegh and Khomeini), Iraq (Qassim and Hussein), and Libya (Qadaffy).[1]
- Fomented coups and coup attempts in Egypt, Iran, Iraq, Lebanon, Libya, Pakistan, Syria and Turkey.
- Deployed our armies and our bombs in Afghanistan, Georgia, Iran, Iraq, Lebanon, Libya and Sudan.
- Paid for proxy wars in Afghanistan, Iran, Iraq, Jordan, Lebanon, Palestine and Sudan.
- Imposed punishing sanctions on Afghanistan, Iran, Iraq, Libya, Pakistan, Sudan and Syria.
- Backed vicious terrorist forces in Afghanistan, Iran, Iraq, Lebanon, Pakistan and Turkey.
- Set up more or less permanent military outposts in Afghanistan, Bahrain, Djibouti, Kazakhstan, Kuwait, Kyrgyzstan, Pakistan, Qatar, Saudi Arabia, Tajikistan, Turkey, Turkmenistan, and Uzbekistan—as well as more than a hundred other countries around the world.
- And supported brutal, undemocratic regimes in, well, every single country discussed in this book, at one time or another.

Some have wondered, in all sincerity, what people in this part of the world could possibly have against us. Throughout this book are possible clues. One imagines that we might hold a bit of a grudge, too, if these sorts of things were done to our country. Suppose the boot were on the other throat—yours. You live in one of these countries, know innocent people who have been killed by these adventures, maybe some are your parents—or children. Maybe you work in a hospital in Iraq, where more than 500,000 children have died of disease and malnutrition from the U.S. embargo.[2] Or you work in Afghanistan, where the U.S. has killed over 200 innocent people for every Taliban leader killed.[3] One day you actually meet a well-meaning American who has an urgent question that pours from the lips of everyone in the U.S.: Why do you hate us? How would you answer?

Since the 9/11 attacks, the U.S. has also sent troops into other countries outside the scope of this book: Indonesia, the Philippines, Somalia and Yemen. Each of these countries has their own history of U.S. intervention. We backed a bloody 1965 coup in Indonesia that led to the deaths of hundreds of thousands, and a 1975 invasion of neighboring East Timor that killed hundreds of thousands more.[4] The U.S. invaded the Philippines in 1898, killing hundreds of thousands of its inhabitants.[5] We then kept it as an outright colony for nearly half a century, before withdrawing to back a ruinous kleptocracy for several decades more. We sent troops into Somalia in 1992 in order to back one set of warlords against another, killing hundreds, perhaps thousands of people on the streets of Mogadishu in the process.[6] And in Yemen, the U.S. sent a flotilla of warships and a half billion dollars in military aid in 1979 to assist one side in a civil war.[7]

But these countries also have something else in common

with those discussed in this book: they either hold significant petroleum reserves, or are strategically important to the world's oil trade by virtue of their geography. As writer Michael Klare has explained,[8] this country's worldwide war on terrorism is inextricably intertwined with our worldwide quest to control the supply of oil. This is, of course, not a recent or unique development; no nation makes war for altruistic reasons. But we are now the most powerful nation in the history of the planet. While many books and articles have focused on whether that power could be or is being used judiciously, the issue I focus on here is different. Namely, that power also means that we have the ability to make a great deal of trouble for ourselves.

Persistent meddling in the affairs of other countries creates enemies for us. And every war plants the seeds of the next one. We may feel we have no choice but to attack our enemies wherever we find them, regardless of what happened in the past. We may feel we have no choice but to use our power to secure the planet's strategic resources for ourselves and our allies, lest they fall into the hands of our enemies. But in fact we do have a choice between widely divergent paths into the future.

To the surprise of many, the people of South Africa chose to back away from the path of confrontation. The ruling white minority attempted to reconcile with their "enemies," to establish a democratic government and to atone for the wrongs in their history. They have been only partially successful, but their example is an inspiration to us all.[9] To the surprise of many, the Soviet Union chose to back away from the military domination of Eastern Europe, and refused to intervene as nearly all of the countries in the Warsaw Pact alliance staged peaceful revolutions to overthrow their one-party governments. Not all the transitions were peaceful, and not all of these countries have prospered, but the Russians could have chosen a starkly different path. Like them, we have both a dark past and uncertain future to confront.

Our government has told us that there are terrorist cells in more than sixty countries and that the present war effort may not end in our lifetimes.[10] If we continue to dominate and kill millions of innocent people, that prediction of a never-ending war cannot help but become a self-fulfilling prophecy. If we choose this path, here's what we can expect:

- **More militarism.** This country is the largest arms merchant on the planet.[11] Our annual defense spending is already bigger than the next 20 largest military budgets combined.[12] Our leaders promise to spend still more, inching up towards a half trillion dollars per year.[13] Combined with the president's $1.35 trillion tax cut, our military spending will crowd out needed services, including education, health care, mass transit and environmental cleanups. If you own stock in defense firms, this is probably the path for you. The rest of us will pay twice: first with our tax returns, and then with a downward spiral of unmet social needs.

- **More dead Americans.** Subsidizing the occupation of Palestine, the oppression of the Uzbeks, the theocracy of the Saudis, and the infant mortality rate of the Iraqis will never end terrorism. On the contrary, it will simply provide an endless supply of new enemies. Bombing wedding parties in Afghanistan and air raid shelters in Baghdad is the single best way to assure more recruits for al-Qaida. If we want to make ourselves more hated, and guarantee that Americans both at home and abroad will be targets, we should focus on an exclusively military approach to the problem of terrorism.

- **More angry allies.** It seems incredible that the administration could have squandered the widespread sympathy and solidarity for our nation in the wake of the 9/11 attacks. But by repudiating treaties on international war crimes, land mines, money laundering, global warming, and arms control, our government has helped to dry up the pool of good will for our country. Allies who used to support us now do so half-heartedly, after being bribed or cajoled, or not at all. As with the first Gulf War,[14] the U.S. twisted arms and cut backroom deals in the UN to produce a new resolution in November 2002,[15] calling for renewed weapons inspections in Iraq.[16] But U.S. officials repeatedly insisted that we retain the authority to launch another Gulf War with or without UN approval.[17] So to the rest of the world the entire exercise looked like a transparent PR ploy, with the U.S. thumbing its nose at the UN. How much longer can we get away with this sort of thing? If some of our allies tire of propping up our trade deficit, or begin to withdraw their investments in our economy, we may find that international good will counts for a great deal.

- **More curtailment of our liberties.** If we're going to be fighting a shadowy enemy for generations to come, we'll be on a permanent war footing. During previous wars our government has suspended the writ of habeas corpus, jailed antiwar writers for sedition, rounded up foreign-born citizens into internment camps, and spied on citizens who dared to dissent.[18] The current administration has shown itself amenable to similar measures. It has backed off on plans to create a nationwide system of domestic informants, a military office of disinformation, and a suspension of the Posse Comitatus Act, only under a barrage of criticism. If the war winds on for many years, expect to see these and other such proposals revived.

- **Many, many more wars.** As mentioned before, every war plants the seeds of the next one. The reparations clamped on Germany after World War I fueled the resurgence of German nationalism and militarism that gave us World War II. The devastation of Europe and the collapse of European colonialism after World War II helped fuel the Cold War rivalry between the victorious Soviets and Americans for control of the resulting power vacuum. The tactics we used in the Cold War, like arming Islamic militants in Afghanistan and backing repressive regimes in the Middle East, have come back to haunt us in the current war. And the enemies we create by stomping over the globe after al-Qaida will surely bring us more wars in the future. We may be sparking new civil wars in Pakistan, Saudi Arabia, Afghanistan, Iraq, Uzbekistan and other countries, and our history suggests we are unlikely to avoid taking sides. The more we intervene abroad, the more we will have to respond to the messes our interventions create.

Luckily, another path is available to us.

- **The path of diplomacy.** Representative Dennis Kucinich (D/OH) has proposed the creation of a cabinet-level Department of Peace.[19] This agency would be given the resources necessary to promote international cooperation through conflict resolution and mediation. The Secretary of Peace would also seek to prevent violent conflicts between nations before they start. A curriculum in peace education would be developed, and international cooperation would be fostered at all levels, from sister cities to international law. It stands to reason that preventing a war is less costly than fighting one. Are we willing to provide, in pursuit of peace, even a fraction of the resources lavished on the Pentagon?

- **The path of reconciliation.** The Marshall Plan was one of the most successful international programs this nation has ever undertaken. Rebuilding Europe engendered generations of good will and helped U.S. businesses as well, by creating export markets—truly a win/win situation. Now the Worldwatch Institute has proposed a Global Marshall Plan for the Third World,[20] and their rationale is worth considering: "A report in 1998 by the United Nations Development Programme estimated the annual cost to achieve universal access to a number of basic social services in all developing countries: $9 billion would provide water and sanitation for all; $12 billion would cover reproductive health for all women; $13 billion would give every person on earth basic health and nutrition; and $6 billion would provide basic education for all. …These social and health expenditures pale in comparison with what is being spent on the military by all nations—some $780 billion each year." Nothing is more likely to ensure success in combating terrorism than to reduce the conditions of human misery that provides endless recruits to the cause of hatred. And given our history of interventions abroad, we have a lot to make up for.

- **The path of cooperation.** Perhaps you noticed that the repudiated treaties mentioned above would all be immensely useful in the fight against terrorism. An international criminal court would help to pursue justice when crimes against all humanity are perpetrated. A land mine treaty would help to reduce civilian casualties; such deaths help to provide more terrorist recruits among the survivors. A money laundering treaty would help to dry up the sources of funding for international terrorist organizations. A global warming treaty would help to reduce dependency on fossil fuels, and tighten the budgets of the oil-rich governments that support terrorist groups. And it goes without saying—or it should—that international cooperation on curtailing both small arms and weapons of mass destruction would help to keep those weapons out of the hands of terrorists. But the key is that in order to foster this international cooperation, we and our client states will have to subject ourselves to the same international laws we expect other nations to follow. How difficult is that?

- **The path of democracy.** To cut down on the burning resentment that provides terrorist recruits throughout the Arab and Muslim world, we have to break ourselves of the habit of backing any repressive regime that proves useful to us. An airtight arms embargo against nations that use them on their own people may cut into the profits of our weapons contractors, but it would also help to prevent any number of future wars. At the same time, a modest improvement in the fuel economy of our domestic automobile fleet would enable us to cut out imports of Middle Eastern oil altogether. This would certainly free us from the perceived necessity of supporting autocratic and murderous governments just because they can keep our SUVs humming along. But if we want to promote democracy abroad, it would help to set a good example at home. Let's show that we can enhance our national security by keeping our Constitution strong. A healthy debate about a more humane foreign policy will not weaken us. Foreign-born citizens are a great asset to this country, and we don't make ourselves more secure by targeting people solely on the basis of their national origin. Nor do we enhance our security by holding people without charging or trying them. If there is a basis for detaining someone, we ought to be able to show why in a court of law. Sticking to our principles at home will give us greater credibility should we choose to encourage some of our client states to derive their authority from the just consent of the governed.

- **The path of peace.** Nobody is suggesting that we sit back and let ourselves be attacked. But it's noteworthy that most of the successes in our struggle against terrorism have come from international police work and cooperation. At the same time, some of the most noteworthy failures—like the scattering of al-Qaida forces across the Pakistani border—have come from our sledgehammer military approach to the problem. Ultimately, there is no military solution to the problem of terrorism. We can defend ourselves best by working to eliminate the root causes of terrorism: hunger, disease, lack of education, repression. It's true that bin Laden himself is neither poor nor uneducated, but millions support him because they perceive him as standing up to the forces that subsidize their oppression. We can combat that perception by showing our willingness to right past wrongs and to work for a more just world order. The al-Qaida network has never once said that they attack us because they envy our freedom. They have said time and again that they oppose our support for the occupation of Palestine, our deadly sanctions against the people of Iraq, and our military alliance with the corrupt monarchy that holds sovereignty over Muslim holy lands. Reversing these policies just happens to be the right thing; we should not stay on this counterproductive path just because our enemies demand otherwise. We can deny them support by proving them wrong about us. And we can defeat them without creating new enemies by taking a multilateral approach to terrorism, cooperating with international law, and ceasing to insist that, as the president's father once crowed, "What we say goes."

Now, if you prefer the path of more war, death, anger and repression, there are some things you can do to help. You can contribute financial support to the most warmongering politicians in the country. They're not hard to find; you can see them on television news programs nearly every day. You can also treat all Arabs and Muslims as enemies, and blame them for the sorry state of their home countries, while making excuses about the role your tax dollars might have played in contributing to the situation. It would also be helpful if you waste as much gasoline and electricity as possible. This country wastes more energy than any other, and if you believe that it's easier to attack foreign countries than to make our country more energy efficient, you have a variety of consumer choices available to you to help further that cause. Finally, it's very important that you attack the patriotism of anyone who questions this path. This has worked well in the past to help create conditions that lead to future wars.

On the other hand, if you would prefer the path of peace, democracy, reconciliation and cooperation, well, you have your work cut out for you. You can find out more about the above proposals of Rep. Kucinich and the Worldwatch Institute, and offer some financial support to their causes. There are a number of other organizations working to promote peace and justice; they are generally not found on your TV screen, but a little diligent internet searching will reveal a wealth of resources.[21] You can also lobby your elected representatives for a more humane foreign policy; some of them will be more reluctant than others, so be persistent. If you would like a more sensible energy policy, you can start by voting with your wallet and buying more efficient vehicles and appliances. Perhaps the most important thing you can do is to educate yourself and your neighbors about the reality and the history of our interventions in the Arab and Muslim world. This book provides just a modest start; you can find much more in the various publications and websites listed in the footnotes.

Of course, you also have the choice to do nothing at all. That's one easy way to guarantee that we stay on the path of war. The old saying is truer than ever: If you want peace, work for justice.

Notes

INTRODUCTION: HELL ON EARTH

1   The single best source on this is Ahmed Rashid, *Taliban: Militant Islam, Oil and Fundamentalism in Central Asia*, Yale University Press, New Haven CT, 2000.

2   See extended discussion in chapter 2, documented by notes 6 through 10.

3   Peter Dale Scott and Jonathan Marshall, *Cocaine Politics*, University of California Press, Berkeley CA, 1991.

4   Stephen Zunes, "The Long and Hidden History of the U.S. in Somalia," from the AlterNet website, January 17, 2002, posted at http://www.alter-net.org/story.html?StoryID=12253; but please see also Mark Fineman, "The Oil Factor in Somalia," *Los Angeles Times*, January 18, 1993.

5   Tim Weiner, "Key Haiti Leaders Said to Have Been in CIA's Pay," *New York Times*, November 1, 1993; see also Dennis Bernstein, "What's Behind Washington's Silence on Haiti's Drug Connection?," Pacific News Service, October 20, 1993.

6   Noam Chomsky, *The New Military Humanism*, Common Courage Press, Monroe ME, 1999.

7   Gareth Jones, "NATO gives green light to Macedonia mission," Reuters, August 22, 2001.

8   See, for instance, Chalmers Johnson, *Blowback: The Costs and Consequences of American Empire*, Henry Holt, New York NY, 2000; see also Christopher Simpson, *Blowback: America's Recruitment of Nazis, and its disastrous effect on our domestic and foreign policy*, Collier/Macmillan, New York NY, 1988.

9   The terrorist who did this has been "harbored" in Florida by the president's brother and was pardoned by the president's father. See Saul Landau, "A Double Standard on Terrorism," *In These Times*, March 4, 2002; see also U.S. House of Representatives Committee on Government Reform, "Examples of Controversial Pardons by Previous Presidents," posted at http://www.house.gov/reform/min/pdfs/pdf_com/pdf_clinton_pardons_past_rep.pdf.

10 Gary Webb, *Dark Alliance: The CIA, the Contras and the Crack Cocaine Explosion*, Seven Stories Press, New York NY, 1998.

11 Interview, *Le Nouvel Observateur*, January 15-21, 1998; see chapter 13 for more on this.

12 See, for instance, Fareed Zakaria, " The Politics of Rage: Why Do They Hate Us?," *Newsweek*, October 15, 2001.

13 George Kennan, PPS/23 (Policy Planning Staff memorandum 23), *Foreign Relations of the United States, 1949, vol. 1*, U.S. Government Printing Office, Washington DC.

14 Barton Gellman, "Keeping the U.S. First; Pentagon Would Preclude a Rival Superpower," *Washington Post*, March 11, 1992.

15 See extended discussion in chapter 2, documented by notes 62 through 69.

Chapter 1: Iran

1   Historical material from Sandra Mackey, *The Iranians: Persia, Islam and the Soul of a Nation*, Dutton, 1996; and from Malcolm B. Russell, *The Middle East and South Asia 2001*, Stryker-Post Publications, Harpers Ferry VA, 2001.

2   Mackey, The Iranians.

3   Russell, Middle East.

4   William Blum, *Killing Hope: U.S. Military and CIA Interventions Since Word War II*, Common Courage Press, Monroe ME, 1995.

5   Blum, Killing Hope.

6   Blum, Killing Hope.

7   Mackey, The Iranians.

8   "The Shah's Last Laugh," *Forbes*, September 19, 1988.

9   "The Secret CIA History of the Iran Coup, 1953," National Security Archive Electronic Briefing Book #28, posted at http://www.gwu.edu/~nsarchive/NSAEBB/NSAEBB28/index.html.

10 David Wise, *The Invisible Government*, Random House, New York, 1964.

11 National Security Archive, Secret CIA History.

12 Mackey, The Iranians.

13 Blum, Killing Hope.

14 Wilbur Crane Eveland, *Ropes of Sand*, Norton, New York NY, 1980.

15 Blum, Killing Hope

16 Blum, Killing Hope.

17 Russell, Middle East.

18 Mackey, The Iranians.

19 Mackey, The Iranians.

20 *Matchbox*, Fall, 1976.

21 Mackey, The Iranians.

22 John Rossant, "How Oil Money Polluted Iran," *Business Week*, June 2, 1997.

23 R. J. Rummel, "Statistics of Democide: Iran," posted at http://www.hawaii.edu/powerkills/SOD.TAB15.1D.GIF.

24 Low estimate: PBS documentary, "Beyond the Veil," transcripts posted at http://www.pbs.org/visavis/BTVPagesTXT/Theislamicrevolution.html#Black Friday; High estimate: Frank E. Smitha, "The Iranian Revolution," posted at http://www.fsmitha.com/h2/ch29ir.html.

25 Mackey, The Iranians.

26 They may have ended up spilling as much as, or more than the hated Shah. See Rummel, Democide.

27   Abolhassan Bani-Sadr, "My Turn to Speak: Iran, the Revolution, and Secret Deals with the U.S.," Brassey's, New York NY, 1991.

28   Mackey, The Iranians.

29   Robin Wright, *Sacred Rage*, Simon & Schuster, New York NY, 1989.

30   These documents were published by the government of Iran in a series extending to 70 volumes. Many are available at the National Security Archive website, http://www.gwu.edu/~nsarchiv/.

31   Robin Wright, *In the Name of God: The Khomeini Decade*, Simon & Schuster, New York NY, 1989.

32   Robert Parry, "Saddam's Green Light," from the Consortium website, 1996, posted at http://www.consortiumnews.com/archive/xfile5.html.

33   John Pike, "Iran-Iraq War: 1980-1988," from the Federation of American Scientists website, posted at http://www.fas.org/man/dod-101/ops/war/iran-iraq.htm.

34   These controversial allegations have been the subject of two books by ex-White House staffers (Gary Sick and Barbara Honneger, both titled *October Surprise*), as well as two congressional investigations (from the House and Senate, each of which declared there was nothing to it). The definitive account of the evidence comes from *Trick or Treason*, by Robert Parry, who has uncovered documents left out of the congressional probes. He maintains an archive of his articles on the topic at http://www.consortiumnews.com/archive/xfile.html.

35   Bani-Sadr, My Turn.

36   Including Bani-Sadr, French intelligence chief Alexandre deMarenches, Iranian businessman Jamshid Hashemi, and Israeli intelligence officer Ari Ben-Menashe (see Parry's articles). In addition, four U.S. intelligence assets, with varying degrees of credibility, claim to have been eyewitnesses to the meetings (see a series of articles by Harry Martin from the *Napa Sentinel*, posted at http://www.sonic.net/sentinel/usa3.html).

37   The closest thing to a smoking gun on this meeting is a Russian intelligence report, supplied to Congressional investigators but suppressed by them; see Parry, "October Surprise: Finally, Time for Truth," from the Consortium website, posted at http://www.consortiumnews.com/archive/xfile9.html.

38   Sick, October Surprise; see also Bani-Sadr, My Turn.

39   Bani-Sadr, My Turn; see also Honegger, October Surprise.

40   Robert Parry, "Russia's Prime Minister and October Surprise," from the Consortium website, May 15, 1999, posted at http://www.consortiumnews.com/1999/051499a.html.

41   Bani-Sadr, My Turn; see also Mackey, The Iranians.

42   Mackey, The Iranians.

43   Stephen R. Shalom, "The United States and the Iran-Iraq War," Z
     Magazine, February 1990.

44   Alan Friedman, *Spider's Web: The Secret History of How the White House
     Illegally Armed Iraq*, Bantam, New York NY, 1993.

45   Shalom, Iran-Iraq War.

46   Mackey, The Iranians; see also Shalom, Iran-Iraq War.

47   Gene I. Rochlin, *Trapped in the Net: The Unanticipated Consequences of
     Computerization*, Princeton University Press, Princeton NJ, 1997.

48   George Wilson, "The Risks of Shooting First," *Washington Post*, January 28,
     1989.

49   Rochlin, Trapped.

50   Mackey, The Iranians.

51   Peter Kornbluh and Malcolm Byrne, *The Iran-Contra Scandal: The
     Declassified History*, New Press, New York NY, 1993.

52   Mackey, The Iranians.

53   Russell, Middle East.

54   Russell, Middle East; see also Camelia Fard and James Ridgeway, "Iran's
     Secret Diplomacy," *Village Voice*, February 20, 2002.

55   Elaine Sciolino and Neil A. Lewis, "Iran Said to Agree to Help U.S. With
     Rescues," *New York Times*, October 16, 2001; see also "Khatami says
     'Radical Warmongers' Drive U.S. Policy," Agence France Presse, April 27,
     2002.

56   Neil King Jr., "Administration Plans Little Action Against Foreign Oil
     Projects in Iran," *Wall Street Journal*, July 12, 2001.

57   Alan Sipress, "Bush Speech Shuts Door on Tenuous Opening to Iran,"
     Washington Post, February 4, 2002.

58   Julian West and Christina Lamb, "Iranian Officials in secret Taliban talks,"
     The Telegraph (UK), April 11, 2001; see also Brian Murphy, "Iran Stakes
     Out Afghanistan Role," *Washington Post*, December 20, 2001.

CHAPTER 2: IRAQ

1   Dilip Hiro, *Desert Shield to Desert Storm*, Routledge, New York NY, 1992.

2   Ramsey Clark and others, *War Crimes: A Report on United States War
     Crimes Against Iraq*, Maisonneuve Press, Washington DC, 1992.

3   Matthew Rothschild, "Interview with Denis Halliday," *The Progressive*,
     February 1999; see also "Iraq says sanctions killed over 1.6 million,"
     Reuters, January 3, 2002.

4   Jim Huck, *200 Years of Imperialism*, online book posted at
     http://www.angelfire.com/ca3/jphuck/BOOK3Ch9.html.

5   Stephen Zunes, "Continuing Storm: The U.S. Role in the Middle East,"
     from the Foreign Policy in Focus website, posted at http://www.foreignpoli-
     cy-infocus.org/papers/mideast/war.html.

6   Said K. Aburish, interview for Frontline documentary "The Survival of
     Saddam," posted at
     http://www.pbs.org/wgbh/pages/frontline/shows/saddam/interviews/aburish.h
     tml.

7   Andrew and Patrick Cockburn, *Out of the Ashes: The Resurrection of Saddam
     Hussein*, Verso, London, 2000.

8   Hiro, Desert Shield.

9   Aburish, Survival.

10   Aburish, Survival.

11   Aburish, Survival.

12   See Huck, Imperialism.

13   William Blum, Killing Hope: *U.S. Military and CIA Interventions Since
     World War II*, Common Courage Press, Monroe ME 1995.

14   "The Pike Report," AKA *Staff Report of the Select Committee on Intelligence*,
     U.S. House of Representatives, 1975.

15   Ralph Schoenman, *Iraq and Kuwait: A History Suppressed*, Veritas Press,
     Santa Barbara CA, 1991.

16   Robert Parry, "Saddam's Green Light," from the Consortium website, 1996,
     posted at http://www.consortiumnews.com/archive/xfile5.html.

17   John Pike, "Iran-Iraq War: 1980-1988," from the Federation of American
     Scientists website, posted at http://www.fas.org/man/dod-101/ops/war/iran-
     iraq.htm.

18   Robert Parry, "Russia's Prime Minister and October Surprise," from the
     Consortium website, May 15, 1999, posted at
     http://www.consortiumnews.com/1999/051499a.html.

19   Or as the ever-compassionate Henry Kissinger put it, "The ultimate
     American interest in the war is that both sides should lose." Quoted by
     Stephanie Reich in "Slow Motion Holocaust: U.S. Designs on Iraq," *Covert
     Action Quarterly*, Spring 2002.

20   Stephen R. Shalom, "The United States and the Iran-Iraq War," *Z
     Magazine*, February 1990.

21   Shalom, Iran-Iraq.

22   Alan Friedman, *Spiders Web: The Secret History of how the White House
     Illegally Armed Iraq*," Bantam, New York NY, 1993.

23   Rodney Stich, *Defrauding America: A Pattern of Related Scandals*, Diablo
     Western Press, Reno NV, 1994.

24   William Blum, "The United States vs. Iraq—A Study in Hypocrisy,"
     February 9, 1998, posted at http://members.aol.com/bblum6/usviraq.htm.

25   Human Rights Watch, "Whatever Happened To The Iraqi Kurds?" special
     report, March 11, 1991, posted at http://www.hrw.org/reports/1991/iraq/.

26   "Iraqgate: Saddam Hussein, U.S. Policy and the Prelude to the Persian Gulf
      War, 1980-1994," from the Digital National Security Archive website, post-
      ed at http://nsarchive.chadwyck.com/igessayx.htm.

27   Hiro, Desert Shield.

28   Brian Becker, "U.S. Conspiracy to Initiate the War Against Iraq," from
      Clark, et al, War Crimes (see note 2 above).

29   Michael Emery, "How the U.S. Avoided Peace," Village Voice, March 5,
      1991.

30   Murray N. Rothbard, Why The War? The Kuwait Connection," from The
      Irrepressible Rothbard, posted at
      http://www.lewrockwell.com/rothbard/ir/Ch27.html.

31   Schoenman, History Suppressed.

32   Craig Hulet, The Secret U.S. Agenda in the Gulf War, Open Magazine
      Pamphlet Series, New Jersey, 1991.

33   Helga Graham, "Exposed: Washington's role in Saddam's oil plot," The
      Observer (UK), October 12, 1990.

34   Emery, Avoided Peace.

35   Murray Waas, "Who Lost Kuwait?" Village Voice, January 22, 1991.

36   Gautam Biswas and Tony Murphy, "Provoking Iraq," from Clark, et al, War
      Crimes (see note 2 above).

37   Ramsey Clark, The Fire This Time: U.S. War Crimes in the Gulf, Thunder's
      Mouth Press, New York NY, 1992.

38   Hiro, Desert Shield.

39   Emery, Avoided Peace.

40   Jean Heller, "Public Doesn't Get Picture with Gulf Satellite Photos," St.
      Petersburg Times, January 6, 1991; see update in Carl Jensen, 20 Years of
      Censored News, Seven Stories Press, New York NY, 1997.

41   Bob Woodward, "Watergate's Shadow on the Bush Presidency," Washington
      Post Magazine, June 20, 1999.

42   Woodward, Bush Presidency.

43   Frontline documentary "The Gulf War," broadcast January 20, 1996; inter-
      view transcript posted at
      http://www.pbs.org/wgbh/pages/frontline/gulf/oral/baker/1.html.

44   Woodward, Bush Presidency.

45   Robert Parry and Norman Solomon, "Behind Colin Powell's Legend: Part
      Four," from the Consortium website, December 26, 2000, posted at
      http://www.consortiumnews.com/2000/122600b.html.

46   Michael Klare, Beyond the "Vietnam Syndrome": U.S. Interventionism in the
      1980s, Institute for Policy Studies, Washington DC, 1981.

47   Wes Janz and Vickie Abrahamson, eds., War of the Words: The Gulf War
      Quote By Quote, Bobbleheads Press, Minneapolis MN, 1991.

48   Quoted by Barton Gellman in "Keeping the U.S. First; Pentagon Would
      Preclude a Rival Superpower," *Washington Post*, March 11, 1992.

49   Clark, Fire This Time.

50   Gen. Carl A. Vuono, "A Strategic Force for the 1990s and Beyond," U.S.
      Army white paper, January 1990.

51   Hiro, Desert Shield.

52   Harry Browne, "Was the Gulf War a Just War?," column, February 20, 1991,
      posted at http://www.harrybrowne.org/articles/pwar.htm.

53   Patrick Sloyan, "Buried Alive," *Newsday*, September 12, 1991.

54   "One of the most terrible harassments of a retreating army from the air in
      the history of warfare," according to reporter Colin Smith of the London
      Observer, quoted in Hiro, Desert Shield.

55   Middle East Watch, *Needless Deaths in the Gulf War: Civilian Casualties
      During the Air Campaign and Violations of the Laws of War*, Human Rights
      Watch, New York, NY, 1991.

56   Clark, Fire This Time.

57   Stephen Zunes, "Why the U.S. Did Not Overthrow Saddam Hussein," from
      the Foreign Policy in Focus website, November 20, 2001, posted at
      http://www.foreignpolicy-infocus.org/commentary/0111gulfwar.html.

58   Strategy described by Denis Halliday, former Assistant Secretary-General of
      the UN, interviewed in *Z Magazine*, March 2000.

59   Huck, Imperialism (note 4 above); see also "Kuwait puts its $100 billion
      war chest to work," *Business Week*, October 1, 1990.

60   Larry Chin, "Enron: Ultimate Agent of the American Empire," from the
      Online Journal website, February 1, 2002, posted at http://www.onlinejour-
      nal.com/Special_Reports/Chin020102/chin020102.html; see also Seymour
      Hersh, "Spoils of the Gulf War," *New Yorker*, September 6, 1993.

61   Halliday, Z Interview.

62   Thomas J. Nagy, "The Secret Behind the Sanctions: How the U.S.
      Intentionally Destroyed Iraq's Water Supply," *The Progressive*, September
      2001, posted at http://www.progressive.org/0901/nagy0901.html.

63   Voices in the Wilderness, "FAQs on Economic Sanctions Against Iraq,"
      October 23, 2001, posted at
      http://www.nonviolence.org/vitw/pages/170.htm.

64   UNICEF figures, cited by Canadian Network to End Sanctions on Iraq,
      posted at http://canesi.org/.

65   *60 Minutes*, May 12, 1996.

66   "I've been using the word 'genocide,' because this is a deliberate policy to
      destroy the people of Iraq."—Denis Halliday, former Assistant Secretary-
      General of the UN, interviewed in *Z Magazine*, March 2000; Halliday's suc-
      cessor, Hans von Sponek, also resigned in protest of Iraq sanctions. Two

days later Julia Burghardt, director of the World Food Program in Iraq, also
resigned for similar reasons.

67   Scott Ritter, "Blinkered Bush Has Got It All Wrong," *The Mirror* (UK),
     March 13, 2002.

68   Geov Parrish, "Selling Round II," from the Working for Change website,
     November 29, 2001, posted at http://www.workingforchange.com/print-
     item.cfm?itemid=12402.

69   Seymour Hersh, "The Iraq Hawks: Can Their Plan Work?," *New Yorker*,
     December 24/31, 2001.

70   "Arab summit rejects any attack on Iraq." CNN website, March 28, 2002,
     posted at
     http://www.cnn.com/2002/WORLD/meast/03/28/summit.iraq/?related.

71   "Attack on Iraq is unavoidable: U.S. official's warning," *Dawn*, (web edi-
     tion), February 5, 2002, posted at
     http://www.dawn.com/2002/02/05/int2.htm.

72   Michael Isikoff, "the Phantom Link to Iraq," *Newsweek* (web edition) April
     28, 2002, posted at http://www.msnbc.com/news/744626.asp; see also
     Robert Novak, "On Atta, Prague and Iraq," *Chicago Sun-Times*, May 13,
     2002.

73   See Halliday, Z Interview.

CHAPTER 3: SYRIA

1   Douglas Little, "Cold War and Covert Action: The U.S. and Syria, 1945-
     1958," *Middle East Journal*, Winter 1990.

2   Historical material from Malcolm B. Russell, *The Middle East and South
     Asia*, Stryker-Post Publications, Harpers Ferry VA, 2001.

3   That is, to restore Syria's historical borders; see Russell.

4   Irene L. Gendzier, *Notes from the Minefield: United States Intervention in
     Lebanon and the Middle East*, Columbia University Press, New York NY,
     1997.

5   Noam Chomsky, "Terrorism Strikes Home," Z *Magazine*, May 1993.
     Interestingly, the Tapline route ran directly through the Golan Heights,
     now occupied by Israel; see Joe Vialls, "Operation Shekhinah, Part Two,"
     posted at http://www.geocities.com/operationshekhinah2/two.html.

6   Eric Margolis, "Not So Fast, Senator Lott," *Toronto Sun*, February 18, 1998.

7   Quoted by Chomsky in Z, May, 93.

8   Russell, Middle East.

9   William Blum, *Killing Hope: U.S. Military and CIA Interventions Since World
     War II*, Common Courage Press, Monroe ME, 1995.

10   Blum, Killing Hope; see also Wilbur Crane Eveland, *Ropes of Sand*, Norton,
     New York NY, 1980.

11   Blum, Killing Hope.

12 Sandra Mackey, *Passion and Politics: The Turbulent World of the Arabs*, Dutton, New York NY, 1992.

13 Bassam Haddad, "Business as Usual in Syria?," *Middle East Report* Press Information Note 66, September 7, 2001.

14 Andrew and Leslie Cockburn, *Dangerous Liaison: The Inside Story of the U.S.-Israeli Covert Relationship*, HarperCollins, New York NY, 1991.

15 Cockburn and Cockburn, Liaison.

16 Mackey, Passion and Politics.

17 Seymour Hersh, *The Price of Power: Kissinger in the Nixon White House*, Summit Books, New York NY, 1983.

18 Richard Pearson, "From Humble Roots to 'Lion of Damascus'," *Washington Post*, June 11, 2000.

19 Cockburn and Cockburn, Liaison.

20 Sandra Mackey, *Lebanon: Death of a Nation*, Congdon & Weed, New York NY, 1989.

21 David Guyatt, "Lockerbie: The Syrian Connection," posted at http://www.deepblacklies.co.uk/lockerbie-the_syrian_connection.htm.

22 Thomas Friedman, "Hama Rules," *New York Times*, September 21, 2001.

23 Regarding U.S. use of Islamic militants as proxies, see Ahmed Rashid, *Taliban: Militant Islam, Oil and Fundamentalism in Central Asia*, Yale University Press, New Haven CT, 2000.

24 Guyatt, Lockerbie.

25 Maggie Mahar, "Unwitting Accomplices?", *Barron's*, December 17, 1990; see also *Time*, April 27, 1992.

26 Quoted by Edward S. Herman in "The New World Order Rule Of Injustice: The Lockerbie Case," *Z Magazine*, December 2001.

27 For a responsible opposing viewpoint, see William Blum, "The Bombing of Pan Am Flight 103: Case Not Closed," posted at http://members.aol.com/bblum6/panam.htm.

28 John Loftus and Mark Aarons, *The Secret War Against the Jews*, St. Martin's Press, New York NY, 1994.

29 Dilip Hiro, *Desert Shield to Desert Storm*, Routledge, New York NY, 1992.

30 Harvey Sicherman, "Hafez al-Assad: The Man Who Waited Too Long," *Peacefacts* (journal of the Foreign Policy Research Institute), July 2000.

31 Richard Z. Chesnoff, "Is Bashar Wimping Out?," *Jewish World Review*, September 13, 2000; see also Donna Abu-Nasr, "Spate of Arrests Disappoints Syrians," AP, October 20, 2001.

32 James Risen and Tim Weiner, "CIA Sought Syrian Aid," *New York Times*, October 31, 2001.

33 Fred Francis, "NBC News Exclusive: The CIA connection to Syria," from the MSNBC website, September 5, 2002, posted at http://www.msnbc.com/news/804153.asp?0cb=41c24124.

33   Judith Miller, "Washington Accuses Cuba Of Germ-Warfare Research," *New York Times*, May 22, 2002.

CHAPTER 4: SUDAN

1   Congressional Research Service, *Sudan: Humanitarian Crisis, Peace Talks, Terrorism and U.S. Policy*, Library of Congress, Washington DC, June 8, 2001.

2   Karl Vick, "Oil Money Supercharges Sudan's Civil War," *International Herald Tribune*, June 13, 2001; see also Mindy Belz, "Blood for Oil," *World Magazine*, March 10, 2001, posted at http://www.vitrade.com/news/210310_blood_for_oil.htm.

3   Historical material from the website "Sudan 101," posted at http://www.sudan101.com/sudan_info.htm.

4   Walid Phares, "The Sudanese Battle for American Opinion," *Middle East Quarterly*, March 1998.

5   Phares, Sudanese Battle.

6   Dan Connell, "Sudan," *Foreign Policy in Focus*, August 1997.

7   Connell, Sudan.

8   Warren P. Strobel, "Oil feeds the fire now in Sudan's long civil war," *Philadelphia Enquirer*, August 4, 2001.

9   BBC World Service, "Sudan branded over slave trade," April 7, 1999.

10   Phillip Smucker, Market thrives for Sudan's 'human capital'," *Christian Science Monitor*, March 21, 2001.

11   Karin Davies, "Slave Trade Thrives in Sudan," AP, posted at http://www.domini.org/openbook/sud80210.htm.

12   "Women and Children as the Spoils of 'Holy War'," posted at http://www.iabolish.com/today/background/sudan.htm.

13' Connell, Sudan.

14   AP, "Bush Extends Sudan Sanctions," November 1, 2001.

15   Middle East Newsline, September 30, 2001.

16   Rory Nugent, "My Lunch With bin Laden," *Rolling Stone*, October 25, 2001.

17   David Rose, "Resentful west spurned Sudan's key terror files," *The Observer* (UK), September 30, 2001.

18   Rose, Resentful west.

19   "U.S. Cruise Missiles Strike Sudan and Afghan Targets Tied to Terrorist Network," *New York Times*, August 21, 1998.

20   Jared Israel, "Credible Deception: The NY Times and the Sudan missile attack," from the Emperor's Clothes website, posted at http://emperors-clothes.com/articles/jared/sudan.html.

21   "U.S. Admits Mistake in Bombing Sudan," May 7, 1999, from the Wisdom
     Fund website, posted at
     http://www.twf.org/News/Y1999/0507-SudanMistake.html.

22   See Noam Chomsky's comments in "Chomsky replies to Hitchens," posted
     on the *Z Magazine* website at http://www.zmag.org/chomskyhitchens.htm.

23   Israel, Credible deception, citing the 8/23/98 *New York Times*.

24   Elizabeth Neuffer, "Critics Decry Oil Investors' Link to Sudan War," *Boston
     Globe*, March 26, 2001.

25   Phares, Sudanese Battle.

26   *The Economist*, March 1998, cited by the European-Sudanese Public Affairs
     Council (ESPAC), "Bush's Sudan Policy Encourages War, Hinders Peace,"
     June 14, 2001 press release, posted at http://www.twf.org/News/Y2001/0614-
     BushSudan.html.

27   Quoted by M. A. Shaikh, "American aid agencies accuse U.S. of deliberate-
     ly prolonging Sudan war," from the Muslimedia website, posted at
     http://www.muslimedia.com/archives/oaw99/sudan-aid.htm.

28   Reuters, April 24, 2001, cited by ESPAC, Bush's Policy.

29   Shaikh, American aid; see also David Hoile of ESPAC, "Delaying Peace in
     Sudan," posted at http://www.mediamonitors.net/espac10.html.

30   U.S. Committee for Refugees, "Crisis in Sudan," posted at
     http://www.refugees.org/news/crisi/sudan.htm.

31   Victoria Brittain and Terry Macalister, "Oil firms stoke up Sudan war," *The
     Guardian* (UK), March 15, 2001.

32   Sudan 101 website; see also Neuffer, Critics decry.

33   ESPAC, Bush's Policy.

34   M. A. Shaikh, "Secession an option in Sudan accord with southern rebels,"
     from the Muslimedia website, posted at
     http://www.muslimedia.com/archives/world98/sudapact.htm.

35   Shaikh, American aid; see also Hoile, Delaying peace.

36   Quoted by Tom Turnipseed, "A Creeping Collapse in Credibility at the
     White House," from the CounterPunch website, January 10, 2002, posted
     at http://www.counterpunch.org/tomenron.html.

37   "Sudanese government accepts U.S. plan for Sudan," Khilafah.com,
     September 10, 2001, posted at
     http://www.khilafah.com/1421/category.php?DocumentD=2150&tagID=11.

38   M. A. Shaikh, "Sudan taking opportunity to improve relations with U.S.,"
     from the Muslimedia website, posted at
     http://www.muslimedia.com/sudan.wtc.htm.

39   Khilafah, Sudanese government.

40   Shaikh, Sudan taking opportunity; see also Jim Lobe, "U.S.-Sudan
     Terrorism Ties Spell Disaster for Anti-Khartoum Activists," Foreign Policy

in Focus website, September 25, 2001, posted at http://www.foreignpolicy-infocus.org/selfdetermination/news/0109sudan_body.html.

41   AP, "UN lifts sanctions from Sudan," September 28, 2001.

42   George Gedda, "U.S.: Sudan Willing to Allow Monitors," AP, March 5, 2002.

43   Reuters, "International monitors deployed in Sudan," April 5, 2002.

44   "Sudan peace talks reach breakthrough," BBC News July 20, 2002.

45   "Khartoum 'suspends' peace talks with rebels," AP, September 2, 2002.

46   "Sudan peace deal falls short: U.S. brokered agreement fails to actually end fighting," from the Strategic Forecasting website http://www.stratfor.com, reposted at http://www.wnd.com/news/article.asp?ARTICLE_ID=28364.

47   U.S. Committee for Refugees, Crisis in Sudan.

48   Strobel, Oil feeds.

CHAPTER 5: LIBYA

1   The man has publicly stated that he doesn't care how his name is spelled in the Roman alphabet, which has led to dozens of variations, thwarting all efforts at web searches; this one, however, is my favorite.

2   Historical material from Stephen R. Shalom, "The United States and Libya," parts 1 and 2, Z Magazine, May and June 1990 issues.

3   Shalom, part 1, citing Lisa Anderson, "Libya and American Foreign Policy," Middle East Journal, vol. 36, Autumn 1982; population figures from http://www.worldinformation.com/World/Africa/Libya/profile.asp?country=218.

4   Shalom, part 1, citing Majid Khadduri, Modern Libya: A Study in Political Development, Baltimore MD, The Johns Hopkins Press, 1963.

5   Shalom, part 1, citing U.S. Department of State, Foreign Relations of the United States: 1949, vol. 4, U.S. Government Printing Office, Washington DC.

6   Shalom, part 1, citing U.S. Department of State, Foreign Relations of the United States: 1951, vol. 5, U.S. Government Printing Office, Washington DC.

7   See Jack Anderson, Fiasco, Times Books, New York NY, 1983.

8   Quoted in Anderson, Fiasco.

9   Daniel Pipes, "No One Likes the Colonel," American Spectator, March 1981.

10   Anderson, Fiasco.

11   Anderson, Fiasco.

12   John M. Blair, The Control of Oil, Vintage Books, New York NY, 1976.

13   Anderson, Fiasco.

14   See V. H. Oppenhem, "Why Oil Prices Go Up," *Foreign Policy*, Winter
      1976-77.

15   Quoted in the London *Observer*, January 14, 2001. Yamani cites the abrupt
      about-face of the Shah, who told him, "Ask Henry Kissinger—he is the one
      who wants a higher price."

16   S. Giovanna Giacomazzi, "Embracing Qadaffi," posted at http://www.gio-
      gia.com/Qadaffi.htm.

17   Samia Nkrumah, "Taking a Trip to Tripoli," *Al-Ahram Weekly*, April 15-21,
      1999.

18   See Seymour Hersh, "The Quadaffi Connection," *New York Times Magazine*,
      6/14/81 and "Exposing the Libyan Link," *New York Times Magazine*,
      6/21/81; see also Ken Silverstein, "Even Spooks Have Rights," *The Nation*,
      October 4, 1999. The Justice Department opened an investigation in 2000
      into Wilson's claims that he had been convicted by perjured testimony,
      claims discussed at length in Mike Ruppert, "Ed Wilson's Revenge," posted
      at http://www.fromthewilderness.com/free/ciadrugs/Ed_Wilson_1.html.

19   Pipes, The Colonel.

20   Shalom, part 2, citing U.S. Senate, Committee on the Judiciary,
      Subcommittee on Security and Terrorism, *Libyan Sponsored Terrorism: A
      Dilemma for Policymakers*, hearings of February 19, 1986.

21   Shalom, part 2, citing David Blundy and Andrew Lycett, *Qaddafi and the
      Libyan Revolution*, Little, Brown, Boston MA, 1987.

22   Shalom, part 2, citing James Kelly, "Searching for Hit Teams," *Time*,
      December 21, 1981; also Duncan Campbell and Patrick Forbes, "Tale of
      anti-Reagan Hit Team was fraud," *New Statesman*, August 16, 1985.

23   Hersh, Target Qaddafi.

24   Shalom, part 2, citing Michael Rubner, "Antiterrorism and the Withering
      of the 1973 War Powers Resolution," *Political Science Quarterly*, Summer
      1987.

25   Noam Chomsky, *Necessary Illusions: Thought Control in Democratic Societies*,
      South End Press, Boston MA, 1989.

26   Hersh, Target Qaddafi.

27   Chomsky, Necessary Illusions.

28   Chomsky, Necessary Illusions.

29   Joel Bainerman, "Bush Administration's Involvement in Bombing Pan Am
      103," *Portland Free Press*, May/June 1997; see also notes 24 through 27 in
      chapter 3.

30   William Blum, "The Bombing of Pan Am Flight 103: Case Not Closed,"
      posted at http://members.aol.com/bblum6/panam.htm; see also "UN moni-
      tor decries Lockerbie judgement," BBC News, March 14, 2002.

31   Neil Mackay, "Lockerbie: CIA witness gagged by U.S. government," *Sunday
      Herald* (UK), May 28, 2000.

32   "Abu Nidal behind Lockerbie plot, says former ally," *Sydney Morning Herald*, August 24, 2002.

33   "U.S. Extends Libya Travel Ban For A Year," Reuters, November 23, 2001.

34   Robert S. Greenberger, "Sept. 11 Girds Gadhafi to Buckle Down In His Work to Get Off U.S. Terror List," *Wall Street Journal Interactive*, January 14, 2002.

35   "U.S. officials differ on Libya policy," AP, February 4, 2002.

36   Dan Chapman and Bob Deans, "8 Aid Workers Held By Taliban Now Safe In Pakistan," Cox News Service, November 15, 2001.

37   David Shayler, "MI6 Plot to assassinate Colonel Gaddafi: Police enquiry confirms plot is not 'fantasy'," posted at http://cryptome.org/shayler-gaddafi.htm.

38   See "Excerpts from News Accounts – Bin Laden in the Balkans," from the Emperor's Clothes website, posted at http://emperorsclothes.com/news/binl.htm.

39   Paul Joseph Watson, "British Press Gagged on Reporting MI6's £100,000 bin Laden Payoff," from the Scoop website (New Zealand), posted at http://www.scoop.co.nz/mason/stories/HL0210/S00061.htm.

40   Richard Norton-Taylor, "Gaddafi seen as ally in war on terrorism," *The Guardian* (UK) August 9, 2002.

CHAPTER 6: LEBANON

1   Historical material from Sandra Mackey, *Lebanon: Death of a Nation*, Congdon & Weed, New York NY, 1989.

2   As'ad Abu Khalil, "Lebanon: Key Battleground for Middle East Policy," *Foreign Policy in Focus*, February 2000.

3   Irene L. Gendzier, "Minority Alliances," *Journal of Palestine Studies*, Winter 1999.

4   David Wise and Thomas Ross, *The Invisible Government*, Random House, New York NY, 1964.

5   William Blum, *Killing Hope: U.S. and CIA Interventions Since World War II*, Common Courage Press, Monroe ME, 1995.

6   Mackey, Lebanon.

7   Blum, Killing Hope.

8   Wilbur Crane Eveland, *Ropes of Sand: America's Failure in the Middle East*, Norton, New York NY, 1980.

9   Malcolm B. Russell, *The Middle East and South Asia*, Stryker-Post Publications, Harpers Ferry VA, 2001.

10   Mackey, Lebanon.

11   Andrew and Leslie Cockburn, *Dangerous Liaison: The Inside Story of the U.S.-Israeli Covert Relationship*, HarperCollins, New York NY, 1991.

12   Noam Chomsky, *Fateful Triangle: The United States, Israel and the Palestinians*, South End Press, Boston MA, 1999 edition.

13   Cockburn and Cockburn, Dangerous Liaison.

14   Neil Macdonald, "The Attitude of Lebanon," CBC Television News, August 29, 2000.

15   Cockburn and Cockburn.

16   Livia Rokach, *Israel's Sacred Terrorism: A Study Based On Moshe Sharett's Personal Diary*, Association of Arab-American University Graduates, Belmont MA, 1986.

17   Chomsky, Fateful Triangle.

18   Noam Chomsky, *Towards a New Cold War: Essays on the Current Crisis and How We Got There*, Random House, New York NY, 1982; see also Robert Fisk, "Israel Opts for a Bloody Retreat," *The Independent* (UK), February 13, 2000.

19   H.D.S. Greenway, *Washington Post*, March 25, 1978.

20   Chomsky, New Cold War.

21   Paraphrased in *Ha'aretz*, May 15, 1978.

22   Chomsky, Fateful Triangle.

23   Mackey, Lebanon.

24   Mackey, Lebanon.

25   Cockburn and Cockburn; see also John H. Kelley, "Lebanon: 1982-1984," Rand Corporation study CF-129, chapter 6.

26   Chomsky, Fateful Triangle.

27   Low estimate: Chomsky, New Cold War; High: Samuel Hazo, "Book Review: Pity the Nation," *Washington Report on Middle East Affairs*, March 1991.

28   Mackey, Lebanon.

29   Arjan El Fassed, citing Robert Fisk and others, in "Historical Myths: The Arabs Started all the Wars," from the Electronic Intifada website, posted at http://www.electronicintifada.net/historicalmyths/1982war.html; Mackey makes the same comparison.

30   Mackey, Lebanon.

31   Cockburn and Cockburn.

32   Russell, Middle East.

33   Robert Fisk, "The Legacy of Ariel Sharon," *The Independent* (UK), February 6, 2001.

34   Comment recorded in Mackey, Lebanon.

35   Abu Khalil, Key Battleground.

36   Kelley, Lebanon 1982-1984.

37   Bob Woodward, *Veil: The Secret Wars of the CIA 1981-1987*, Simon & Schuster, New York NY, 1987.

38   Fisk, Bloody Retreat.

39   Robert Fisk, "Occupied Lebanon," *The Nation*, May 13, 1996.

40   Ghasan Bishara, "Lebanon's Most Dangerous Summer," MERIP Press
      Information Notes, April 25, 2000.

41   "The Syrian Ethnic Cleansing of Lebanon, Year 1999," posted at http://gen-
      eralaoun.simplanet.com/freedomwriter40.html.

42   Juan A. Lozano, "U.S., Syria Seek Common Ground," AP, May 23, 2002.

CHAPTER 7: JORDAN

1   Andrew and Leslie Cockburn, *Dangerous Liaison: The Inside Story of the
      U.S.-Israeli Covert Relationship*, HarperCollins, New York NY, 1991.

2   Edward Said, "Deconstructing King Hussein," posted at http://www.geoci-
      ties.com/capitolhill/lobby/6814/theking.html.

3   See, for instance, "The ruling family of Jordan – a family of treason!", post-
      ed at http://www.geocities.com/arabicpaper911/hus.html.

4   Historical material from Malcolm B. Russell, *The Middle East and South
      Asia*, Stryker-Post Publications, Harpers Ferry VA, 2001.

5   Richard Becker, "Why four presidents went to Jordan," *Worker's World*,
      February 18, 1999.

6   William Blum, *Killing Hope: U.S. and CIA Interventions Since World War II*,
      Common Courage Press, Monroe ME, 1995.

7   Becker, Four presidents.

8   As'sad AbuKhalil, "Home View of King Hussein Does Not See a Friendly
      Democrat," *Jinn Magazine*, February 2, 1999.

9   "King Hussein of Jordan," *Socialism Today*, Issue 36, March 1999.

10   Russell, Middle East.

11   Cockburn and Cockburn, Liaison.

12   Andrew Kilgore, "The Late King Hussein of Jordan (A Reminicence),"
      Washington Report on Middle East Affairs, April/May 1999.

13   Cockburn and Cockburn, Liaison.

14   Cockburn and Cockburn, Liaison.

15   *Socialism Today*, King Hussein

16   "King Husain: a loyal royal," from the Muslimedia website, November 16-
      30, 1997, posted at http://www.muslimedia.com/archives/oaw98/husain.htm.

17   *Socialism Today*, King Hussein

18   Donald Neff, "Nixon's Middle East Policy," *Arab Studies Quarterly*,
      Winter/Spring 1990.

19   "Hussein of Jordan: The Bloody King of Black September," *Revolutionary
      Worker* #995, February 21, 1999.

20   *Revolutionary Worker*, Bloody King.

21   Low estimate: *Socialism Today*; medium: Russell; high: Becker.

22   Said, Deconstructing, citing the BBC.

23   Roger Matthews and David Gardner, "Jordan: The chameleon king," posted
      at http://www.library.cornell.edu/colldev/mideast/huss4.htm.

24   *Socialism Today*, King Hussein.

25   Becker, Four presidents.

26   Russell, Middle East.

27   Matthews and Gardner, Chameleon; see also Russell and AbuKhalil.

28   "Dangerous game in Jordan," *Le Monde Diplomatique*, March 1999; see also
      Jim Hoagland, "Hussein's Royal Mistake," *Washington Post*, January 31,
      1999.

29   Anne-Marie O'Connor and Dana Calvo, "A Day Fit for a Queen and
      King," *Los Angeles Times*, March 20, 2002.

30   Family of treason, at http://www.geocities.com/arabicpaper911/hus.html.

31   Becker, Four presidents.

32   "Resurgent Palestinian Group Test Kingdom," Free intelligence brief from
      the Strategic Forecasting website, posted at
      http://www.stratfor.com/fib/fib_view.php?ID=204298.

CHAPTER 8: EGYPT

1   Hizb ut-Tahir, "Was Nasser a CIA Agent?", *Khilafah* magazine, April 1991,
      posted at http://msanews.mynet.MSANEWS/199903/1990321.27.html.

2   Donald Neff, "Nasser Comes to Power," *Washington Report on Middle East
      Affairs*, July 1996, posted at http://www.washington-
      report.org/backissues/0796/9607083.htm.

3   Andrew and Leslie Cockburn, *Dangerous Liaison: The Inside Story of the
      U.S.-Israeli Covert Relationship*, HarperCollins, New York NY, 1991.

4   Cockburn and Cockburn.

5   Ehud Yaari, cited by Noam Chomsky in *The New Cold War: Essays on the
      Current Crisis and How We Got There*, Pantheon, New York NY, 1982.

6   Cited by Chomsky, as well as by Arjan El Fassed in "Historical Myths: The
      Arabs Started All the Wars," posted at
      http://www.electronicintifada.com/historicalmyths/1956war.html.

7   Kenneth Love, *Suez: The Twice Fought War*, McGraw-Hill, New York NY,
      1969.

8   Cockburn and Cockburn, Liaison.

9   Cockburn and Cockburn, Liaison.

10   Malcolm B. Russell, *The Middle East and South Asia*, Stryker-Post
      Publications, Harpers Ferry VA, 2001.

11   Chomsky, New Cold War.

12   William Blum, *Killing Hope: U.S. and CIA Interventions Since World War II*,
      Common Courage Press, Monroe ME, 1995.

13   Wilbur Crane Eveland, *Ropes of Sand*, Norton, New York NY, 1980.

14   Eyewitnesses have noted Eisenhower's less ambiguous orders to "liquidate" Congolese Prime Minister Patrice Lumumba, as mentioned by Stanley Crouch in "Ignore the Guilt Trip Some Want to Lay on Us," *Arizona Daily Star*, 09/19/01. A similar "changed my mind" explanation was used to obfuscate U.S. complicity in the assassination of Chilean general Rene Schneider in 1970; see Christopher Hitchens, "The Case Against Henry Kissinger," *Harpers*, March 2001.

15   For other Western assassination plots against Nasser see http://www.wake-upmag.co.uk/articles/sstate2.htm.

16   Cited by Jews for Justice in the Middle East, The Origin of the Palestine-Israel Conflict, third edition, posted at http://www.cactus48.com/truth.html.

17   Cockburn and Cockburn, Liaison.

18   El Fassed, posted at http://www.electronicintifada.com/historicalmyths/1967war.html.

19   Cited by Jews for Justice and El Fassed.

20   Sheldon Richman, "U.S. Policy in the Middle East Since World War II and the Folly of Intervention," Cato Institute Policy Analysis #159, August 16 91.

21   Cited by Suzy Hansen in "Assault on the U.S.S Liberty," posted at http://www.salon.com/books/feature/2001/04/25/liberty/.

22   Richman, U.S. Policy.

23   Chomsky, New Cold War.

24   Eveland, Ropes.

25   Eric Margolis, "Not So Fast, Sen. Lott," *Toronto Sun*, 02/16/98.

26   George Szamuely, "Israel's Hamas," *New York Press*, April 27, 2002.

27   Chomsky, New Cold War.

28   Edward Said, "Deconstructing King Hussein," posted at http://www.geocities.com/capitolhill/lobby/6814/theking.html.

29   Chomsky, New Cold War.

30   Noam Chomsky, *Fateful Triangle*, South End Press, Boston MA, 1999 (updated edition of 1983 work).

31   Richman, U.S. Policy.

32   Chomsky, Fateful Triangle.

33   Douglas Valentine, "Homeland Insecurity, part 5," CounterPunch.org, November 8, 2001, posted at http://www.counterpunch.org/homeland5.html.

34   Dave McGowan, "Lies My Psychology Professors Taught Me," *The Konformist*, August 2000, posted at http://davesweb.cnchost.com/psych.htm; also at http://www.konformist.com/2000/psych-lies.htm.

35 Foreign Policy in Focus special report, "Continuing Storm: The U.S. Role in the Middle East," posted at http://www.foreignpolicy-infocus.org/papers/mideast/islam.html.

36 Federation of American Scientists, "Arab Veterans of Afghanistan War Lead New Islamic Holy War," October 28, 1994, posted at http://wwwfas.org/irp/news/1994/afghan_war_vetrans.html.

37 Amnesty International report 2001: Egypt, posted at http://www.web.amnesty.org/web/ar2001.nsf/webmepcountries/Egypt?OpenDocument.

38 "Egypt History," posted at http://www.arabnet/egypt/history/et_mubarak.html.

CHAPTER 9: PALESTINE

1   Jews for Justice in the Middle East, "Origins of the Palestine-Israel Conflict," third edition, published online at http://www.cactus48.com/truth.html.

2   Quoted by Noam Chomsky in *Deterring Democracy*, Hill and Wang, New York NY, 1992.

3   Edward Said, "What Israel Has Done," *The Nation*, May 6, 2002; see also notes 90-92 below.

4   Ramit Plushnick-Masti, "Amnesty Accuses Israel of War Crimes," AP, November 4, 2002.

5   Amos Harel, "Peres Calls IDF Operation in Jenin a 'Massacre'," *Haaretz*, April 9, 2002.

6   Phil Reeves and Justin Huggler, "Once upon a time in Jenin," *The Independent* (UK), April 25, 2002.

7   By Joshua Brilliant, " Hostilities ebb as Powell arrives," *Washington Times*, April 11, 2002.

8   Tanya Reinhart, "Jenin: The Propaganda Battle," *Dissident Voice*, April 24, 2002.

9   Amira Haas, "What kind of war is this?" *Haaretz*, April 20, 2002.

10 "Powell: No Evidence Yet of Massacre in Jenin," UPI, April 25, 2002; see also 'Massacre' mystery: What really happened in Jenin?," ABC News online, May 2, 2002.

11 Ben Lynfield and Rory Macmillan, "Are the Israelis guilty of mass murder?," *The Scotsman*, April 19, 2002.

12 Dina Shiloh, "U.S. Promise on Jenin Won Arafat's Freedom," *San Francisco Chronicle*, April 30, 2002.

13 "Israelis Re-enter Ramallah," UPI, June 10, 2002; see also Janine Zacharia, "Bush backing IDF West Bank operations," July 9, 2002.

14 "Jenin deaths video implicates army," BBC News, July 5, 2002.

15 Rita Hauser, "Future Visions of the Middle East," remarks to the Foreign Policy Association, April 30, 2002, transcript posted at http://www.fpa.org/topics_info2414/topics_info_show.htm?doc_id=109837.

See also Natan Sachs, "The Intra-Likud Power Struggle And Israeli National Elections," Peacewatch Number 381, May 10, 2002, posted at http://www.washingtoninstitute.org/watch/Peacewatch/peace-watch2002/381.htm.

16   Historical material from Malcolm B. Russell, *The Middle East and South Asia*, Stryker-Post Publications, Harpers Ferry VA, 2001.

17   Benjamin Beit-Hallahmi, *Original Sins*, Olive Branch Press, New York NY, 1993.

18   Noam Chomsky, *Fateful Triangle: The United States, Israel and the Palestinians*, updated edition, South End Press, Boston MA, 1999.

19   Jews for Justice, citing Don Peretz, *The Arab-Israeli Dispute*.

20   Chomsky, Fateful Triangle.

21   Khalil Osman, "Zionist terrorism," from the Muslimedia website, posted at http://www.muslimedia.com/archives/special-edition/terrorism50/zionterr.htm.

22   Chomsky, Fateful Triangle; see also Jason Vest, "The Rich History of Jewish Terrorism," *Village Voice*, December 21, 2001.

23   Lernni Brenner, *Zionism in the Age of Dictators*, Laurence Hill, Westport CT, 1983; see also Vest, Jewish Terrorism.

24   Jews for Justice, citing Teikener, et al, *Anti Zionism*.

25   Jews for Justice, citing John Quigley, *Palestine and Israel: A Challenge for Peace*. Authors John Loftus and Mark Aarons argue that the Zionists were able to blackmail Nelson Rockefeller, by threatening to reveal his wartime collaboration with Hitler's Nazi regime, into using his influence to sway decisive South American votes. John Loftus and Mark Aarons, *The Secret War Against the Jews*, St. Martin's Press, New York NY, 1994.

26   Loftus & Aarons, Secret War.

27   Chomsky, Fateful Triangle.

28   Andrew and Leslie Cockburn, *Dangerous Liaison: The Inside Story of the U.S.-Israeli Covert Relationship*, HarperCollins, New York, 1991.

29   Russell, Middle East; see also Loftus & Aarons.

30   David Ben-Gurion, *Rebirth and Destiny of Israel*, Philosophical Library, New York NY, 1954.

31   Arjan El-Fassed, "Historical Myths: The Arabs Started All the Wars: 1948," from the Electronic Intifada website, posted at http://www.electron-icintifada.net/historicalmyths/1948war.html, citing the *New York Times*.

32   "The Deir Yessin Massacre," from the Jerusalemites website, posted at http://www.jerusalemites.org/yassin2.html; see also Jews for Justice.

33   El-Fassed, Historical Myths.

34   Quoted by Norman Finkelstein in *Image and Reality of the Israel-Palestine Conflict*, Verso, New York NY, 1995.

35   Chomsky, Fateful Triangle.

36   Joel Beinin and Lisa Hajjar, "Palestine, Israel and the Arab-Israeli Conflict: A Primer," from the Middle East Research and Information Project (MERIP) website, posted at www.merip.org/palestine-israel_primer/

intro-pal-isr-primer.html.

37 Beinin and Hajjar, A Primer.

38 700,000 out of 1,269,000, the prewar Arab population cited by Beinin and Hajjar.

39 Jews for Justice, citing Israeli historian Benny Morris, *The Birth of the Palestinian Refugee Problem, 1947-1949*.

40 Loftus and Aarons.

41 See Loftus and Aarons, Secret War.

42 Cockburn & Cockburn, Dangerous Liaison; see also Jonathan Marshall, Peter Dale Scott and Jane Hunter, *The Iran Contra-Connection: Secret Teams and Covert Operations in the Reagan Era*, South End Press, Boston MA, 1988.

43 "…if the matter were delicately handled." Cockburn & Cockburn, Dangerous Liaison.

44 Quoted by Donald Neff in "Nasser Comes to Power in Egypt, Frightening Britain, France and Israel," *Washington Report on Middle East Affairs*, July 1996.

45 Cockburn & Cockburn, Dangerous Liaison.

46 Loftus and Aarons.

47 Wilbur Crane Eveland, *Ropes of Sand*, Norton, New York NY, 1980.

48 Chomsky, Fateful Triangle.

49 Jews for Justice, quoting Edward Said, *The Question of Palestine*.

50 "Palestine and the United Nations," posted at http://www.palestine-un.org.

51 Beinin and Hajjar, A Primer; see also Amira Haas, "Just for one week," *Ha'aretz*, September 27, 2001.

52 Derek Brown, "Israel and the Middle East: Key Events," *The Guardian* (UK), January 2, 2002.

53 Emphasis in original. Paraphrased by former Prime Minister Moshe Sharett, quoted in Livia Rokach, *Israel's Sacred Terrorism*, Association of Arab-American University Graduates, Belmont MA, 1980.

54 John Steinbach, "Palestine in the Crosshairs," *Covert Action Quarterly*, Spring 2002; see also Ali Abunimah and Hussein Ibish, "Debunking 6 common Israeli myths," from the Electronic Intifada website, posted at http://electronic intifada.net/coveragetrends/6mythsprint.shtml.

55 Rokach, Sacred Terrorism.

56 Quoted in Palestine Center Fact Sheet #1, posted at http://www.palestine-center.org/cpap/pubs/20001127fs.html.

57 See David Hirst, "Where terror begins: Arabs are asking why Israeli brutality is deemed self-defence while Palestinians are vilified as terrorists," *The Guardian* (UK), October 26, 2001; see also Elijah Ward, "The Suicide Bombers Lie," from the AlterNet website, April 3, 2002, posted at http://www.alternet.org/story.html?StoryID=12772.

58 Kathleen Christison, "The Full Story of Resolution 242: How the U.S. Sold Out the Palestinians," *Palestine Chronicle*, July 2, 2002, posted at http://www.palestinechronicle.org/article.php?story=20020702071406432.

59   Chomsky, Fateful Triangle.

60   Chomsky, Fateful Triangle.

61   As quoted by Ze'ev Schiff in *Haaretz,* May 15, 1978.

62   Kathryn Casa, "Water: The Real Reason Behind Israeli Occupations,"
      Washington Report on Middle East Affairs, July 1991.

63   Discussed in the diaries of former Prime Minister Moshe Sharett, as
      excerpted in Rokach, *Sacred Terrorism.*

64   Chomsky, Fateful Triangle.

65   Chomsky, Fateful Triangle; see also chapter 6, note 27.

66   Foundation for Middle East Peace (FMEP), "Israeli Settlements in the
      Occupied Territories," a special report, published March 2002, posted at
      http://www.fmep.org/reports/2002/sr0203.html.

67   FMEP, Israeli Settlements.

68   Chomsky, Fateful Triangle.

69   Edward S. Herman, "Israeli Apartheid and Terrorism," Z *Magazine,* May
      1994.

70   Chomsky, Fateful Triangle.

71   Richard Sale, "Hamas history tied to Israel," UPI, June 18, 2002; see also
      George Szamuely, "Israel's Hamas," *New York Press,* volume 15, number 17,
      posted at http://www.nypress.com/15/17/taki/2.cfm.

72   Ray Hanania, "How Sharon and the Likud party nurtured the rise of
      Hamas," Middle East News online, posted at
      http://www.middleeastwire.com:8080/printarticle.jsp?id=10540.

73   Laiala A. Nazzal and Nafez Y. Nazzal, *Historical Dictionary of Palestine,*
      Scarecrow Press, Latham MD, 1996.

74   Tarik Kafala, "Intifada: Then and Now," BBC, December 8, 2000.

75   U.S. State Department Country Report on Human Rights Practices in
      Israel, 1988, notes dryly that "Many avoidable deaths and injuries occurred
      because Israeli soldiers frequently used gunfire in situations that did not
      present mortal danger to troops…"

76   Chomsky, Fateful Triangle.

77   James Bennet, "Narrowing death ratio raises heat on Sharon," *New York
      Times,* March 12, 2002.

78   U.S. State Department Country Report on Human Rights Practices in
      Israel, 1991: "Human rights groups charged that plainclothes security per-
      sonnel acted as death squads who killed Palestinian activists without warn-
      ing…"

79   Nazzal and Nazzal, Dictionary of Palestine.

80   Beinin and Hajjar, A Primer.

81   1407, according to B'Tselem, "The Israeli Information Center for Human
      Rights in the Occupied Territories," posted at
      http://www.palestinecenter.org/cpap/pubs/20001127fs.html. In the same
      period 405 Israelis were killed by Palestinians.

82   Chomsky, Fateful Triangle.

83   Jim Hoagland, "Friends of the CIA," *Washington Post,* April 7, 2002.

84   Quoted by Rahul Sigar in an interview posted at http://www.india-semi-
      nar.com/2001/506/506%20interview%20with%20rahul%20sagar.htm.

85   Abunimah and Ibish, 6 common myths; see also the map of the so-called
      "Area A Territories" under full Palestinian control, posted by the Global
      Policy Forum at http://www.globalpolicy.org/security/issues/israel-
      palestine/land/2001/large.htm.

86   Richard H. Curtiss, "Rabin Assassination Sharpens Choice Facing His
      Country," *Washington Report on Middle East Affairs*, December 1995.

87   FMEP, Israeli Settlements.

88   Nissar Hoath, "Israel 'usurping Arab water resources'," *Gulf News*, April
      15, 2002.

89   Ilene R. Prusher, "Israel Dodges U.S. Deadline," *Christian Science Monitor*,
      December 19, 1997; see also H.D.S. Greenway, "How Middle East peace
      process was killed," *Boston Globe*, May 3, 2002.

90   Robert Wright, "Was Arafat the Problem?," *Slate*, April 18, 2002.

91   Foundation for Middle East Peace (FMEP), "West Bank Final Status Map
      Presented by Israel – May 2000," posted at
      http://www.fmep.org/images/maps/map0007_2.jpg.

92   The best and most detailed examination of this matter is "Camp David:
      Tragedy of Errors," by Hussein Agha and Robert Malley, (who participated
      in the negotiations), in the *New York Review of Books*, August 9, 2001.
      Barak replied twice to their article and was twice rebutted.

93   Agha and Malley, "Camp David and After: An Exchange (A Reply to
      Ehud Barak)," *New York Review of Books*, June 13, 2001.

94   Stephen Shalom, "Background to the Israel-Palestine Crisis," *Z Magazine*,
      May 2002.

95   Agha and Malley, Camp David and After.

96   Julian Borger, Anger at peace talks 'meddling'," *The Guardian* (UK), July
      13, 2000.

97   Lee Hockstader, "Sharon's Year in Power has Been Israel's Bloodiest in a
      Generation," *International Herald Tribune*, February 7, 2002; see also Hamza
      Hendawai, "Hamas Threatens Deadlier Attacks," AP, April 19, 2002.

98   Steve Weizman, "West Bank Settlements Increasing," AP, October 4,
      2001.

99   Justin Huggler, "Israeli Attack Ruins Deal to End Suicide Bombings," *The
      Independent* (UK), July 25, 2002; see also Amos Harel, "Security brass:
      Targeted killings don't work; no military solution to terror," *Haaretz*,
      January 7, 2002.

100   "Israelis demolishing Palestinian government infrastructure," CBC News,
      April 11, 2002; see also Amira Haas, "Operation Destroy the Data,"
      Haaretz, April 24, 2002; see also Betsy Pisik, "Palestinians say troops van-
      dalized, looted West Bank," *Washington Times*, April 23, 2002.

101   Flore de Préneuf, "Sharon's war," from the Buzzle.com website, posted at
      http://www.buzzle.com/editorials/4-18-2002-16801.asp?viewPage=4; see
      also "Palestine Under Fire," from Revolutionary Worker #1111, July 22,

2001, posted at http://www.rwor.org.

102   Gil Hoffman, "Arafat said to endorse Saudi plan," *Jerusalem Post*, February 26, 2002.

103   Gideon Levy, "Building the Terror Infrastructure," *Ha'aretz*, April 22, 2002; see also Lucy Winkett, "I Watched a Soldier Shoot at Children," *The Guardian* (UK), February 14, 2002.

104   Phil Reeves and Justin Huggler, "From the Ruins of Jenin, the truth about an atrocity," *The Independent* (UK), April 20, 2002; see also Phil Reeves, "Fresh Evidence of Jenin atrocities," *The Independent* (UK), April 18, 2002; see also Phil Reeves, "Amid the ruins of Jenin, the grisly evidence of a war crime," *The Independent* (UK), April 16, 2002.

105   Robert Fisk, "Mr. Powell must see for himself what Israel inflicted on Jenin, *The Independent* (UK), April 14, 2002.

106   Jim Lobe, "Hawks Control U.S. Mideast Policy," from the AlterNet website, April 2, 2002, posted at http://www.alternet.org/print.html?StoryID=12765.

107   Adam B. Kushner, "Mideast Misstep: Bush's dismal foray into peacemaking," from the *American Prospect* website, June 27, 2002, posted at http://www.prospect.org/webfeatures/2002/06/kushner-a-06-27.html.

108   Jim Lobe, "Hawks. See also Eric Margolis, "Why Bush dances to Sharon's Tune," *Toronto Sun*, April 14, 2002.

109   From *Ha'aretz*, reposted at the Middle East Information Center website, at http://www.middleeastinfo.org/print.php?sid=253.

110   Martin van Creveld, "Sharon's plan is to drive Palestinians across the Jordan," *The Telegraph* (UK), April 28, 2002; see also Inigo Gilmore and David Wastell, "Sharon plans to annex half the West Bank, says coalition ally," *The Telegraph* (UK), April 21, 2002.

111   "West Bank fence plan makes strange bedfellows," CNN, July 4, 2002.

112   Quoted by Noam Chomsky in *Deterring Democracy*, Hill and Wang, New York NY, 1992.

113   Generally $3 billion a year in aid and another $2-3 billion in other assistance such as loan guarantees and special grants, according to Max Elbaum and Hany Khalil, "War on Terrorism or Illegal Occupation?: The U.S. has given $14 million a day to Israel for 25 years," from the *War Times* website, posted at http://www.wartimes.org.

114   Frida Berrigan and William D. Hartung, "U.S. Arms Transfers and Security Assistance to Israel," from the Antiwar.com website, posted at http://antiwar.com/orig/israelweapons.html.

CHAPTER 10: TURKEY

1   Anne Applebaum, "Talking Turkey," *Slate*, November 19, 2001, posted at http://slate.msn.com/?id=2058813.

2   Historical material from Malcolm B. Russell, *The Middle East and South Asia*, Stryker-Post Publications, Harpers Ferry VA, 2001.

3   Christopher Simpson, *The Splendid Blond Beast*, Common Courage Press, Monroe ME, 1995; see also Ian Urbina, "U.S. Bows to Turkey," *The Nation*, November 12, 2001.
4   Nicole and Hugh Pope, *Turkey Unveiled: A History of Modern Turkey*, Overlook Press, Woodstock NY, 1997.
5   Urbina, U.S. Bows.
6   Ertugrul Kurkcu, "Turkey's Web of Covert Killers," *Covert Action Quarterly*, Summer 1997.
7   Pope and Pope, Turkey Unveiled.
8   Kurkcu, Covert Killers.
9   Martin A. Lee, "On the Trail of Turkey's Terrorist Grey Wolves," from the Consortium website, posted at http://www.consortiumnews.com/archive/story33.html; see also Scott Anderson and Jon Lee Anderson, *Inside the League*, Dodd, Mead, New York NY, 1986.
10   Levant Basturk, "The Praetorian Turkish State and Its Crisis of Hegemony," Anadolu (http://www.wakeup.org/anadolu), Winter 1998; reposted at http://msanews.mynet.net/Scholars/Basturk/praetorian.html.
11   Christopher Hitchens, "The Case Against Henry Kissinger, Part Two," *Harper's*, March 2001.
12   Hitchens, The Case.
13   Christopher Deliso, "Turkey's Eclipse: Earthquakes, Armenians and the Loss of Cyprus," from the Antiwar.com website, October 4, 2001, posted at http://www.antiwar.com/orig/deliso9.html.
14   Kurkcu, Covert Killers.
15   Husayn al-Kurdi, "The CIA in Kurdistan," *Z Magazine*, December 1996.
16   Ayse Ozdemir, "Not Talking Turkey," *Extra!*, July/August 2001; see also Jennifer Washburn, "Power Bloc: Turkey and Israel Lock Arms," *The Progressive*, December 1998.
17   "Fast Facts," from the Federation of American Scientists website, posted at http://www.fas.org/asmp/fast_facts.htm.
18   Noam Chomsky, *The New Military Humanism: Lessons from Kosovo*, Common Courage Press, Monroe ME, 1999.
19   Ozdemir, Not Talking.
20   Basturk, Praetorian State.
21   Y. Altintas, "Critical Review of PKK History," posted at http:www.turkiye.net/konuk/yusuf3.htm.
22   Kurkcu, Covert Killers.
23   Ozdemir, Not Talking.
24   Husayn al-Kurdi, "The CIA in Kurdistan," *Z Magazine*, December 1996.
25   Washburn, Power Bloc.
26   Kurkcu, Covert Killers; see also Tamar Gabelnick, "Turkey: Arms and Human Rights," *Foreign Policy in Focus*, May 1999.
27   Urbina, U.S. Bows.
28   Ozdemir, Not Talking.

29   Chomsky, Military Humanism.
30   Kani Xulam, "Smashing the Kurds: CIA Role in Kidnapping Abdullah
      Ocalan," Covert Action, Fall 2002.
31   Gareth Jenkins, "Scramble for Caspian oil," Al-Ahram Weekly, December
      2-8, 1999.
32   Urbina, U.S. Bows.
33   "U.S. lawmakers call for erasing $5 billion in military debt of key U.S. ally
      Turkey," Agence France Presse, October 3, 2001.
34   Urbina, U.S. Bows.
35   Urbina, U.S. Bows.
36   Washburn, Power Bloc.
37   Russell, Middle East.
38   Tabitha Morgan, "Turkey and Greece in Mid-East effort," BBC News,
      April 25, 2002.
39   Deliso, Turkey's Eclipse.
40   "U.S. defense official seeks to ease Turkish concerns over regime change in
      Iraq," AP, July 14, 2002.
41   Amberin Zaman, "Islamic 'clean' party sweeping board in Turkey," The
      Telegraph (UK), November 4, 2002.

CHAPTER 11: SAUDI ARABIA

1   Tariq Ali, "The Saudi Connection: The Kingdom of Corruption," from the
      CounterPunch website, September 24, 2001, posted at http://www.counter-
      punch.org/tariq3.html.
2   David Leigh and Richard Norton-Taylor, "House of Saud looks close to col-
      lapse," The Guardian (UK), November 21, 2001.
3   Nicolas Pelham, "Saudi clerics issue edicts against helping 'infidels',"
      Christian Science Monitor, October 12, 2001.
4   Zafar Bangash, "Occupation of the Arabian Peninsula by the Al-e Saud,"
      from the Muslimedia website, posted at
      http://www.muslimedia.com/archives/special96/saud.htm.
5   Zafar Bangash, "Foreign hand behind the emergence of the Saud family,"
      from the Muslimedia website, posted at
      http://www.muslimedia.com/archives/features98/saud1.htm.
6   Bangash, Foreign hand.
7   John Loftus and Mark Aarons, The Secret War Against the Jews, St. Martin's,
      New York NY, 1994.
8   "The House of Saud," New Internationalist, August 2000.
9   Bryan Curtis, "Dossier: The Saudi Royal Family," Slate, September 28, 2001;
      see also "Saudi Royal Politics Are Quicksand for U.S.," from the Strategic
      Forecasting website, September 26, 2001, posted at
      http://www.stratfor.com/home/0109262300.htm.

10   Seymour Hersh, "King's Ransom: How Vulnerable Are the Saudi Royals?" *New Yorker*, October 22, 2001.

11   James Ridgeway, "Why the U.S. Can't Lean on Saudi Arabia," *Village Voice*, October 12, 2001.

12   Scott Armstrong, "A Decade of Deception," *Mother Jones*, November/December 1991.

13   Armstrong, Deception.

14   Armstrong, Deception.

15   Dilip Hiro, *Desert Shield to Desert Storm*, Routledge, New York NY, 1992.

16   Jean Heller, "Public doesn't get picture with Gulf satellite photos," *In These Times*, February 27, 1991.

17   According to Middle East Newsline, October 18, 2001; the more commonly cited figure is about 5000 troops – which doesn't count accompanying "staff."

18   Dan Morgan, "Apparent Role of Saudis Brings the Kingdom's Tensions Into Focus," *Washington Post*, September 22, 2001.

19   "A Look at U.S. Role in Saudi Arabia," AP, January 18, 2002.

20   Morgan, Role of Saudis; see also Robert G. Kaiser, "Royal family's wealth invested in West," *Seattle Times*, February 18, 2002.

21   Charles J. Handley, "U.S.-Saudi Relations Face Challenges," AP, January 27, 2002.

22   Amnesty International Report 2001: Saudi Arabia.

23   "On U.S.-Saudi Relations: With Us… Or Against?," *San Francisco Chronicle*, November 18, 2001.

24   Nick Fielding, "Bin Laden's Sister Implicates Arab Royals," *Sunday Times* (UK), October 28, 2001; see also Jonathan Wells, Jack Meyers and Maggie Mulvihill, "Saudi elite linked to bin Laden financial empire," *Boston Herald*, October 14, 2001.

25   Neela Banerjee, "The High, Hidden Cost of Saudi Arabian Oil," *New York Times*, October 21, 2001.

26   Wells, Meyers and Mulvihill, Saudi elite.

27   David B. Ottaway and Dan Morgan, "Muslim Charities Under Scrutiny," *Washington Post*, September 29, 2001.

28   "Gulf War radicalized bin Laden – former spy chief," Reuters, November 6, 2001.

29   Robert G. Kaiser and David Ottaway, "Oil for Security Fueled Close Ties," *Washington Post*, February 11, 2002.

30   Daniel Schorr, "Louis Freeh's Final Act," *Christian Science Monitor*, May 11, 2001.

31   "J.B.," "The Saudi Question," from the Democratic Underground website, October 17, 2001, posted at http://www.democraticunderground.com/whopper/01/10/p/17_saudi.html.

32   Daniel Golden, James Bandler and Marcus Walker, "Bin Laden Family
      Could Profit From a Jump In Defense Spending Due to Ties to U.S. Bank,"
      Wall Street Journal, September 27, 2001. Supposedly the bin Laden family
      has cut all ties to the black sheep Osama; for evidence to the contrary see
      note 24.

33   Tom Brazaitis, "A strange intersection of Bushes, bin Ladens," *Cleveland
      Plain Dealer*, November 11, 2001. Bin Mahfouz links to Bush family inter-
      ests not only through the notorious criminal bank BCCI but also through
      current pipeline deals in the Caspian region. See "George W. Bush's
      Dubious Friends," *Intelligence Newsletter*, March 2, 2000; see also Jack
      Meyers, Jonathan Wells and Maggie Mulvihill, "Saudi clans working with
      U.S. oil firms may be tied to bin Laden," *Boston Herald*, December 10,
      2001.

34   Maggie Mulvihill, Jonathan Wells and Jack Meyers, "Saudi 'agents' close
      Bush friends," *Boston Herald*, December 11, 2001; see also Wayne Madsen,
      "Questionable Ties: Tracking bin Laden's money flow leads back to
      Midland, Texas," *In These Times*, November 12, 2001.

35   Maggie Mulvihill, Jonathan Wells and Jack Meyers, "Bush advisers cashed
      in on Saudi gravy train," *Boston Herald*, December 11, 2001.

36   Gregory Palast, "FBI and U.S. Spy Agents Say Bush Spiked bin Laden
      Probes Before 11 September," *The Guardian* (UK), November 7, 2001.

37   Stephen Schwartz, "Wahhabis in the Old Dominion," *The Weekly Standard*,
      April 8, 2002.

38   Rob Morse, "Bin Laden's relatives made a first-class escape," *San Francisco
      Chronicle*, November 9, 2001.

39   From the French book "Bin Laden: the Forbidden Truth," by Jean-Charles
      Brisard and Guillaume Dasquie, cited by Martin Yant in "Bushwhacked
      again?", *Columbus Alive*, December 6, 2001. Note that O'Neill perished in
      the WTC attacks shortly after his interview with the French authors.

40   Saudi Royal Politics, Stratfor.com, September 26, 2001.

CHAPTER 12: PAKISTAN

1   See Gerald F. Seib, "Why U.S. History of Friendship Raises Pakistani
      Skepticism," *Asian Wall Street Journal*, November 1, 2001; see also
      "Pakistan: America's Most Sanctioned Ally & Friend," posted at
      http://www.pakistanlink.com/Opinion/2001.Nov/02/05.html.

2   Historical material from Malcolm B. Russell, *The Middle East and South
      Asia*, Stryker-Post Publications, Harpers Ferry VA, 2001.

3   Low estimate: Russell; high: Philip Goodheart, "The Double Exodus," *The
      Scribe*, August 2001.

4   Low estimate: Russell; high: Lal Khan, "Pakistan—Futile crusades of a failed
      state," *New Youth* magazine, July 2000.

5   Kashmir: over 3000 (both sides), according to Amnesty International press release, posted at http://www.amnesty-usa.org/news/2002/india12112001.html; West Bank: over 1000 (both sides), according to Palestine Intifada fact sheet, posted at http://www.hdip.org/reports/PalestinainIntifadaFactSheet.htm.

6   Ahmed Rashid, *Taliban*, Yale University Press, New Haven CT, 2000.

7   See Tahira Mazhar Ali, "50 Years of Human Rights in Pakistan: A Women's Perspective," in Asian Human Rights Commission's journal *Human Rights Solidarity*, September 1998, posted at http://www.ahrchk.net/solidarity/199809/v89 09.htm.

8   Alexander Cockburn and Jeffrey St. Clair, "The Empire Strikes Back," from the CounterPunch website, October 9, 2001, posted at http://www.counterpunch.org/empire1.html.

9   Vijay Prashad, "The 'Americanization' of South Asia," *Sangat Review*, Summer 1998.

10 Russell, Middle East.

11 Stephen R. Shalom, "The U.S. Response to Humanitarian Crises: Bangladesh," *Z Magazine*, September 1991.

12 R. J. Rummel, "Statistics of Democide: Pakistan," posted at http://www.hawaii.edu/powerkills/SOD.CHAP8.HTM.

13 Rummel, Democide.

14 Christopher Hitchens, "The Case Against Henry Kissinger, Part Two, "*Harper's*, March 2001.

15 Shalom, U.S. Response.

16 Shishir Thadani, "Undermining Indian Sovereignty: U.S. Policy in the Indian Subcontinent," *Covert Action Quarterly*, Spring/Summer 2000.

17 From the PPP website's biography of Bhutto at http://www.ppp.org.pk/zab.html.

18 Michael Parenti, *Against Empire*, City Lights Books, San Francisco CA, 1995.

19 Anthony Davis and Jabal Saraj, "A Brotherly Vendetta," *Asiaweek*, December 6, 1996.

20 Janette Rainwater, Ph.D., "Afghanistan, 'Terrorism' and Blowback: A Chronology," posted at http://www.infowar.com/class 3/01/class3 110201a j.shtml.

21 "Arabs contributed $1.5 billion to Pakistan nuclear bomb in 1970s," *The Nation* (Pakistan), July 6, 1998.

22 Henry Kissinger, *Years of Upheaval* (which may well make you want to upheave) Little, Brown, Boston MA, 1982.

23 Quoted in Zafar Agha, "America's fear: short fuse of the Islamic bomb," posted at the Tehelka.com website, http://www.tehelka.com/channels/commentary/2001/oct/27/printable/com102701islamicpr.htm.

24   See Harold Gould, "Coup in Pakistan: An Expert's Initial Observations," posted at
http://www.d-n-i.net/FCS_Folder/comments/c325.htm.

25   Al Martin, in an excerpt from his book *The Conspirators: Secrets of an Iran-Contra Insider*, posted at http://home.talkcity.com/ReportersAlley/thecat-birdseat/CrouchingDragon.htm; see also Ben C. Vigden, "A State of Terror," *Nexus Magazine*, February-March 1996.

26   Interview with Brzezinski in *Le Nouvel Observateur* (France), January 15-21, 1998; he explicitly states that "I wrote a note to the president in which I explained to him that in my opinion this aid was going to induce a Soviet military intervention."

27   At least $3 billion from Washington and an equal amount in matching funds from Saudi Arabia, according to Steve Coll, "Anatomy of a Victory: CIA's Covert Afghan War," *Washington Post*, July 19, 1992.

28   See Alfred McCoy's indispensable study *The Politics of Heroin*, Lawrence Hill Books, New York NY, 1991.

29   See Khan, Futile crusades.

30   Ali, 50 years; see also Eqbal Ahmad, "The Roots of Violence in Contemporary Pakistan," posted at
http://members.tripod.com/~no_nukes_sa/chapter_1.html.

31   McCoy, The Politics of Heroin,

32   Vigden, State of terror; see also Benazir Bhutto, "The Rise of the Intelligence Officer and His Friends," from the PPP website, posted at http://www.ppp.org.pk/articles/article21.html.

33   Hasan Askari Rizvi, "Civil Military Relations in Contemporary Pakistan," from the Defence Journal (UK) website, posted at http://www.defencejour-nal.com/july98/civilianmilitary4.htm.

34   Rizvi, Civil military relations; see also Russell, Middle East.

35   "Anatomy of a coup foretold," Labour Left Briefing (UK), February 2000, posted at http://www.solidarity.freeserve.uk/campaign/lableft.htm.

36   Russell, Middle East.

37   Zafar Bangash, "Military coup brings short-term relief but little hope to Pakistan's weary people," from the Muslimedia website, November 1-15, 1999, posted at http://www.muslimedia.com/archives/world99/pak-coup2.htm.

38   Human Rights Watch World Report 2000, "Pakistan," posted at http://www.hrw.org/wr2k1/asia/pakistan/html.

39   "Pakistan: America's Most Sanctioned Ally & Friend," posted at http://www.pakistanlink.com/Opinion/2001.Nov/02/05.html; see also Bhutto, Intelligence officer, and Rizvi, Civil military relations.

40   The single most vital source on this is Ahmed Rashid's *Taliban* (note 6).

41   See Vijay Prashad, "Pakistan's Vise," from the CounterPunch website,
      September 19, 2001, posted at http://www.counterpunch.org/prashad2.html.

42   "Pipeline dreams one of the factors which led to throwing Ms. Benazir
      Bhutto out of power," *The Herald*, June 1997, posted at http://www.nowar-
      collective.com/pipeline.htm; see also Rashid, *Taliban*, for more detail.

43   To say the least. Larry Chin, "Players on a rigged grand chessboard: Bridas,
      Unocal and the Afghanistan pipeline," from the Online Journal website,
      posted at http://www.onlinejournal.com/Special_Reports/Chin030602/chi...

44   Bill Gertz, "Pakistan sends supplies to Taliban," *Washington Times*,
      November 1, 2001.

45   Ahmed Rashid, "Pakistan, the Taliban and the U.S.," *The Nation*, October
      8, 2001; see also Syed Saleem Shahzad, "Pakistan Boxed into a Corner,"
      Asia Times Online, November 14, 2001, posted at
      http://www.alternet.org/print.html?StoryID=11920.

46   Robert Fisk, "Farewell to Democracy in Pakistan," *The Independent* (UK),
      October 26, 2001; see also Amir Zia, "U.S. Vows to Help Pakistan Debt,"
      AP, October 21, 2001.

47   Khan, Futile crusades.

48   Ken Silverstein, "When Osama Met the Taliban," *Slate*, October 9, 2001;
      see also "Pakistan Detains Nuclear Scientists," AP, November 27, 2001;
      also Swati, "Pak Nukes under de facto control of the fundamentalist clergy,"
      posted at http://www.sreevideos.com/southasia/

49   Michel Chossudovsky, "The role of Pakistan's Military Intelligence (ISI) in
      the September 11 attacks," posted at
      http://globalresearch.ca/articles/CHO111A.html; see also "India helped FBI
      trace ISI-terrorist links," *Times of India*, October 9, 2001. Atta was linked to
      al-Qaida by Attorney General John Ashcroft in his December 11, 2001
      press conference, but his actual role in the organization remains unknown,
      see transcript at http://www.usdoj.gov/ag/speeches/2001/agcrisisre-
      marks12_11.htm.

50   James Risen and Judith Miller, "Pakistani Intelligence Had Links to Al
      Qaeda, U.S. Officials Say," *New York Times*, October 29, 2001.

51   Richard Reeves, "The Indian Scenario: From Bad to Worse," *Yahoo! News*,
      December 21, 2001; see also Chidanand Rajghatta, "U.S. to India: Beware,
      nukes ahead," Times of India Online, December 18, 2001.

52   Tariq Ali, "Who really killed Danny Pearl?," *The Guardian* (UK), April 5,
      2002; see also Vijay Dutt, "Omar double agent for ISI and Osama,"
      Hindustan Times, April 21, 2002. Pearl had been poking around on stories
      related to Enron's activities in India as well as to the Afghan pipeline deal
      and ISI links to terrorism; who benefited most from his death is an open
      question. See Mark Zepezauer, "Enron Body Count," posted at
      http://iwhome.com/ComicNews.

53   Naveed Miraj, "Pak-U.S. operation in tribal areas troubles Islamabad,"
     Frontier Post, May 1, 2002; see also Riaz Khan, "U.S. Forces Under Fire in
     Pakistan,' AP, May 1, 2002.

54   Zahid Hussain, "Opposition cries foul over Musharraf's 98% victory," *The
     Times* (UK), May 2, 2002.

55   "Musharraf, Karzai agree major oil pipeline in co-operation pact," Reuters,
     February 10, 2002; see also "U.S. seeks Pakistan's oil nod," January 26,
     2002, from the "This is Pakistan" website, posted at
     http://www.pakwatan.com/main/article_detail.php3?t1+402.

56   Kathy Gannon, "Cleric Could Be Next Pakistan Leader," AP, November 7,
     2002.

57   Paul Watson, "War on Terrorism Stirs Anger of Pakistani Tribe," *Los
     Angeles Times*, October 4, 2002; see also David Rohde, "Pakistani
     Fudamentalists Do Well in Election," *New York Times*, October 11, 2002.

58   Gretchen Peters, "Pakistan tilts towards extremism?," *Christian Science
     Monitor*, October 15, 2002.

59   Luke Harding, "Islamists on brink of Power in Pakistan," *The Guardian*
     (UK), November 6, 2002.

60   Ahmed Rashid, "'Fix' backfires as army halts Pakistan assembly," *The
     Telegraph* (UK), November 7, 2002.

61   Rohan Sullivan, "Musharraf Ally Elected Pakistan PM," AP, November
     23, 2002.

62   Rohde, Fundamentalists.

CHAPTER 13: AFGHANISTAN

1   Ethnolinguistic information from G2mil, a Magazine of Future Warfare,
     October 2001, at http://www.g2mil.com/militaryoptions.htm.

2   Historical data from *Random House Concise Encyclopedia*, Random House,
     New York NY, 1996.

3   William Blum, *Rogue State: A Guide to the World's Only Superpower*,
     Common Courage Press, Monroe ME, 2000.

4   Digital National Security Archive, "Afghanistan: The Making of U.S.
     Policy (1973-1990)," posted at http://192.195.245.32/alessayx.htm.

5   Quoted by Alexander Cockburn and Jeffrey St. Clair, "The Price," from
     the CounterPunch website, September 25, 2001, posted at
     http://www.counterpunch.org/theprice.html.

6   Vijay Prashad, "War Against the Planet," from the CounterPunch website,
     September 15, 2001, posted at http://www.counterpunch.org/prashad.html.

7   Interview, *Le Nouvel Observateur*, January 15-21, 1998.

8   Digital National Security Archive, Afghanistan.

9   Odd Arne Westad, "New Russian Evidence on the Soviet Intervention in
     Afghanistan," from the Digital National Security Archive.

10   Interview, *Le Nouvel Observateur*.

11   Ramzi Kysia, "Unleashing Hell." From the Common Dreams website, October 17, 2001, posted at http://www.commondreams.org/views01/1017-09.htm; see also John F. Burns, "Afghans: Now They Blame America," *New York Times*, February 4, 1990.

12   Interview, *Le Nouvel Observateur*.

13   Cockburn and St. Clair, The Price.

14   Digital National Security Archive, Afghanistan.

15   Westad, New Russian Evidence.

16   Prashad, War Against the Planet.

17   Amitabh Pal, "The Islamic Ghandi," *The Progressive*, February 2002.

18   Pankaj Mishra, "The Making of Afghanistan," *New York Review of Books*, November 15, 2001; see also David Gibbs, "Forgotten Coverage of Afghan 'Freedom Fighters'," *Extra!*, January/February 2002.

19   Michael Ruppert, "A War in the Planning for Four Years: How Stupid Do They Think We Are?," from the From the Wilderness website, November 9, 2001, posted at
     http://www.fromthewilderness.com/free/ww3/11_09_01_zbig.html.

20   Ahmed Rashid, *Taliban: Militant Islam, Oil and Fundamentalism in Central Asia*, Yale University Press, New Haven CT, 2000.

21   Veronique Maurus and Marc Rock, "The Most Dreaded Man of the United States," *Le Monde*, September 15, 2001.

22   Rashid, Taliban.

23   Steve Coll, "Anatomy of a Victory: The CIA's Covert Afghan War," *Washington Post*, July 19, 1992.

24   Burns, Blame America.

25   Patricia Gossman, "Afghanistan in the Balance," *Middle East Report*, Winter 2001.

26   Rashid, Taliban.

27   John J. Maresca, "Testimony to House Committee on International Relations, Subcommittee on Asia and the Pacific, February 12, 1998, posted at
     http://www.house.gov/international_relations/105th/ap/wsap212982.htm.

28   Wayne Madsen, "No Warning: Bush and the Taliban," *In These Times*, October 15, 2001.

29   Camelia Fard and James Ridgeway, "The Accidental Operative," *Village Voice*, June 6, 2001.

30   Madsen, No Warning.

31   Robert Scheer, "Bush's Faustian Deal With the Taliban," *Los Angeles Times*, May 22, 2001.

32   Rep. Ron Paul, "Underwriting the Taliban," from the CounterPunch website, November 6, 2001, posted at
     http://www.counterpunch.org/paul2.html.

33   Rashid, Taliban.

34   See "Excerpts from News Accounts—Bin Laden in the Balkans," from the Emperor's Clothes website, posted at http://emperors-

clothes.com/news/binl.htm.
35   John K. Cooley, *Unholy Wars: Afghanistan, America and International Terrorism*, Pluto Press, London, 2000.
36   Cooley, Unholy Wars.
37   Madsen, No Warning.
38   Patrick Martin, "U.S. planned war in Afghanistan long before September 11," from the World Socialist Website, posted at http://www.wsws.org/articles/2001/nov2001/afgh-n20_prn.shmtl.
39   Jean-Charles Brisard and Guillaume Dasquie, *Ben Laden: La Verite Interdite*, Denoel Impacts, Paris, 2001.
40   Rashid, Taliban.
41   Brisard and Dasquie, ben Laden.
42   George Armey, "U.S. 'planned attack on Taleban'," BBC, September 18, 2001, posted at http://news.bbc.co.uk/1/hi/world/south_asia/1550366.stm.
43   Patrick Martin, U.S. Planned War, citing *The Guardian* (UK) of September 22, 2001.
44   "U.S. planned for attack on al-Qaida: White House given strategy two days before Sept. 11," MSNBC, May 16, 2002.
45   Randy Fabi, "Aid Groups Urge U.S. to Not Worsen Afghan Disaster," Reuters, November 1, 2001.
46   Marc W. Herold, " A Dossier on Civilian Victims of United States' Aerial Bombing of Afghanistan: A Comprehensive Accounting [revised]," from the cursor.org website, posted at http://www.cursor.org/stories/civilian_deaths.htm. Herold estimates civilian deaths of 3000-3400 through March 2002. See also Jonathan Steele, "Forgotten Victims," *The Guardian* (UK), May 20, 2002. Steele cites a *Guardian* report of 1300 to 8000 deaths from bombing alone, and as much as an additional 20,000 from the exacerbation of the refugee crisis during a time of famine.
47   Christina Lamb, "They call this 'the slaughterhouse'," *The Telegraph* (UK), December 9, 2001; see also Marc W. Herold, "Rubble Rousers: U.S. Bombing and the Afghan Refugee Crisis," March 16, 2002, from the cursor.org website, posted at www.cursor.org/stories/rubble.htm.
48   Philip Smucker, "Taliban rule as darkness descends," *Scotland on Sunday*, May 28, 2002.
49   Felicity Lawrence and Jonathan Steele, "Most Afghans Don't Share This Optimism," *The Guardian* (UK), November 14, 2001; see also Charles M. Sennet, "A dark side to the Northern Alliance," *Boston Globe*, October 6, 2001.
50   Jennifer Van Bergen, "Zalmay Khalilzad and the Bush Agenda," from the truthout website, January 13, 2001, posted at http://www.truthout.org/docs_01/01.14A.Zalmay.Oil.htm.
51   "Afghanistan plans gas pipeline," BBC, May 13, 2002.
52   Eric Margolis, "U.S. Hit Squads Signal New Twist to Afghan War," *Toronto Sun*, May 12, 2002.

53   Kandea Mosley, "Fresh memories of war," *Ithaca Journal*, May 25, 2002,
       posted at http://www.theithacajournal.com/news/stories/20020525/topsto-
       ries/380284.html. The soldier later clarified his statement to say that he
       had been ordered only to kill women and children with "hostile intent."

54   "'Scores killed' in U.S. Afghan raid," BBC, July 1, 2002. This is far from
       the only such incident, though it may be the worst; see also "Mistaken
       U.S. Attacks in Afghanistan," AP, July 1, 2002.

55   Burt Herman, "Afghans Fight Against Locusts," AP, April 19, 2002.

56   "Afghanistan earthquake," BBC, April 4, 2002.

57   Christina Lamb, "Blair's aides denounce U.S. 'blundering' in Afghan war,"
       The Telegraph (UK), June 30, 2002.

58   Ken Silverstein, "No War for Oil! Is the United States really after
       Afghanistan's resources? Not a chance," The *American Prospect*, August 12,
       2002, posted at http://www.prospect.org/print/V13/14/silverstein-k.html.
       For a detailed response from a writer attacked by Silverstein, please see
       Patrick Martin, "Oil and 'conspiracy theories:' a reply to a liberal apologist
       for the U.S. war in Afghanistan (parts one and two)," from the World
       Socialist Web Site, posted at
       http://www.mehring.com/articles/2002/sep2002/oil1-s20_prn.shtml and
       http://www.mehring.com/articles/2002/sep2002/oil2-s21_prn.shtml.

59   "Turkmenistan: Asian Development Bank Backs Afghan Pipeline Project,"
       Radio Free Europe/Radio Liberty, July 9, 2002, posted at
       http://www.rferl.org/nca/features/2002/07/09072002133612.asp.

60   Jean Serror, "Expert claims oil interests ruined U.S.-Taliban talks," *The
       Daily Yomiuri*, November 28, 2001, posted at
       http://www.co.jp/newse/20011128wo41.htm.

61   Aaron Marr, "Softer on Terrorism? Why Bush deserves his share of the
       9/11 blame," *The American Prospect* web exclusive, January 28, 2002, post-
       ed at http://www.prospect.org/webfeatures/2002/01/page-a-01-23.html. See
       also Barton Gellman, "A Strategy's Cautious Evolution: Before Sept. 11,
       the Bush Anti-Terror Effort Was Mostly Ambition," *Washington Post*,
       January 20, 2002, posted at http://www.washingtonpost.com/ac2/wp-
       dyn?pagename=article&node=&contentId=A8734-
       2002Jan19&notFound=true.

62   Gregory Palast, "FBI and U.S. Spy Agents Say Bush Spiked bin Laden
       Probes Before 11 September," *The Guardian* (UK), November 7, 2001.

63   Byron York, "the bin Ladens' Great Escape," *National Review Online*,
       September 11, 2002, posted at
       http://www.nationalreview.com/york/york091102.asp.

64   Armey, U.S. planned attack.

65   John Omicinki, "General: Capturing bin Laden is not part of mission,"
       USA Today, November 8, 2001.

66   Seymour M. Hersh, "The Getaway," *The New Yorker*, January 28, 2002,
       posted at http://www.newyorker.com/fact/content/?020128fa_FACT.

67   See Amir Mateen, "U.S. preparing for long stay in Central Asia," *The

News International (Pakistan), January 5, 2002.

68   "General Suggests Extending U.S. Campaign to Afghan Neighbors," *New York Times*, August 25, 2002.

69   See William Branigan, "Unocal 'Smoking Gun' Alleged," *Washington Post*, May 2, 2000.

70   According to geologist Dale Allen Pfeiffer, "The Forging of 'Pipelineistan'," from the From The Wilderness website, posted at http://www.fromthewilderness.com/free/ww3/071102_pipelineistan.html. You can follow links to his sources, chiefly from the industry newsletter *Alexander's Gas and Oil Connections*, or root around there yourself at http://www.gasandoil.com.

71   See Martin, Oil and conspiracy theories, part one.

72   "Growing U.S. Military Presence Since 9/11/01," *The Nation*, October 21, 2002.

73   See, for instance, Andrew I. Kilgore, "Why Israel's Latest Power Play in Washington, the Baku-Ceyhan Oil Pipeline, Will Fail," *Washington Report on Middle East Affairs*, June 2000, posted at http://www.washington-report.org/backissues/062000/0006028.html. Or note the usually reliable private intelligence service, Stratfor, in its January 26, 2000 report, predicting that Baku-Ceyhan, "despite having U.S. support… is one of the least likely to be built."

74   Rashid, Taliban.

75   Brisard and Dasquie, ben Laden.

76   See Stan Goff, "The Unseen Conflict," from the From the Wilderness website, posted at http://www.fromthewilderness.com/free/ww3/101802_the_unseen.html. See also Dale Allen Pfeiffer, "Is the Empire About Oil?," from the From The Wilderness website, posted at http://www.fromthewilderness.com/free/ww3/080802_oil_empire.html.

77   Pfeiffer, Pipelineistan.

CHAPTER 14: CASPIAN REGION

1   Low estimate: Brooke Shelby Biggs, "Pipe Dreams," from the Mother Jones website, October 12, 2001, posted at http://www.motherjones.com/web_exclusives/features/news/pipedreams.html ; medium: Sitram Yechury, "America, oil and Afghanistan," *The Hindu*, October 13, 2001; high: Pepe Escobar, "Pipelineistan, Part 1: The rules of the game," *Asia Times Online*, January 25, 2002, posted at http://www.atimes.com/c-asia/DA25Ag01.html.

2   Quoted by Tom Turnipseed, "A Creeping Collapse in Credibility at the White House," from the CounterPunch website, January 10, 2002, posted at http://www.counterpunch.org/tomenron.html.

3   Stephen Gowans, "Getting the Pipeline Map and Politics Right," from the
     Swans website, November 12, 2001, posted at
     http://www.swans.com/library/art7/gowans10.html.

4   Again, the prime source on this story is Ahmed Rashid's *Taliban: Militant
     Islam, Oil and Fundamentalism in Central Asia*, Yale University Press, New
     Haven CT, 2000; see also Biggs, Pipe dreams; plus "Consortium formed to
     build Central Asia gas pipeline," from Unocal's website, October 27, 1997,
     posted at http://www.unocal.com/uclnews/97news/102797a.htm; and John J.
     Maresca, "Testimony to House Committee on International Relations,
     Subcommittee on Asia and the Pacific, February 12, 1998, posted at
     http://www.house.gov/international_relations/105th/ap/wsap212982.htm.

5   Christopher Deliso, "But Would it be an Evil Axis?," from the Antiwar.com
     website, February 2, 2002, posted at
     http://www.antiwar.com/orig/deliso30.html ; see also "U.S. Caspian envoy
     pushes pipelines outside Iran," Reuters, March 12, 2002.

6   Vladimir Georgiyev, " Russian Military Intelligence: The War on Iraq Will
     Be Launched in September," from the CounterPunch website, February 6,
     2002, posted at http://www.counterpunch.org/georgiyev.html; see also
     Armen Georgian, "U.S. Eyes Caspian Oil in "War on Terror," from the
     Foreign Policy in Focus website, April 30, 2002, posted at www.foreignpoli-
     cy-infocus.org/outside/ commentary/2002/0204oil_body.html.

7   George Monbiot, "A Discreet Deal in the Pipeline," *The Guardian* (UK),
     February 15, 2001.

8   "United States Deploys Aircraft in Bulgaria," Balkan Times, November 26,
     2001, posted at http://www.balkantimes.com/html2/english/011126-IVAN-
     004.htm# ; see also Michel Chossudovsky, "America at War in Macedonia,"
     originally from the Emperor's Clothes website, reposted at
     www.antiwar.com/rep/chuss5.html; also, please, Paul Stuart, " Camp
     Bondsteel and America's plans to control Caspian oil," from the World
     Socialist Web Site, April 29, 2002, posted at http://www.wsws.org/arti-
     cles/2002/apr2002/oil-a29_prn.shtml.

9   See "Was Europe the real target in the bombing of Serbia?," Tanjug news
     service (Yugoslavia), September 17, 1999, posted at http:///emperors-
     clothes.com/analysis/corridor.htm ; see also Arben Kola, "Corridor Eight:
     Dreams and Interests," AIM press service (France), April 17, 1998, posted
     at http://www.aimpress.org/dyn/trae/archive/data/199804/80426-005-trae-
     tir.htm.

10   William Arkin, "U.S. risks Arab backlash with ring of military bases,"
     Sydney Morning Herald, January 7, 2002.

11   Attributed.

12   Robyn Dixon, "Officials believe bin Laden linked to blasts in Russia," *Los
     Angeles Times*, September 27, 1999; see also Dave Montgomery, "Bin Laden

helped bankroll Dagestan war, expert says," *San Jose Mercury News*, September 10, 1999.

13   Fred Weir, "Terror war fallout could create several fronts in Central Asia,"*Christian Science Monitor*, October 8, 2001; see also Abid Aslam, "Central Asia: On the Periphery of a New Global war," from the Foreign Policy in Focus website, September 24, 2001, posted at www.foreignpolicy-infocus.org/outside/ commentary/0109istans_body.html.

14   Jan Knippers Black, "Carpetbaggers & Suits in Central Asia," *Z Magazine*, February 1995; see also Richard Norton-Taylor, "The New Great Game," *The Guardian* (UK), March 5, 2001; plus Franz Schurmann's well-timed piece, "Conflict Building Up in Oil-Rich Caspian, New California Media Online, September 6, 2001, posted at

15   John Pilger, "The Colder War," *The Mirror* (UK), January 29, 2002, posted at http://pilger.carlton.com/print/94988; see also Michael Ruppert, "A War in the Planning for Four Years: How Stupid Do They Think We Are?," from the From the Wilderness website, November 9, 2001, posted at http://www.fromthewilderness.com/free/ww3/11_09_01_zbig.html; see also Rashid, *Taliban*.

16   Frederick Starr, "GUUAM: What is the Future?," from the website of the Center for Strategic and International Studies, July 11, 2001, posted at http://www.csis.org/energy/ga_010711star.htm.

17   Thomas E. Ricks and Susan B. Glasser, "U.S. Operated Secret Alliance With Uzbekistan," *Washington Post*, October 14, 2001.

18   Anssi Kullberg, "Shanghai vs. the West," *The Eurasian Politician*, June 2001, posted at http://www.cc.jyu.fi/~aphamala/pe/issue4/shanghai-en.htm.

19   Igor Torbakov, "GUUAM's Loss is Russia's Gain," *Eurasia Insight*, April 18, 2001 posted at http://www.eurasianet.org/departments/insight/articles/eav041801.shtml.

20   Rashid, Taliban.

21   Amir Mateen, U.S. preparing for long stay in Central Asia," *The News International* (Pakistan), January 5, 2002; see also Michael Richardson, "U.S. Wants More Use of Central Asia Bases," *International Herald Tribune*, February 8, 2002; and don't miss Zoltan Grossman, "New U.S. Military Bases: Side Effects or Causes of War?," from the CounterPunch website, February2, 2002, posted at http://www.counterpunch.org/zoltanbases.html.

22   Monique Mekenkamp, "Nagorno-Karabakh—Pawn in the major power game," from the website of the European Platform for Conflict Prevention and Transformation, posted at http://www.euconflict.org/euconflict/guides/surveys/arm.at.htm.

23   Mekenkamp, Nagorno-Karabakh.

24   Indeed, Bush personally involved himself in diplomacy on Nagorno-Karabakh early in his term while putting the Israeli-Palestinian issue on the back burner. See Wayne Madsen, " Is Big Oil Calling the Shots in

Washington?," *In These Times*, August 6, 2001; see also Steven R. Mann, "American diplomat sees encouraging signs on Baku-Ceyhan pipeline," from the Eurasianet website, November 20, 2001, posted at http://www.eurasianet.org .

25 Afshin Molavi, "Caspian Basin Competition Kicking Into High Gear," from the Eurasianet website, March 14, 2001, posted at http://www.eurasianet.org .

26 BBC News, "Armenian killers' family connection," October 29, 1999.

27 See Ara Sanjian, "Murder in the Parliament: Who? Why? And what next?," Armenian News Network, November 1, 1999, posted at http://groong.usc.edu/ro/ro-19991101.html; see also Haroutiun Khachatrian, "Parliament Shooting Trial Poses Challenge for Armenian Political Institution," from the Eurasianet website, June 13, 2001, posted at http://www.eurasianet.org/departments/insight/articles/eav062101.shtm.

28 BBC News, Armenian killers.

29 BBC News, "Country Profile: Armenia," posted at http://news.bbc.co.uk/hi/english/world/europe/country_profiles/newsid_1108 000/1108052.stm.

30 "Armenia turns away from Russia," from the Strategic Forecasting website, November 25, 1999, reposted at http://www.atimes.com/c-asia/AK26Ag01.html.

31 Khachatrian, Parliament Shooting.

32 "Armenia, NATO discuss cooperation," ITAR-Tass news agency, March 13, 2001.

33 Emil Danielyan, "Armenia: Westward Foreign-Policy Shift Brings Unease in Iran," from the Eurasianet website, November 6, 2001, posted at http://www.eurasianet.org/departments/business/articles/eav100502.shtml.

34 Susan Smith Nash, Ph.D., "Land of Fire: Azerbaijan and the Caspian Continue to Burn Hot with Potential," posted at http://www.geocities.com/beyondutopia/azerbaijan-oil-and-pipelines/land-of-fire.htm.

35 M. A. Shaikh, "Bush Administration's interest in Azeri-Armenian conflict bodes ill for Baku," from the Muslimedia website, posted at http://www.mus-limedia.com/archives/special01/azer-bush.htm.

36 Mekenkamp, Nagorno-Karabakh.

37 Kenan Aliyev, "Azerbaijan Engaged In Balancing Act That Could Influence Oil & Gas Development," from the Eurasianet website, November 6, 2001, posted at http://www.eurasianet.org/departments/busi-ness/articles/eav110601.shtml.

38 Afshin Molavi, "Caspian Basin Competition Kicking Into High Gear," from the Eurasianet website, March 14, 2001, posted at http://www.eurasianet.org/departments/business/articles/eav031401.shtml.

39   "The Great Game in Azerbaijan and Beyond," from the Aliyev.com web-
      site, posted at http://www.aliyev.com/aliyev/fact_07.htm.

40   See note 5 above; see also George Monbiot, "America's Pipe Dream," *The
      Guardian* (UK), October 23, 2001.

41   The Great Game, from Aliyev.com.

42   "Redrawing the Caucasus," from the Transitions Online website, October
      23, 2001, reposted at http://www.eurasianet.org/departments/insight/arti-
      cles/pp112701.shtml.

43   Mamed Suleimanov, "Baku Alarmed Over 'Wahhabi Menace'," CRS news
      service, September 7, 2001, posted at
      http://www.ipr.net/index.pl?archive/cau/cau200109_97_1_eng.txt.

44   Vafa Gulazadeh, "Expert Expects Russia to Get Tough With Azerbaijan,"
      from the Eurasianet website, October 24, 2001, posted at
      http://www.eurasianet.org/departments/qanda/articles/eav102401.shtml.

45   Mevlut Katik, "Caucasus Summit Cements Cooperation Among Turkey,
      Azerbaijan and Georgia," from the Eurasianet website, May 3, 2002, posted
      at http://www.eurasianet.org/departments/insight/articles/eav050302.shtm.

46   Haroutiun Khachatrian, "Security Interests in the South Caucasus Begin to
      Gel," from the Eurasianet website, June 13, 2002, posted at
      http://www.eurasianet.org/departments/insight/articles/eav061302.shtm.

47   Michael Lelyveld, "U.S. Rejects Military Involvement in Caspian Dispute,"
      from the Eurasianet website, March 17, 2002, posted at
      http://www.eurasianet.org/departments/insight/articles/pp031702.shtml .

48   Martha Brill Olcott, "Revisiting the Twelve Myths of Central Asia,"
      Carnegie Endowment for International Peace, Russian/Eurasian Working
      Paper #23, September 2001.

49   Aida Sultanova, "Azerbaijan Referendum Change on Hold," AP, August
      23, 2002.

50   Azerbaijan Dissention Slides into Violence," from the Eurasianet website,
      October 3, 2002, posted at
      http://www.eurasianet.org/departments/rights/articles/eav100302.shtml.

51   Michael Specter, "Rainy nights in Georgia, The *New Yorker*, December 18,
      2000.

52   Human Rights Watch World Report 2001: Georgia, posted at
      http://www.hrw.org/wr2k1/europe/georgia.html ; see also British Helsinki
      Human Rights Group (BHHRG), "Human rights abuses including torture
      in Georgia today," posted at
      http://www.bhhrg.org/georgia/georgia1992/humanrights.htm.

53   BHHRG, Human rights abuses; see also Specter, Rainy nights.

54   Vladimir Volkov, "The elections in Georgia: an analysis of Shevardnadze's
      victory,' from the World Socialist Web Site, May 2, 2000, posted at
      http://www.wsws.org/articles/2000/may2000/geor-m02.shtml.

55 Chad Nagle, "The Betrayal of Democracy in Post-Soviet Georgia," from the Antiwar.com website, November 30, 1999, posted at http://www.antiwar.com/orig/nagle1.html.

56 Christopher Deliso, "A Quiet Battle in the Caucasus: Georgia Between Russia and NATO," from the Antiwar.com website, September 26, 2001, posted at http://www.antiwar.com/orig/deliso7.html.

57 Floriana Fossato, "Georgia: President Supports NATO Air Campaign; Draws Parallels With Abkhazia," Radio Free Europe/Radio Liberty, May 11, 1999, posted at http://www.rferl.org/nca/features/1999/05/F.RU.990511133219.html.

58 Volkov, Elections in Georgia.

59 Volkov, Elections in Georgia.

60 Against all odds, the Baku-Ceyhan pipeline began construction in June 2002, with an estimated completion date sometime in 2005. See Aynura Akhmedova, "Azerbaijan, Georgia Move to Secure Oil Pipelines," from the Eurasianet website, April 21, 2002, posted at http://www.eurasianet.org/departments/insight/articles/pp042102.shtml .

61 Todd Diamond, "UN Secretary-General Reports on Abkhazia, as Georgia Unravels," from the Eurasianet website, November 1, 2001, posted at http://www.eurasianet.org/departments/insight/articles/eav110101.shtml ; see also Patrick Cockburn, "Collapse of Georgia is Ignored by the World," *The Independent t* (UK), January 14, 2002.

62 Ariel Cohen, "Azerbaijan and Georgia Face Succession Conundrum," from the Eurasianet website, September 11, 2001, posted at http://www.eurasianet.org/departments/insight/articles/eav091101.shtm.

63 Deliso, A Quiet Battle.

64 Misha Dzhindzhikhashvili, "14 Said Killed in Georgia Raid," AP, October 9, 2001.

65 Cockburn, Collapse of Georgia.

66 Ian Traynor, "Georgia: U.S. opens new front in war on terror," *The Guardian* (UK), March 20, 2002.

67 Armen Khanbabyan, "Georgia is Only the Beginning: The American Presence in the Transcaucasus will Quickly Expand," from the CounterPunch website, March 18, 2002, posted at http://www.counterpunch.org/georgia2.html ; see also Tony Karon, "Why U.S. Arrival in Georgia Has Moscow Hopping Mad," *Time*, February 27, 2002.

68 Saadet Oruc, "U.S. military in Georgia will increase Baku-Tbilisi-Ceyhan security," *Turkish Daily News*, March 7, 2002; see also Peter Dale Scott, "Pipeline Politics—Oil Behind Plan for U.S. Troops in Georgia," Pacific News Service, March 1, 2002.

69 See note 44 above; see also Igor Torbakov, "Russia Struggles to Counterbalance Rising U.S. Influence in the Caucasus," from the

Eurasianet website, April 8, 2002, posted at
http://www.eurasianet.org/departments/insight/articles/eav040802.shtml

70   "Putin warns of 'self-defence' strikes," BBC News, September 11, 2002; see
      also Jim Heintz, "Russia May Intervene in Georgia," AP, March 22, 2002.

71   "Possible Iraq-for-Georgia Deal Could Seal Baghdad's Fate," from the
      Strategic Forecasting website http://www.startfor.com, September 17, 2002.

72   Jaba Devdariani, "U.S. Proposes New Trilateral Security Arrangement for
      Georgia," from the Eurasianet website, April 8, 2002, posted at
      http://www.eurasianet.org/departments/insight/articles/eav092402.shtml

73   Black, Carpetbaggers & Suits (note 14 above).

74   Rall, New Great Game; see also "Caspian Sea Oil: By 2015, Kazakhstan
      hopes to be a major oil producer," from the Odessa American website,
      August 27, 2001, posted at http://www.oaoa.com/oil/oil082701a.htm.

75   Black, Carpetbaggers & suits.

76   Human Rights Watch World Report 2001: Kazakhstan, posted at
      http://www.hrw.org/wr2k1/europe/kazakhstan.html ;

77   Patrick E. Tyler, "Kazakh Leader Urges Iran Pipeline Route," *New York
      Times*, December 10, 2002.

78   Elaine Monaghan, "Bush, Kazakh Declare Longterm Strategic Partnership,"
      Reuters, December 21, 2001; see also Rall, New Great Game.

79   Black, Carpetbaggers & Suits.

80   Mara Bellaby, "Russian, U.S. officials officially open Caspian pipeline," AP,
      November 28, 2001.

81   Ben Aris and Ahmed Rashid, "Russia Anxious over grip on oil as U.S. firms
      join Great Game," *The Telegraph* (UK), October 21, 2001.

82   AP, "Ex-Soviet Republics in Central Asia," September 23, 2001.

83   Alima Bisenova, "Kazakhstan Tries to balance Disparate Interests," from the
      Eurasianet website, October 9, 2001, posted at
      http://www.eurasianet.org/departments/insight/articles/eav100901.shtml.

84   Bruce Pannier, "Kzakhs, Kyrgyz Opt for Stricter Security Measures," from
      the Eurasianet website, October 17, 2001, posted at
      http://www.eurasianet.org/departments/insight/articles/eav101701.shtm.

85   "Growing U.S. Military Presence Since 9/11/01," *The Nation*, October 21,
      2002; see also Bisenova, Disparate Interests.

86   Rall, New Great Game.

87   "Political Turmoil Hits Kazakhstan as Nazarbayev Sacks Top Officials,"
      from the Eurasianet website, November 27, 2001, posted at
      http://www.eurasianet.org/departments/insight/articles/eav112701.shtm.

88   Ahmed Rashid, "Central Asia Elites, Suddenly, Shift Into Revolt," from the
      Eurasianet website, May 2, 2002, posted at
      http://www.eurasianet.org/departments/insight/articles/eav050202.shtm.

89   Cheney sat on Nazarbayev's own Oil Advisory Board, according to The
     Public I, website of the Center for Public Integrity (citing *Business Week*),
     posted at http://www.public-i.org/story_04_031500.htm; Rice was the main
     Kazakhstan expert on Chevron's board of directors, according to Escobar,
     Pipelineistan (see note 1 above).

90   Larry Chin, "Big Oil, the United States and corruption in Kazakhstan, parts
     one and two" from the Online Journal website, May 12 and 16, 2002.

91   Human Rights Watch World Report 2001: Kyrgyzstan, posted at
     http://www.hrw.org/wr2k1/europe/kyrgyzstan.html.

92   Chris Schuepp, "Democracy Gets a Makeover in Kyrgyzstan," from the
     Eurasianet website, August 30, 2001, posted at
     http://www.eurasianet.org/departments/insight/articles/eav083001.shtml

93   "4 Die in Regional Riots Called a Coup Attempt," *International Herald
     Tribune*, March 19, 2002; see also Elena Listvennaya, "Kyrgyzstan
     Opposition Leader Freed," AP, March 19, 2002.

94   Elenea Listvennaya, "Kyrgyzstan's Government Resigns," AP, May 22, 2002.

95   Anatol Lieven, "The Causasus and Central Asia Ten Years After the Soviet
     Collapse," from the Eurasianet website, August 21, 2001, posted at
     http://www.eurasianet.org/departments/insight/articles/eav082101.shtml

96   Black, Carpetbaggers & Suits.

97   "Kyrgyzstan: Future Front in Anti-Terrorism war," from the Strategic
     Forecasting website Stratfor.com, October 10, 2001.

98   Abid Aslam, "Central Asia: On the Periphery of a New Global War," from
     the Foreign Policy in Focus website, September 24, 2001, posted at
     http://www.foreignpolicyinfocus.org/commentary/0109istans_body.html.

99   See note 78 above: Pannier, Kzakhs, Kyrgyz.

100 "Uzbekistan Seeking Regional Dominance," from the Strategic Forecasting
     website Stratfor.com, October 17, 2001.

101 Beatrice Hogan, "Kyrgyz Authorities Concerned About Retaliatory Raids
     Against Central Asian Reservoirs," from the Eurasianet website, October
     16, 2001, posted at
     http://www.eurasianet.org/departments/insight/articles/eav101601.shtml

102 Aslam, Central Asia.

103 Beatrice Hogan, "Tightened Security in Ferghana valley Pinches
     Residents," from the Eurasianet website, November 27, 2001, posted at
     http://www.eurasianet.org/departments/insight/articles/eav112701.shtml

104 Stratfor.com, Uzbekistan, October 17, 2001.

105 Hogan, Kyrgyz Authorities.

106 Human Rights Watch, Kyrgyzstan.

107 Stratfor.com, Kyrgyzstan, October 10, 2001.

108 Robert Burns, Rumsfeld Visits Central Asia Base," AP April 26, 2002.

109 Kari Huus, "Kyrgysz president faces harsh criticism on rights," MSNBC, September 24, 2002.

110 "U.S. Troops to Stay in Kyrgyzstan", BBC News, March 3, 2002.

111 World Bank, 2002 World Economic Indicators, posted at http://www.world-bank.org/data/wdi2002/tables/table1-1.pdf.

112 World Bank, 2002 Indicators.

113 Konstantin Parshin, "Tajikistan Gains Global Prominence, Yet Fights Regional Isolation," from the Eurasianet website, November 14, 2001, posted at
http://www.eurasianet.org/departments/insight/articles/eav111401.shtm.

114 Asian Development Bank, "Tajikistan in Transition," posted at http://www.adb.org/Documents/Books/Country_Briefing_Papers/Women_in_Tajikistan/chap_01.pdf.

115 Olcott, Twelve Myths (see note 47 above).

116 Karen Talbot, "Chechnya: More Blood for Oil," Covert Action Quarterly, Spring/Summer 2000.

117 Quoted by Talbot, Chechnya.

118 Stephen Franklin and Colin McMahon, "Tajiks wary of chaos across their border," Chicago Tribune, October 19, 2001; see also Talbot., Chechnya.

119 Franklin and McMahon, Tajiks wary.

120 Talbot, Chechnya.

121 William O. Beeman, "The Tajikistan Connection—A Tenuous Proposition," Pacific News Service, November 7, 2001.

122 Human Rights Watch World Report 2001: Tajikistan, posted at http://www.hrw.org/wr2k1/europe/tajikistan.html.

123 Human Rights Watch, Tajikistan; see also Talbot., Chechnya.

124 Beeman, Tajikistan Connection.

125 Parshin, Tajikistan Gains; see also Pannier, Kazakhs, Kyrgyz (note 78 above).

126 Franklin and McMahon, Tajiks wary.

127 Bruce Pannier, "Tajikistan, Kyrgyzstan Balancing Relations with West, Russia," from the Eurasianet website, December 8, 2001, posted at http://www.eurasianet.org/departments/insight/articles/eav120801.shtm.

128 Tajikistan is the last former Soviet republic (other than Russia) to do so. BBC World Service, "Tajikistan joins NATO peace," February 20, 2002.

129 Davron Vali, "IMU Movements May Press Tajikistan to Forefront of Security Concerns," from the Eurasianet website, December 8, 2001, posted at http://www.eurasianet.org/departments/insight/articles/eav120801.shtm.

130 Rustem Safronov, "Turkmenistan: A Question Mark in Central Asia's Security Framework," from the Eurasianet website, September 21, 2001, posted at
http://www.eurasianet.org/departments/insight/articles/eav092101.shtm.

131 Human Rights Watch World Report 2001: Turkmenistan, posted at http://www.hrw.org/wr2k1/europe/turkmenistan.html.

132 Kullberg, Shanghai vs. the West (see note 18 above).

133 Officially Turkmenistan is still protective of its neutrality, offering use of its airspace and territory only for "humanitarian assistance" to suffering Afghanistan. The private intelligence service DEBKA reported on November 7, 2001 that the U.S. was looking at three specific bases on Turkmen territory, but no announcements have been made. Curiously, though, *Stars and Stripes* reported on April 11, 2002, that the U.S. had established an (unnamed) military base in Turkmenistan after several of Turkmen military and civilian leaders had attended "training sessions" at a U.S. think tank in Germany. See David Josar, "Marshall Center ties prove valuable in forging alliances for war on terror," *Stars and Stripes*, European edition, April 11, 2002.

134 Safronov, A Question Mark; see also Talbot, Chechnya.

135 Safronov, A Question Mark.

136 Bagila Bukharbayeva, "Caspian States Consider Oil Issues," AP, April 23, 2002.

137 See note 4 above.

138 Starting in 1997 the U.S. publicly opposed the Taliban, ostensibly due to human rights concerns. Ahmed Rashid, in *Taliban*, describes how negotiations foundered on the Taliban's insistence on infrastructure projects in Afghanistan as a condition of the pipeline transit. French authors Jean-Charles Brisard and Guillaume Dasquie report that the U.S. clumsily demanded the return of exiled King Zahir Shah as a condition of recognition, enraging the Taliban; see Nina Burleigh, "Bush, oil and the Taliban," Salon.com website, February 8, 2002.

139 In his 1998 congressional testimony (referenced above in note 4), Unocal vice president John J. Maresca stated that "construction of our pipeline cannot begin until a recognized government is in place."

140 See chronology at http://www.worldpress.org/specials/pp/pipeline_timeline.htm; see also Caspian News Agency, "Turkmen President and head of Afghan interim government discussed perspective of Turkmenistan-Afghanistan-Pakistan pipeline construction," March 7, 2002.

141 Rustem Safronov, "Niyazov's Latest Purge Reveals a Regime on the Brink," from the Eurasianet website, April 16, 2002, posted at http://www.eurasianet.org/departments/insight/articles/eav041602.shtml

142 Alec Applebaum, "Turkmenistan's Niyazov Lambasted by Former Minister," from the Eurasianet website, November 2, 2001, posted at http://www.eurasianet.org/departments/insight/articles/eav110201.shtml

143 Ahmed Rashid, "Central Asian Elites, Suddenly, Shift into Revolt," from the Eurasianet website, May 2, 2002, posted at http://www.eurasianet.org/departments/insight/articles/eav050202.shtml

144 Roger N. McDermott, "Shakeup in Turmen Spy Agency Hints at Pending Crisis," from the Eurasianet website, May 2, 2002, posted at http://www.eurasianet.org/departments/insight/articles/eav093002.shtml

145 Alexander Vershinin, "Shots fired at car carrying president of Turkmenistan," AP, November 25,2002.

146 Human Rights Watch World Report 2001: Uzbekistan, posted at http://www.hrw.org/wr2k1/europe/uzbekistan.html.

147 Dilip Hiro, "Bush's Uzbek Bargain," *The Nation*, online report, from http://www.thenation.com.

148 Quoted in Ruppert, How Stupid (see note 15 above).

149 Frida Berrigan, "Uzbekistan: Bush's New Best Friend," from the Common Dreams website, November 8, 2001, posted at http://www.commondreams.org/views01/1108-02.htm.

150 Berrigan, Uzbekistan.

151 Thomas E. Ricks and Susan B. Glasser, "U.S. Operated Secret Alliance with Uzbekistan," *Washington Post*, October 14, 2001.

152 Ricks and Glasser, Secret Alliance.

153 Priscilla Patton, "America Turns a Blind Eye to its Uzbek Host," Globalvision News Network, November 13, 2001.

154 Human Rights Watch, Uzbekistan.

155 Human Rights Watch, Uzbekistan.

156 Human Rights Watch, Uzbekistan.

157 Burt Herman, "Uzbekistan a Key Military Locale," AP, October 2, 2001.

158 Human Rights Watch, Uzbekistan; see also Patton, Blind Eye.

159 Patton, Blind Eye; see also Davron Val, "IMU Movements May Press Tajikistan To Forefront Of Security Concerns," from the Eurasianet website, April 18, 2002, posted at http://www.eurasianet.org/departments/insight/articles/eav041802.shtml.

160 Patrick Martin, "U.S. bases pave the way for long-term intervention in Central Asia," World Socialist Web Site, January 11, 2002.

161 Stratfor.com, "Uzbekistan Seeking Regional Dominance" (see note 92 above).

162 William O. Beeman, "America's Uzbek Connection May Inflame All of Central Asia," Pacific News Service, October 8, 2001.

163 Jeff Gerth and Don Van Natta Jr., "In Tough Times, a Company Finds Profits in Terror War," *New York Times*, July 13, 2002; with supplemental material at http://cryptome.org/dod-kbr.htm.

164 Robert G. Kaiser, "U.S.-Uzbek Declaration Kept Secret," Washington Post, July 1, 2002.

165   Elver Ramazano, "Fresh Allegations Continue Pattern of Repression in Uzbekistan," from the Eurasianet website, May 1, 2002, posted at http://www.eurasianet.org/departments/rights/articles/eav050102.shtml.

AFTERWORD

1   For details see William Blum, *Killing Hope*, Common Courage Press, Monroe ME, 1995.

2   Anthony Arnove, *Iraq Under Seige*, updated edition, South End Press, Boston MA, 2002.

3   Marc Herold, "Archivistan," a collection of articles posted at http://www.cursor.org/stories/archivistan.htm; see also his forthcoming book: *Blown Away: The Myth and Reality of Precision Bombing*, Common Courage Press, 2003.

4   Blum, Killing Hope.

5   Gore Vidal and David Nielson, "Death in the Philippines," *New York Review of Books*, December 17, 1981, posted at http://www.nybooks.com/articles/6787.

6   Larry Chin, "Hollywood drags the bloody corpse of truth across movie screens," from the Online Journal website, January 3, 2002, posted at www.onlinejournal.com/01-03-02_Chin.pdf.

7   Stephen Zunes, "Yemen, The United States, and al-Qaida," from the Foreign Policy in Focus website, December 19, 2001, posted at http://www.foreignpolicy-infocus.org/commentary/0112yemen.html; see also Zunes' excellent book *Tinderbox: U.S. Middle East Policy and the Roots of Terrorism*, Common Courage Press, Monroe ME, 2002.

8   Michael Klare, "Oil moves the War Machine," *The Progressive*, June 2002, posted at http://www.progressive.org/June%202002/klare0602.html; see also his book *Resource Wars: The New Landscape of Global Conflict*, Metropolitan Books, New York NY, 2001.

9   For a compelling account of this process please see Joel Garreau, "Conspiracy of Heretics," *Wired*, November 1994, posted at http://www.wired.com/wired/archive/2.11/gbn.html?topic=investing_ipos&topic_set=neweconomy.

10   Quoted by Peace Action at http://www.peace-action.org/camp/justice/jnwquestions.pdf.

11   Ben Partridge , "East: Changes In Militaries In Europe, Russia, And Others Analyzed," Radio Free Europe/Radio Liberty, October 31, 1999, posted at http://www.rferl.org/nca/features/1999/10/F.RU.991021132449.html.

12   If you count non-Pentagon military spending at the Department of Energy and elsewhere; see "The 20 Power Standard," from the Defense and the National Interest website, posted at http://www.d-n-i.net/charts_data/20_power_standard.htm.

13   Arms Trade Resource Center, "Increases in Military Spending and Security Assistance Since 9/11/01, posted at

http://www.tompaine.com/feature.cfm/ID/6504/view/print.

14   Ramsey Clark and others, *War Crimes: A Report on United States War
      Crimes Against Iraq*, Maisonneuve Press, Washington DC, 1992.

15   Thalif Deen, "U.S. Dollars Yielded Unanimous UN Vote Against Iraq,"
      Inter Press Service, November 11, 2002, posted at http://www.common-
      dreams.org/headlines02/1111-02.htm

16   Ramsey Clark, et al, *War Crimes: A Report on United States War Crimes
      Against Iraq*, Maisonneuve Press, Washington DC, 1992.

17   Scott Lindlaw, "Iraq watched closely for compliance," AP, November 11,
      2002.

18   Bud and Ruth Schultz, *It Did Happen Here: Recollections of Political
      Repression in America*, University of California Press, Berkeley CA, 1989.

19   Posted at http://www.house.gov/kucinich/action/peace_legis_summary.htm.

20   Richard C. Bell and Michael Renner, "A Global Marshall Plan to Fight
      Terrorism," Worldwatch Institute, Washington, DC, from the Common
      Dreams website, October 6, 2001, posted at
      http://www.commondreams.org/views01/1006-06.htm.

21   Dilip Hiro, *Desert Shield to Desert Storm*, Routledge, New York NY, 1992.

Index

About the Author

Author/cartoonist Mark Zepezauer was raised amidst the peaceful semiconductor farms of Silicon Valley, the son of immigrants from Milwaukee and Chicago. After graduating from UC Santa Cruz, he worked for several newspapers there, creating the cartoon panel *U.S. History Backwards*. In 1989 he produced a limited edition art book, *The Nixon Saga*, now found in more than two museum collections. He moved to Arizona in 1993, publishing the *Tucson Comic News*, a monthly compendium of political cartoons, until 2000. He is the author of *The CIA's Greatest Hits* (1994) and *Take the Rich Off Welfare* (1996, appearing soon in an updated edition). Most of his columns and essays are archived at his website, http://iwhome.com/ComicNews. Zepezauer lives in Tucson with his splendid wife and miraculous baby daughter and four recalcitrant cats.